POWER, POLITICS AND PHARMACEUTICALS

Power, Politics and Pharmaceuticals

Drug Regulation in Ireland in the Global Context

Edited by Orla O'Donovan
and Kathy Glavanis-Grantham

CORK UNIVERSITY PRESS

First published in 2008 by
Cork University Press
Youngline Industrial Estate
Pouladuff Road, Togher
Cork, Ireland

British Library Cataloguing in Publication Data
A CIP catalogue record for this book is available from the British Library.

ISBN 978-1-85918-419-6

Typesetting by Red Barn Publishing, Skeagh, Skibbereen, Co. Cork
Printed by ColourBooks Ltd., Baldoyle, Dublin

www.corkuniversitypress.com

Published with the support of the Arts Faculty, University College Cork and the National
University of Ireland

The editors gratefully acknowledge permission to publish a modified version of the article, 'Is
Australia's National Medicines Policy Failing? The Case of COX-2 Inhibitors' by Agnes Vitry, Joel
Lexchin and Peter R. Mansfield originally published in *International Journal of Health Services*, vol.
37, no. 4, 2007, pp. 735–744.

CONTENTS

Acronyms

ABPI	Association of British Pharmaceutical Industry
ADRs	Adverse drug reactions
CHM	Commission on Human Medicines (Britain)
CSM	Committee on Safety of Medicines (Britain)
DoHC	Department of Health and Children (Ireland)
DPS	Drugs Payment Scheme (Ireland)
DTCA	Direct to Consumer Advertising
EMEA	European Agency for the Evaluation of Medicinal Products
EU	European Union
FDA	Food and Drug Administration (USA)
GATS	General Agreement on Trade in Services
GATT	General Agreement on Tariffs and Trade
GMS	General Medical Service (Ireland)
GP	General practitioner
HIV	Human Immunodeficiency Virus
HSE	Health Services Executive (Ireland)
ICH	International Conference on Harmonisation of Technical Requirements for Registration of Pharmaceuticals for Human Use
IDA	Industrial Development Authority (Ireland)
IFPMA	International Federation of Pharmaceutical Manufacturers' Associations
IMB	Irish Medicines Board
IMF	International Monetary Fund
IP	Intellectual property
IPHA	Irish Pharmaceutical Healthcare Association
MCA	Medicines Control Agency (Britain)
MHRA	Medicines and Healthcare Products Regulatory Agency (Britain)
NDA	New Drug Application
NDAB	National Drugs Advisory Board (Ireland)
NGOs	Non-governmental organisations
NMEs	New molecular entities

NSAID	Non-Steroidal Anti-Inflammatory Drug
OECD	Organisation for Economic Co-operation and Development
OTC	Over the counter medicines
PHARM	Pharmaceutical Health and Rational Use of Medicines (Australia)
PhRMA	Pharmaceutical Research and Manufacturers of America
R&D	Research and development
SSRIs	Selective Serotonin Re-uptake Inhibitors
TGA	Therapeutic Goods Administration (Australia)
TNCs	Transnational corporations
TPD	Therapeutic Products Directorate (Canada)
TPI	Transnational pharmaceutical industry
TRIPs	Trade-Related Aspects of Intellectual Property Rights Agreement
WIPO	World Intellectual Property Organisation
WTO	World Trade Organisation

INTRODUCTION

Orla O'Donovan

Aims and arguments of the book

In December 2003, Niall O'Mahony took his own life in what his wife, Nuria, believes was a drug-induced suicide. Following a bout of mild depression, Niall was prescribed the antidepressant Seroxat, and thirteen days later he was dead. Driven by the conviction that the antidepressant played a role in the deterioration of Niall's health, culminating in his suicide, Nuria began an Irish campaign for stricter state regulation of SSRIs (Selective Serotonin Re-uptake Inhibitors, the group of antidepressants that includes Seroxat) and, more generally, for greater public awareness of the potential harmful effects of pharmaceutical drugs.[1] This is just one of a number of similar campaigns that have been mobilised internationally due to apprehensions about the safety of SSRIs. Equally, the dispute about SSRIs is just one example of a drug controversy that has generated public concern about the safety of medicines. The controversy over rofecoxib (Vioxx), the arthritis drug and painkiller withdrawn from the global market in 2004 that by some accounts had an estimated death toll in the US alone of over 35,000 people, is a further case in point.[2] By the time Vioxx was withdrawn from the market, it was earning its manufacturer, Merck, $2.5 billion a year.[3] Campaigns mounted by people harmed by drugs form just one strand of a broader field of political mobilisation that is intensifying around the globe, provoked by concerns about regulation of the pharmaceutical industry.[4] Paradoxically, these concerns centre on the over-consumption of medicines of dubious benefit in Western societies, the 'pharmaceuticalisation of life',[5] and lack of access to essential medicines in the Global South, which constitutes a 'war on the poor'.[6] This collection of essays both reflects on and aims to contribute to the growing attention being paid to the power relations and political processes that have led to this paradoxical state of affairs.

Nuria O'Mahony's campaign received considerable attention from the Irish mass media. An article in *The Irish Times,* published on 28 June 2005,

1

detailed some of the specific changes called for by O'Mahony; these include greater monitoring of the way in which SSRIs are prescribed in Ireland, public access to full and impartial information about their potential adverse effects, public access to full clinical trial data and the establishment of a public pharmacovigilance[7] system that would allow users of medicines to report adverse reactions directly. Furthermore, she called for the establishment of a new regulatory body, separate from the existing regulatory authority, the Irish Medicines Board (IMB), that would differ in its source funding; namely, that it would be wholly publicly funded rather than derive its income from fees paid by pharmaceutical corporations. This campaign succeeded in attracting the support of some influential and what some may regard as improbable allies. The article reported the endorsement of the campaign in respect of SSRIs by Pat Bracken, a consultant psychiatrist. Bracken added: 'As medical practitioners, I feel we need to become more aware of how corporate interests can sometimes dominate agendas within medicine, in a way that isn't necessarily always in the best interest of patients.' The article concluded with a response from the IMB to the concerns raised in respect of Seroxat; a spokesperson stated that the IMB had participated in a series of reviews of Seroxat through its membership of the European Agency for the Evaluation of Medicinal Products (EMEA), the EU agency established in 1995 to coordinate the evaluation and supervision of pharmaceuticals throughout Europe. The conclusion of these reviews, completed in April 2004, was that the benefits of Seroxat outweighed the risks associated with the use of the product.

This single newspaper article about Nuria O'Mahony's campaign encapsulates the central questions explored in this collection of essays; namely, what are the implications for health of existing systems of pharmaceutical drug regulation, and what do the systems of drug regulation in Ireland and internationally reveal about the power of transnational pharmaceutical corporations to shape regulatory and other policies? The article also highlights some of the main players in the politics of drug regulation who are the subject of analysis; these actors, organisations and institutions include drug regulatory agencies at the nation state and supranational levels, pharmaceutical corporations, patients or the users of medicines, medical professionals, and social movements and user groups who strive to have an impact on regulatory policies. Other players can be added to this list, including supranational bodies with a broader regulatory remit, such as the World Trade Organisation, governments, journalists and the mass media.

The assembled chapters are written by an international and multidisciplinary group of contributors with varying perspectives, but all of whom question aspects of existing systems of medicines regulation. The analyses of trends in medicines regulation offered by many of the contributors resemble the argument developed by Ivan Illich in his classic text on modern biomedicine, in which he points to its paradoxical counterproductivity.[8] Just as Illich sought to reveal how many modern institutions end up taking away from society the very things they claim to provide, several of the essays here consider how medicines regulation has come to put people's health in jeopardy rather than protect it. In addition to contributions from people in disciplines conventionally associated with publications about drug regulation, such as medicine, pharmacology and pharmacoeconomics, the volume also includes chapters written by social scientists. Some of the contributors cross these disciplinary boundaries and the analysis of others is informed by their involvement in health advocacy organisations, such as Health Action International[9] and Healthy Skepticism[10].

The volume is primarily focused on the analysis of pharmaceutical drug regulation in the Republic of Ireland, a country that has embraced neo-liberalism to such an extent that in the early years of the twenty-first century it was deemed to be the most 'globalised' of all economies and the fifth 'freest' economy in the world (see the chapter in this volume by O'Hearn and McCloskey). A low corporate tax rate, combined with government initiatives such as ensuring the availability of well-serviced industrial sites with high 'assimilative capacity' (i.e. effluent disposal facilities), have made Ireland a very attractive location in recent decades for footloose transnational corporation investment.[11] In 2005, eighty-three foreign-owned pharmaceutical companies had bases in Ireland, including fourteen of the world's largest fifteen corporations.[12] These foreign corporations, which accounted for 93 per cent of pharmaceutical industry employment in 2003, dominate the sector. Ireland is also a country that has witnessed a dramatic expansion in patienthood, evident in the escalation of the consumption of medicines by more and more people for a widening array of health conditions. Public expenditure on medicines has grown dramatically in Ireland in recent years, and by 2005 it exceeded 15 per cent of total state spending on healthcare. The public drug bill grew by over 600 per cent between 1993 and 2005 and significant proportions of this expenditure were for medications lacking a strong 'scientific evidence base' supporting their use (see the chapter by Barry,

Tilson and Ryan in this volume). Critical analysis of the Irish regulatory regime requires broader contextualisation and is enriched by reference to debates in social theory and comparisons with drug regulation systems elsewhere. The volume is structured in such a way that the discussion moves from the global to the Irish context, and then, having familiarised the reader with the situation in Ireland, provides commentaries on the drug regulation systems in three other countries that serve as comparators. We begin with three chapters on the theme 'Globalisation, Power and the Politics of Science'. In this first section, theoretical debates about the nature of capitalist globalisation, the alleged eclipsing of the nation state by supranational authorities, neo-liberalism, the power of transnational corporations and the distinctive features of 'scientific' knowledge are surveyed. These debates provide a backdrop for the analysis of sites for resisting corporate power (O'Hearn and McCloskey), the pharmaceutical industry's success in formulating a new normative framework that has shaped international intellectual property law (Downes), and evidence of bias towards the commercial interests of the pharmaceutical industry in the science of drug regulation (Abraham).

In the second section, 'Medicines Regulation in Ireland: Health and Democracy at Risk?', five chapters address aspects of the Irish regulatory system. Here, contributors consider the historical resituating of the Irish state in respect of protecting the public from unsafe medicines and the emergence of 'regulation for competition' (O'Donovan), and the context within which the pharmaceutical industry in Ireland has come to play a prominent role in the economy and the wider society (Glavanis-Grantham). Explanations for the dramatic escalation in drug consumption and public expenditure on medicines in Ireland are addressed (Barry, Tilson and Ryan), as is the entanglement of the medical profession and the pharmaceutical industry (Bradley) and the dominance of drug-based mental healthcare (Lynch).

The third section, 'Controversy and Change: Medicines Regulation in Canada, Britain and Australia', contains three chapters that trace altercations about drug regulation in three Western countries. The first of these considers how the push for 'smart regulation' has resulted in the reorientation of the Canadian regulatory system in favour of the interests of private industry (Lexchin), whereas the second considers how the 'stink' about SSRIs revealed serious deficiencies and triggered a reshaping of the British regulatory regime (Herxheimer). The final chapter examines how the Australian drug regulation system failed to protect citizens from the

Vioxx drug disaster (Vitry, Lexchin and Mansfield) and provides a salutary discussion of the core elements of the drugs policy necessary if we want to avoid similar disasters in the future.

This is by no means an exhaustive overview of contemporary debates about pharmaceutical drug regulation. We do not, for example, consider the industry's compliance with environmental regulations, which in recent times has been shown to be lax; for example, a Shannon-based company, Schwarz Pharma, was fined in 2006 for eleven breaches of its pollution control licence that included air emissions containing thirty-five times the legal limit of a suspected cancer-causing substance.[13] However, we hope there is ample stimulus in these pages to contribute to the imagination of alternative and better ways of regulating medicines.

High time for public debate about medicines regulation

In the foreword to the Irish government's 2002 public consultation document, *Towards Better Regulation,* the Taoiseach, Bertie Ahern, states: 'Very little debate has taken place so far in Ireland about how regulation is made, who is best placed to regulate, what makes a bad law, what might constitute a good law and what other tools exist for the achievement of policy goals.'[14] Pharmaceutical drug regulation is an extreme example of this absence of debate. With some notable exceptions,[15] internationally pharmaceutical drug regulation has not attracted the attention of many social scientists, despite the widespread and dramatic increase in the consumption of pharmaceutical industry products, both drugs and so called 'health literacy' messages. The scarcity of critical commentaries on medicines regulation and the pharmaceutical industry in Ireland is particularly remarkable, given the country's economic reliance on the industry (by 2005, 44 per cent of the country's annual exports were pharmaceutical industry products[16]).

There are a number of possible explanations for the poverty of public debate about medicines regulation in Ireland, not least of which is that secrecy pervades this policy domain. The enactment of a freedom of information law in 1997 opened up the policy process to greater scrutiny, but the exemption of 'commercially sensitive' information, which prioritises private property rights over democratic rights, is a serious limitation. Another explanation is the tendency in the Irish public's imagination to view the pharmaceutical industry as a wholly positive force in Irish society and further afield. The pharmaceutical industry has been central to the transformation of the Irish economy into one of Europe's 'star performers' in terms of growth rates, evident in the fact that in 2005 Ireland was the biggest net exporter of pharmaceuticals in the world. Celebrities who champion 'conscientious commerce' and argue that the profit motive can be harnessed to redress global inequities in access to medicines have contributed to the now pervasive denial of the inherent conflicts between the goals of corporate wealth and public health.[17]

The low level of democratic deliberation in general in Irish society is a further explanation for the poverty of public debate about drug regulation, a feature of Irish life that the Democracy Commission views as being intensified by the concentration of media ownership.[18] In 2002 approximately 80 per cent of Irish newspapers sold in Ireland were sold by companies which are fully or partially owned by one 'media giant', Independent Newspapers PLC. The increasing privatisation of healthcare, together with the restructuring of the health services in 2005 (that involved the replacement of ten regional health boards, which had a majority of local public representatives, by the single Health Services Executive, all of whose members are ministerial appointees), are also identified by the Democracy Commission as changes that have further weakened the public accountability and transparency of state healthcare, with the latter contributing to increased executive dominance and the bolstering of what the journalist John Healy referred to as 'the permanent government'. But perhaps the strongest explanation for the lack of public debate about medicines regulation is that it is a realm of public policy that is intensely 'scientized'.[19] It is widely represented as a policy domain in which power and politics are sublimated and replaced by apolitical technical scientific knowledge. Such technocratic representations of policy-making undermine a role for citizens who lack specialist scientific expertise. As many contributors to this volume argue, drug regulation epitomises this technocratic construction of the policy process. However, campaigners such as Nuria O'Mahony and advocacy organisations that call for a radical rethinking of drug regulation bring the ethical and political dimensions of drug regulation to public attention. By demonstrating how the analysis of pharmaceutical drug regulation can provide rich insights into the operation of power and politics in contemporary society, this book challenges the prevailing construction of drug regulation as a sphere of 'policy without politics'.[20]

PART ONE

Globalisation, Power and the Politics of Science

CHAPTER I

Globalisation and Pharmaceuticals:
Where is the Power? Where to Resist?

Denis O'Hearn and Stephen McCloskey

Introduction

It has become common knowledge that we are living in an era of globalisation, in which the numbers and importance of international relations and networks that we all experience exceed previous historical periods. Like most common knowledges, however, there is little agreement or even understanding of what this means (or even questioning about whether it is actually true). Yet the character of global institutions and processes has an essential impact on the exercise of power and how power affects different regions, social groups and classes. In the context of the international pharmaceutical industry, globalisation affects (1) the developmental trajectories of regions or countries within which large transnational drug companies operate and (2) the ability of regions and groups within regions to access drugs as well as different forms of healthcare within which certain drugs may or may not be a component. It *matters,* for example, whether certain kinds of power reside in transnational corporations, nation states, or global institutions, because different policy outcomes that arise from the exercise of power are literally matters of life and death for billions of people across the globe.

Our first question about globalisation, therefore, is whether it is a historically new phase in the history of capitalism and, if so, what is its nature? Robinson argues that globalisation is a distinct new 'epoch of modern world history' after monopoly capitalism. Not only has the tempo of change speeded up and the global scope of change intensified, but also the chief loci of power under globalisation have now transcended the nation state. Economic globalisation has created the material basis for the 'emergence of a single global society, marked by the transnationalization of civil society and political processes, the global integration of social life, and a global culture'.[1] Robinson thus takes things much further than Sklair,[2] who develops a concept of a global capitalist class. He insists that the unification of the world into a single mode of production and the organic integration of regions/countries into a single global economy means that we should stop using the nation state as a unit of analysis, as it has been transcended and superseded by 'a truly transnational social structure'.[3] Economic activities (such as the production and distribution of drugs) are global; economic and political elites are global rather than nation-based; and, most importantly, political systems and civil societies have become transnationalised. Although social movements may lag behind, they must recognise the global character of power institutions or they will focus their activities on the wrong targets. States have become integrated externally into supranational institutions and forums that are assuming more and more functions that used to be in the domain of the nation state.[4] Thus, not only is capital international, but its regulation is international and the only way social movements and user groups can have an impact on regulation and other policies is by addressing institutions at that global level.

Other perspectives, however, argue that analyses such as Robinson's underestimate the degree to which the nation state remains a key structure through which globalisation is managed and enforced. For example, those who refer to 'hegemony' within the context of the world-system analyse how certain countries aspire to and collect overwhelming power in the global polity and economy, and how they exercise this power on behalf of corporations and corporate sectors which, in turn, reinforce their economic power.[5] Key trade agreements are sponsored and imposed primarily by powerful nations, particularly the US, and in the interests of 'their' corporations. In extreme cases, wars are fought against those who interfere with economic expansion from the hegemon. Moreover, although the economic structures of regions have been transformed towards so-called 'transnational' forms like 'maquiladora'[6] manufacturing and non-traditional agricultural exports that are embedded in global commodity chains, the transnational corporations (TNCs) that are involved in these commodity chains retain a national character to the degree that their key activities are located in core states and their global activities are supported and protected by their sponsor governments (particularly the US).[7] Many key economic relations that appear to be global actually have national or bilateral characters. Not only are bilateral or regional trade agreements still important, but also international agencies may act primarily, if not exclusively, in the interest of key nation states and their corporations.

Strategies

The debate over the loci of power raises a more concrete question: what are the key elements of globalisation? Here, we may speak of institutions and of strategies. There is some agreement that the key strategy of the current phase of globalisation is a set of policies that have become known as the 'Washington Consensus'. Economist John Williamson coined this phrase in 1990 to refer to policies being promoted (or, in some cases, imposed) in Latin-American countries by Washington-based international institutions including the International Monetary Fund (IMF), the World Bank and US administrations (both Democrat and Republican).[8] While there is debate about how this 'consensus' is defined, it usually includes the following:

- Fiscal discipline (reduced public spending, balanced budgets, paying off public debt)
- Redirecting public expenditures away from social welfare and local subsidies
- Reducing tax rates
- Liberalising interest rates and exchange rates
- Free trade
- Liberalising inflows of foreign direct investment
- Privatising public companies (including services and utilities)
- Deregulating corporate activities
- Securing private property rights[9]

To this list of essential elements of the Washington Consensus, we may also add policies that create 'flexible labour markets' by reducing workers' rights/protection.

The phrase 'Washington Consensus' is often used interchangeably with the phrase 'neo-liberal policies'. Although Williamson insists that he never intended this when he coined the term, there is a clear connection between his list of policies under the Washington Consensus and the essential elements of neo-liberalism, including the deregulation of business, monetarist economics, and reducing the state's role in welfare provision, income redistribution and the provision of services and basic goods such as energy (privatisation). The Washington Consensus clearly intends to advance the role of markets at the expense of social institutions.

In providing a high level of freedom to market participants, particularly to transnational corporations and financial institutions, it advantages the preferences of those firms over the general preferences of the public.

Critics claim that the economic process encompassed under the Washington Consensus forces poor countries to reduce tariffs and barriers to trade. To pay for Western imports and loans, their governments must cut spending on welfare and social services while privatising public utilities. According to the Jubilee Debt Campaign,[10] the total external debt of low-income countries is $523 billion (€433 billion), with $100 billion (€83 billion) being paid every day in debt servicing. Africa's total external debt is approximately £300 billion (€451 billion), with many African states spending more on debt servicing than on health or education. For example, Zambia's debt repayments to the IMF alone total £25 million (€38 million), which exceeds its education budget, despite 40 per cent illiteracy rates among rural women.[11]

Meanwhile, many African states are contending with a worsening HIV/AIDS problem. The UN estimates that 25 million people in Africa are living with HIV out of a global total of 37.8 million.[12] The AIDS crisis, therefore, looks set to compound the problems created by debt servicing. According to UNAIDS, an additional $22 billion (18.2 billion) is needed by 2008 to combat the spread of AIDS in the developing world, but with many basic medicines already beyond the reach of the poorest peoples in regions like sub-Saharan Africa, the HIV/AIDS crisis will worsen without meaningful debt cancellation.[13] Debt is siphoning off invaluable economic resources required by the poorest countries for the detection and prevention of AIDS and provision of appropriate treatment for the virus. External debt is also reducing the impact of overseas development aid. For every dollar (€0.82) that is received in grants by donors in the developed world, poor countries return $2.30 (€1.90) in debt repayments.[14] The conclusions of this statistic are clear: if poor countries pay more than double their level of incoming aid on debt repayments, they will struggle to introduce development programmes that will address significant deficits in expenditure on health and education. Debt cancellation is therefore an essential first step in enabling poor countries to expand their economies and address their social needs.[15] This situation has often been worsened where countries compete for transnational corporate investments. Many deregulate corporate activities with regard to the environment and otherwise in order to attract or retain investment projects.

Together, the effects of these economic policies have accentuated inequalities between developed and developing countries, while impeding the capacity of poor nations to introduce meaningful development programmes through investment in vital areas, including health and education.[16] As a result, the incidence of poverty has increased to a level where, according to the United Nations *Human Development Report* (HDR), 1.2 billion of the world's people live on less than $1 a day; 2.4 billion people lack basic sanitation; and 11 million children under five die each year from preventable causes, the equivalent of 30,000 a day.[17] Yet, even in comparatively wealthy countries like the Irish Republic, dependence on foreign investment has forced governments to create an attractive environment for investors by adhering strictly to 'sound macroeconomic policies', which often means that they severely curtail public spending on health, education, housing and social welfare.

Institutions

The major institutions that enforce this increasing global inequality run from the large transnational corporations and banks, in whose interests the system is maintained, to a series of international institutions that are managed jointly (perhaps primarily) by the United States along with other Western powers.

The literature on transnational corporations (TNCs) is so vast and familiar that it hardly bears a lengthy review here. TNCs have assumed increasing economic wealth and political influence in the period of renewed globalisation since the end of the Cold War. TNCs are companies that have holdings or operations in more than one country, but are usually headquartered in one of the leading developed countries in North America, Europe or Japan. Because of the dispersed nature of their activities and, even, their directors, it is debatable whether or not TNCs have essentially transcended identity with nation states. Sklair and Robinson, for example, argue that there is now a transnational capitalist class and, therefore, that it makes no sense to speak of 'US capital' or 'Japanese capital'. Their apparent power is reflected in the fact that many leading TNCs boast an annual sales turnover in excess of the national incomes of mid-size developed countries. Others, however, believe that TNCs are still quite rooted in nation states and that they often call on their sponsorship and protection where necessary to maintain market access or to obtain raw materials or labour power. Again, the nature of corporate power is important for movements and states that might want to regulate TNCs or to get around their controls over the distribution of key products such as important drugs. Key concerns regarding TNCs include the treatment of their workers, particularly where exploitative practices include excessively long shifts and low wages; preventing the unionisation of staff, especially in so-called industrial processing zones where labour-intensive industries often exploit female workers; the relocation of TNC profits from developing countries to headquarters or tax havens; breaching environment and labour standards in developing countries; engaging in biopiracy (the theft of native knowledge and genetic resources) and accessing resources without sufficient compensation; and relocating their operations from one country to another, thus creating unemployment and economic depression.

The pharmaceutical industry is highly globalised (both in terms of production and distribution). The industry is also concentrated among a relatively few giant companies. Not only do the largest ten transnational pharmaceutical companies control nearly half of the world market for drugs, in 2002 the sector also had the highest average profit rates of any major manufacturing sector in the world (Table 1.1). This makes these companies very powerful globally, but it also means that they can have strong and even distorting social and economic effects in the regions where they operate.

The Republic of Ireland, for example, is the key producing and exporting region in Europe for most of the transnational drugs producers. Along with computers and software, the rapidly growing activities of pharmaceutical companies there since 1990 have been largely responsible for its emergence as the 'Celtic Tiger', the most rapid-growth economy in the Organisation for Economic Co-operation and Development (OECD) since 1994. Indeed, although computers and software have been more high profile in the Irish media, output growth in pharmaceuticals has been nearly twice as rapid as in those sectors (over 20 per cent since 1997). By 2004, the (overwhelmingly US-owned) drug industry in Ireland was the largest net exporter of medicines in the world, exporting drugs worth €13.3 billion each year. On the surface, US computer and pharmaceutical companies appear to have made Ireland extremely wealthy: in terms of Gross Domestic Product (GDP) per capita it was the second wealthiest country in the European Union by 2004. On the other hand, Ireland was also by far the most distorted economy in the EU if not in the world. Gross *National* Product (GDP *minus* repatriated transnational corporate profits) is nearly a quarter less than GDP. Thus,

Table 1.1. Top ten pharmaceutical companies, 2002

Company	Sales (US Millions) 2002	Profit Margin 2002	% Share of World Market
1. Pfizer/Pharmacia	$42,281	46% (Pfizer only)	12%
2. Glaxo Smith Kline	$26,979	29%	8%
3. Merck & Co. (incl. Warner Lambert)	$21,631	47%	6%
4. AstraZeneca	$17,841	22%	5%
5. Johnson & Johnson	$17,151	34%	5%
6. Aventis	$15,705	19%	5%
7. Bristol-Myers Squibb	$14,705	16%	4%
8. Novartis	$13,497	29%	4%
9. Hoffman-La Roche	$12,630	19%	4%
10. Wyeth	$12,387	28%	4%

Source: ETC Group (2003); based on data provided by Scrip's Pharmaceutical League Table, 2003.

a major part of the fruits of rapid growth simply leak abroad, up to half of it to pharmaceutical companies alone. In terms of actual *national* wealth, then, Ireland is much less wealthy than it appears to be. It is much closer to Spain than to Luxembourg.

Nor are TNCs normal in their productive structures. Pharmaceutical companies, especially, are very capital intensive and hire little labour. In Ireland, the wage bill in the sector is less than 5 per cent of sales. One extreme case is Pfizer, whose introduction of one Irish-produced product, Viagra, led in 1996/97 to a 70 per cent rise in the country's output of organic chemicals without adding a single new worker.[18] Thus, the Irish-based (but US-owned) pharmaceutical sector appears to be extremely dynamic, rapidly growing and largely responsible for the fact that Ireland is considered to be such a successful model of economic development.

On the other hand, the southern Irish state has introduced extreme neo-liberal measures to attract companies such as Pfizer. In order to become the 'most globalised economy in the world',[19] Ireland has introduced policies that make it the fifth 'freest' economy in the world (according to the Heritage Foundation/*Wall Street Journal* 2005). These anti-interventionist policies include a near tax-free corporate environment (profits taxes are 12.5 per cent compared to 30–40 per cent on average throughout the EU), deregulation, fiscal conservatism, and so on – in short, most of the characteristics of the 'Washington Consensus' are found in Ireland. As a result, successive Irish governments have been either unwilling or unable to use newly created wealth on behalf of the Irish people. The country has the lowest per student spend on primary education and at the end of the 1990s it had the second lowest per capita expenditure on health in the EU.[20] Despite the fact that it exports more drugs than any country in the world and the fact that Irish pharmacies' profit rates are the highest in the EU, Irish people spend nearly a third less per person on medicines than the European average.[21] Moreover, during the period of the Celtic Tiger (since 1994), Ireland has experienced rapidly growing inequality, poverty rates and rates of homelessness. It is now the second most unequal country in the OECD, with the second highest poverty rates.[22]

While the size and corporate power of the giant pharmaceutical companies can have a significant impact on the regions where they locate their production, a particularly important aspect of TNC behaviour with respect to drug access and regulation is their ability to control or distort local markets in ways that contradict social welfare. Within the World Trade Organization, for instance, they engage political lobbyists and lawyers to argue their case for the further relaxation of trade barriers and easing of national legislation that protects local markets. With the support of leading Western countries, they promote global trade legislation like the General Agreement on Trade in Services (GATS)[23] that aims to open up public utilities and services to private takeover (see below). The implementation of GATS would be disastrous for poorer countries where severe shortages of clean water, medicines and sanitation are already resulting in high rates of infant mortality, shorter life expectancies and increased poverty.

The question of how to regulate the activities of TNCs preoccupies many non-governmental organisations (NGOs), social movements and even states. Evidence from the World Development Movement suggests that many of the leading corporations contravene international labour standards and environmental protection codes. Therefore, it has called for independent monitoring of TNCs and enforcement of sanctions against offending companies by an international body with teeth, such as the International Labour Organization. They and other NGOs have also called for the introduction of binding global regulations that properly police TNC activities under the auspices of an International Investment Treaty that promotes 'quality investment and core standards for corporate responsibility'.[24] Unfortunately, the track record of international institutions, which have gained in strength under globalisation, has had the opposite effect: promoting rather than regulating transnational corporate power.

International financial institution

The IMF and the World Bank

The Bretton Woods Institutions, the International Monetary Fund (IMF) and the World Bank, were established in 1944 to support post-war rehabilitation and promote international trade. These bodies have been the vanguard of globalisation for almost sixty years, primarily through the disbursement of conditional loans to developing countries. The World Bank was charged at Bretton Woods with providing longer-term loans to developing countries to support their development, while the IMF was given the role of supporting an orderly international monetary system. The rhetoric of Bretton Woods promised greater development for poor countries, but the reality of IMF and World Bank policies has been an orchestrated economic indebtedness throughout the Third World.

While the IMF has been integral to the 'bonanza' of irresponsible borrowing by Third World countries in the 1970s that sowed the seeds of today's crippling debt crisis, the World Bank has largely been associated with high-profile development projects such as dam construction. These projects are often developed without consulting local people in the areas most affected by reconstruction, yet the Bank considers the poor to be the primary beneficiaries of its policies. Many World Bank programmes, which regularly involve the disbursement of valuable construction contracts to Western corporations, have been highly insensitive to the needs of the poor. The operations of the World Bank and the IMF exacerbate poverty levels in the developing world because they fail to address the specific economic and social needs of poor countries. Instead they attempt to impose a 'one size fits all' solution to underdevelopment based on the ideology that the interests of giant corporations are equivalent to the interests of poor nations and that the strong medicine of neo-liberalism is the only solution to slow economic growth in developing countries.

A key difficulty with the current IMF/World Bank structures is their dominance by leading developed countries, particularly the United States, and by leading corporations in those countries. This scenario ensures that IMF/World Bank policies strategically favour the interests of the developed world and maintains the dominance of its economic hegemony over alternative models of development. The democratisation of the IMF/World Bank is an absolute prerequisite to social and economic development in Third World countries. It is important that developing countries play a full and equal role in determining how multilateral finance and development programmes are rolled out in the Third World. This can only be achieved through a democratisation of the international financial institutions and a genuine commitment to partnership by developed countries with the developing world.

World Trade Organization

The triumvirate of key international financial institutions was completed in 1995 by the establishment of the World Trade Organization (WTO), which effectively controls the policy agenda for global trade. The WTO was established as a successor to the General Agreement on Tariffs and Trade (GATT) with the aim of deregulating trade and rolling back state protection of markets. While GATT only dealt with manufactured products, the WTO's remit includes agriculture, services and intellectual property rights.

The WTO is an institution with teeth. It has the power to arbitrate in trading disputes between its members and, if necessary, impose sanctions on nations in breach of its regulations. Moreover, in negotiating and implementing the rules of global trade, the WTO has enormous influence over the economic development of Third World countries. Many development NGOs consider the WTO an undemocratic institution designed to bully poor countries into accepting agreements that will damage their economies. With 151 members, the WTO should, in theory, arrive at decisions favouring developing countries, which represent a majority of members and some 80 per cent of the world's population. In practice, however, negotiations are mostly conducted behind closed doors with developing country representatives confronted by a plethora of experts and consultants who specialise in one area of policy.

Almost half of the world's poorest countries are not represented at the

WTO headquarters in Geneva, while developed countries can ensure permanent representation as well as drawing on other experts during negotiations on specific issues.[25] The imbalance in negotiations is reflected in the unfair agreements reached in the WTO despite the democratic pledges and language used by the organisation in public. The bruising exchanges in negotiations result in poorer nations being arm-twisted into bad agreements.

The September 2003 WTO Ministerial Council meeting held in Cancun, Mexico, collapsed in acrimony and underlined the need for a reconfiguration of WTO operations. Developing countries are particularly concerned at the millions of dollars of subsidies given to farmers in Western countries. These subsidies result in the flooding of markets in the developing world with cheap produce that undercuts local commodities and puts local farmers and producers out of business. According to the United Nations (UN), this form of protectionism in developed countries costs the Third World an export income of $2 billion a day, which is many times more than the total inflows of aid. Poor countries rightly point to the anomaly of developed countries urging deregulation and proclaiming the advantages of free trade, while protecting their own agricultural markets from developing world imports. For example, cheap maize imports from the US into Mexico have wiped out the livelihoods of small-scale Mexican farmers, while maize prices received for exports have been halved.[26]

Another point of contention at Cancun were plans to introduce new investment laws known as the 'Singapore Issues' to the WTO agenda. These issues include new proposed agreements in:

- Investment – designed to undermine the capacity of governments to regulate foreign investors in areas like manufacturing and agriculture
- Competition policy – with the aim of enhancing market access in the developing world to transnational corporations
- Transparency in government procurement – which will require countries to publish details of government procurement contracts
- Trade facilitation agreement – which will require countries to improve their customs procedures.[27]

If introduced, these agreements would further undermine developing countries' control over inward investments and prevent their full participation in the WTO, which would be bogged down in 'regulatory spaghetti'. It was, therefore, highly significant to see the Singapore Issues defeated at Cancun by a new coalition of poorer countries, the G20+, which has the potential to act as a progressive counterbalance in trade negotiations against the policies of the powerful G8 countries, led by the United States.

International (multilateral) agreements
GATS
Towards the end of the 1990s, the WTO attempted to introduce a new privatisation agreement called the Multilateral Agreement on Investment (MAI), which offered virtual economic impunity to TNCs investing in developing countries. The MAI was defeated in December 1998 through the vigorous and sustained campaigning efforts of hundreds of NGOs around the world, but its privatising agenda has been resurrected in the guise of the General Agreement on Trade in Services (GATS). The aim of GATS is to remove any restrictions and internal government regulations in the area of service delivery that are considered to be 'barriers to trade'.[28] In other words, GATS will identify hitherto public services that are liable to privatisation and ownership by corporations.

The services vulnerable to privatisation under the GATS agreement include education, health, and municipal services such as the supply of water. The main danger for the poor lies in public services becoming profit-making entities under the control of TNCs that will demand payment at the point of delivery. It is likely that the quality of essential services will steadily decline without government intervention and be priced beyond the reach of the poorest communities in developing countries.

Like many other issues related to globalisation, GATS is not just an issue for the 'developing countries'. It has also been used in the EU to drive an agenda towards privatising public services so that they can be taken over by profit-making private companies against the interests of those who most need the services. In February 2003, the European Commission announced its intention to further open postal, environmental, telecommunications, retail, transport and financial services to foreign competition. It was only the protests of a strong alliance of trade unions and other campaigners that stopped the Commission from making further commitments to apply the free trade rules of GATS to health and education in the EU countries. Nevertheless, privatisation is being brought into health and education by the Irish and British governments even in the absence of EU regulations.

In Ireland, north and south, Public Private Partnerships (PPPs) and Private Finance Initiatives (PFIs) are facilitating the private takeover of schools and hospitals.

The same privatising agenda is at work in both local and international contexts. GATS is meeting strong opposition in the WTO from developing countries and around the world from civil society movements and NGOs. Successes in 2004/05 of grassroots campaigns against water and gas privatisation in Latin-American countries such as Bolivia and Uruguay provide some hope.

TRIPs

The control of international markets by TNCs and their increasing foothold in the economies of developing countries are also underpinned by the Agreement on Trade-Related Intellectual Property Rights (TRIPs), one of the main outcomes of the Uruguay Round of trade talks.[29]

TRIPs is a particularly insidious and damaging agreement for developing countries because it enables TNCs 'to patent life forms and genetic sequences and increases corporate control over access to seeds, which is a vital issue in developing countries'.[30] TRIPs patenting rights include vital resources such as medicines and agricultural seeds that are indigenous to the Global South. This agreement effectively represents the economic piracy of eco-systems in developing countries whereby corporations assume intellectual ownership of resources indigenous to poor countries. These resources are patented by TNCs and then marketed as 'new' corporate products, which means that developing countries are being invited to buy back their own intellectual property at inflated prices.

TRIPs enables Western-based corporations to monopolise new technologies and stifle indigenous industrial development in developing countries. Most crucially, however, this agreement will hinder food and commodity production, and exacerbate medicinal shortages in developing countries. Countries have difficulty producing cheaper generic drugs[31] even where they would save thousands of people, because doing so would violate the intellectual property rights of giant pharmaceutical companies. With the spiralling AIDS crisis reaching epidemic proportions in many parts of the Global South, the TRIPs agreement has already caused thousands of deaths. By protecting intellectual property, it has kept the price of life-saving drugs beyond what poorer countries can pay in order to save the lives of their citizens.

The stated rationale behind TRIPs is that the research and development costs behind many new products such as drugs is so high that the companies that bear these costs must secure inflated returns for a new product over a certain number of years in order to make the research worthwhile. Thus, a drug company must have a patent guarantee for twenty years or they will not invest in the development and testing processes that must precede a new drug's entry into the market.[32] This thinking, however, creates a further problem in drugs access because it privatises the research process and ensures that only drugs that are demanded in wealthy countries with large potential markets will be developed. As Velásquez points out, under the privatised research environment of the past twenty years, hardly any research has gone into developing drugs for diseases that affect mainly poor people of the Global South, such as Chagas' disease, schistosomiasis or sleeping sickness.[33]

Another key threat posed by TRIPs is against global biodiversity. The world's biodiversity is concentrated in a surprisingly small group of areas in the world that also coincides with the areas of highest indigenous cultural diversity. This coincidence of some of the world's most valuable resources in areas that are populated by the world's least powerful people has disastrous outcomes. The world's richest nations and their giant corporations, protected by international agreements such as TRIPs, have been responsible for biopiracy in these fragile zones while, ironically, supporting their ruination by deforestation and the intrusion of cattle ranching and other damaging practices. Their power to do so has been enhanced by regional trade agreements such as the North American Free Trade Agreement, and by the neo-liberal policies that local governments have followed in order to abide by these agreements. The Lacandon Jungle in southern Mexico, for instance, has the world's highest concentration of biodiversity and an impressive store of indigenous knowledge about its uses. Yet, its biodiversity and the lives of its inhabitants have been threatened by changes to the Mexican constitution,[34] made in preparation for joining NAFTA, which removed the rights of indigenous people to communal lands, rights that had been guaranteed since the Mexican revolution.

The interplay between vanishing bio resources, life-dominating new technologies and the emergence of ever more powerful concentrations of economic control is driving social and political change around the globe. 'New technologies' lean heavily on biological materials, yet their use is regulated not by the good of the indigenous custodians of bio resources or even by the wider public good, but by the requirements of private profits through the patent system and the protection of intellectual property rights. Aided by international agreements such as TRIPs, these rights have been increasingly concentrated in the hands of high-tech corporations based in a few rich countries. The removal of land from the common ownership of indigenous people not only creates genetic erosion and the attrition of species, soils and the atmosphere, but also the erosion of knowledge and of global equality among regions and groups of people. We are losing both our biological resources and our eco-specific knowledge of those resources. Ecological destruction increases the commercial importance of dwindling genetic 'raw materials'. Paradoxically, this is occurring just when new technologies need (and can utilise) the endangered biomaterials, but can only do so to the general good if they are used under principles other than those of free trade and the profit motive.[35]

Bilateral agreements

Despite its potential threat to the well-being of poor regions, TRIPs also provided an arena for one of the most hopeful victories of forces opposed to the excesses of globalisation. The November 2001 Ministerial Conference in Doha adopted a declaration on the TRIPs agreement that conceded that access to life-saving drugs is not a commercial issue. This provided the possibility that countries could access generic drugs or cheaper re-exports from a third country ('parallel imports') if it was in the interest of public health. The ability of the large (especially US-based) corporations, with government sponsorship, to avoid these exceptions and to impose trade regimes that surpass even TRIPs indicates the continued importance of the nation state even under globalisation.

The main mechanism whereby the US, beginning under Clinton and intensifying under the Bush administration, imposes its power over the countries of the Global South is the bilateral Free Trade Agreement. The bilateral strategy is to weaken the power of poor countries by fragmenting the coalitions they pursue in multilateral trade negotiations. Once the US cajoles one country or region into agreeing to unfavourable issues in a trade treaty, it uses the treaty as a template for establishing further bilateral agreements with other countries or regions. Having agreed to unfavourable stipulations in a bilateral deal with the US, countries can hardly pursue them in WTO negotiations.

The economists Jagdish Bhagwati and Arvind Panagariya give an example of this strategy in a stinging critique of bilateral free trade agreements. During negotiations over the North America Free Trade

Figure 1.1. Evolution of regional trade agreements in the world, 1948–2007

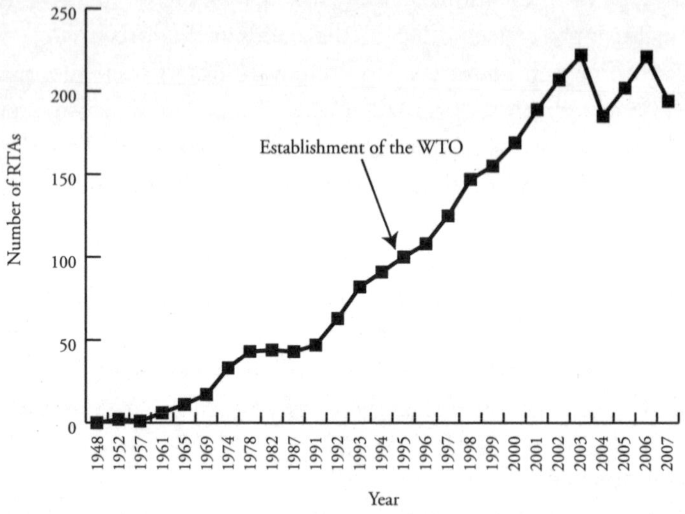

Source: WTO Secretariat.

Agreement (NAFTA), Mexico was told that the price of a deal was acceptance of intellectual property protection provisions. Then, the US demanded that other countries accept similar provisions or face retaliatory tariffs. Subsequently, the US was able to insert TRIPs into the WTO, 'even though no intellectual case had ever been made that TRIPs, which is about royalty collection and not trade, should be included'.[36] Moreover, provisions on environmental and labour standards that were forced on Mexico were then drafted into free trade agreements with Jordan and, later, into the Central American-Dominican Republic Free Trade Agreement (CAFTA).

It is no wonder that by the end of 2002, more than 250 bilateral free trade agreements had been notified to the WTO, more then triple the number in 1994 (Figure 1.1). Most were initiated by the US, which boldly states that it:

> pursues comprehensive free trade agreements on a bilateral basis to expand opportunities for American workers, farmers and ranchers. In 2004, the U.S. completed free trade agreements with Australia, Morocco, in addition to the DR-CAFTA, deepening U.S. strategic and economic interests in Asia, the Middle East and Latin America.[37]

Bilateral FTAs between the US and Costa Rica, Morocco, Chile, Jordan, Singapore and Sri Lanka (as well as CAFTA) threaten the concessions on health that were won at Doha. They include clauses on intellectual property that go beyond the TRIPs requirements, including extension of patent protection beyond twenty years and, crucially, restrictions on the use of compulsory licences or parallel imports to protect health. In this way, say Bhagwati and Panagariya, 'thanks to the myopic and self-serving policies of the world's only superpower, bilateral free trade agreements . . . have become a vehicle for introducing extraneous issues into the WTO for the benefit of narrow US domestic interests'.[38]

Conclusions

Globalisation is more than a buzzword. It is a worldwide regime wherein corporate power is exercised in imperfect ways, but with the main objective of maintaining corporate power and profit. Yet, that does not tell us a lot, because that goal involves strategies and institutions that are complex and sometimes contradictory. As we have seen, institutions can have either a national or global character or both. Corporations, and the states with which they associate (and by which they are sponsored and protected), use a variety of strategies to attain goals. When one strategy is insufficient, they may move to another. Such flexibility is at the base of their ability not just to attain, but also to maintain, power.

The institutions of globalisation – the World Bank, IMF and WTO – and associated multilateral agreements such as TRIPs and GATS are so crucial to the regime that they may appear to transcend and subsume the nation state. TNCs, including drug companies, often use these institutions and agreements to maintain their global reach, and to achieve favourable investment and distribution outcomes. And the results of their activities can be detrimental to the social well-being, including the health, of the majority of people, particularly in the poorer regions of the Global South, where diseases like HIV/AIDS, malaria and tuberculosis are endemic.

Yet people can be powerful. For example, NGOs and states that represent the poorer regions of the world attained a partial victory when the Doha Agreement blunted TRIPs as an instrument whereby large TNCs could limit public access to drugs. However, the reaction of the powers of the Global North, particularly the US and US-based corporations, demonstrated their ability to change tack in the face of concerted opposition. US trade authorities have used bilateral free trade agreements to undercut the progressive amendments to TRIPs, inserting clauses that are even more favourable to the owners of 'intellectual property' and detrimental to large sections of the world's population, and then using one such agreement as leverage against further countries and groups of countries.

In terms of globalisation, the conclusion is not just theoretical but highly practical: it is insufficient to resist the global strategies of capital only at the level of global institutions. Nation states, particularly a hegemon like the US, still have perceived 'national interests' and exercise raw power on their behalf, usually in favour of their most influential TNCs and, coincidentially, in favour of corporate interests from other countries. If there is a 'global capitalist class', it finds sponsorship at all levels, including the nation state. The agents of progressive change, like popular movements in the Global South, that campaign on crucial issues like access to drugs and adequate healthcare must resist at all levels.

CHAPTER 2

The Pharmaceutical Industry and the World Trade Organisation's TRIPs Agreement:

Intellectual Property, Global Governance and Health

Gerard Downes

Introduction

Throughout the 1980s and early 1990s, the pharmaceutical industry in the United States accomplished a spectacular victory in policy-making that will have profound consequences for public health policy on a global scale. Although the industry was heavily criticised domestically during the 1980s for maintaining inflated prices on prescription drugs, a coterie of pharmaceutical firms successfully campaigned throughout the decade for the US government to adopt the industry's international objectives in the area of intellectual property rights.[1] Their campaign culminated in the signing of the Trade Related Aspects of Intellectual Property Rights Agreement (TRIPs) by contracting parties to the General Agreement on Tariffs and Trade (GATT)[2] in Marrakech, Morocco, on 15 April 1994. The globalisation of intellectual property rights, as embodied in TRIPs, was the most significant change in intellectual property laws enacted in the twentieth century.

This chapter examines why countries ceded sovereignty over an issue as fundamental as the intellectual property laws which determine who gains control of information and technologies. It also assesses the implications of TRIPs for World Trade Organisation (WTO) member states in the area of public health policy.

Intellectual property and TRIPs

TRIPs is one of the three pillars of the WTO and was negotiated during the Uruguay Round of trade talks that took place from 1986 to 1994 under the auspices of the GATT. TRIPs came into being with the establishment of the WTO on 1 January 1995. Under TRIPs all WTO members[3] must introduce legislation that complies with the provisions of the agreement. For many WTO members, the TRIPs agreement has ushered in a period of profound change as a large number of countries have amended their existing legislation or drafted completely new laws pertaining to intellectual property rights.[4]

Intellectual property rights are the rights given to persons over creations of the mind such as inventions, works of art and literature and designs. Intellectual property rights, such as patents, trade marks and copyright, grant the creators of an object an exclusive right over the use of their creation for a certain period of time, usually twenty years. In order for a patent to be granted, the invention must fulfil the criteria of being novel, innovative and useful.[5]

TRIPs was framed with the intention of protecting intellectual property on a global scale by making the practice of intellectual property piracy punishable by a penalty such as economic or trade sanctions in the WTO's Dispute Settlement Understanding (DSU), a body which effectively acts as the WTO's court of arbitration. In July 2007, the WTO consisted of 151 members. If a member state perceives that a fellow WTO member is transgressing its intellectual property rights, the aggrieved party may bring a case to the DSU and seek redress therein. The DSU is a particularly significant development in global governance, as it gives the WTO enforcement powers that its predecessor institution, the GATT, inherently lacked.[6] Under TRIPs, all members must provide a minimum of twenty-year patents on pharmaceutical processes and products. The holder of the patent has exclusive rights to manufacture, sell and distribute the drug during that time-span. At the time of the WTO's inception, the organisation had ninety-eight 'developing' country members. Twenty-five of those countries did not provide any patent protection for pharmaceutical products. Among those developing country members that had such laws in place, the length of patent protection in fifty-six of them was much shorter than twenty years.[7]

Why the necessity for TRIPs?

Rapid changes in technology and transformations in the structure of global capitalism in the 1980s helped to propel the issue of intellectual property rights from what was 'an arcane area of legal analysis and a policy backwater' to the forefront of global economic policymaking.[8]

International trade in goods embodying intellectual property increased substantially with the rapid expansion of knowledge-based industries from the early 1980s onwards. As the USA's comparative advantage began to shift away from industrial manufacturing to high-technology industries such as pharmaceuticals, the protection of intellectual property became a fundamental tenet of the United States' economic foreign policy.[9] Concomitant to profound technological change was the perception among business leaders in many industrialised countries that inadequate protection of intellectual property (IP) in technology-importing countries was detrimental to their competitiveness.[10] This was an argument that found much resonance in the US Congress throughout the 1980s. Despite the fact that trade in counterfeit goods had been ongoing for centuries, the ease with which intellectual property-embodied goods, such as software and pharmaceutical products, could be replicated led to a call for a global IP protection regime.[11]

Barry MacTaggart, the then chairman and president of Pfizer International, first articulated the pharmaceutical industry's frustration with intellectual property piracy with an opinion piece in *The New York Times* in July 1982. In an article entitled 'Stealing from the Mind', MacTaggart accused a plethora of foreign governments of stealing knowledge and inventions that had been generated in the USA.[12] MacTaggart asserted that, as more and more countries strive to industrialise, it is ironic that little or no respect is accorded the laws and principles that helped to bring about industrialisation, particularly in the area of patent protection, for high technology.[13] The Pfizer chairman neglected to relate how the piracy of intellectual property had been pivotal to the industrial development of countries as diverse as the United States, the Netherlands, Switzerland and the 'Tiger' economies of south-east Asia.[14]

The ire of Pfizer and other major pharmaceutical firms was primarily focused on the Indian Patents Act of 1970, which exempted pharmaceutical products from patenting and provided for compulsory licensing, a strategy which allows a government to issue a licence to a domestic manufacturer to manufacture a drug without the consent of the patent holder.[15] Protection of its intellectual property interests is central to the international economic strategy of the United States, as goods embodying IP have been calculated to comprise almost half of its annual exports. However, intellectual property 'piracy' remains an all-pervasive problem. The International Anti-Counterfeiting Coalition (IACC)[16] calculated in 1993 that the US economy loses about $US200 billion each year and 750,000 jobs annually from piracy.[17] An earlier study into US losses from intellectual property piracy played a seminal role in fomenting political support for what later became the TRIPs agreement.

In 1987, President Reagan commissioned the United States International Trade Commission (ITC)[18] to undertake a study with the aim of quantifying losses to the US economy from intellectual property piracy. Questionnaires were dispatched to affected industries. Firms with an interest in a trade-based approach to intellectual property rights had, according to Susan Sell, 'plenty of incentive to overestimate the losses knowing that the ITC report would be used by politicians and economists in Washington when they debated whether or not IP should become a major issue in international trade negotiations'.[19] The ITC study found that the cost of all intellectual property violations to US industry was between $US43 and $US61 billion per annum. This figure included not only the cost of generic drugs to US pharmaceutical firms, but also copyright violations and trademark infringements.[20] The findings of the study were particularly crucial because they galvanised the attitudes of policy-makers on Capitol Hill who hitherto had been either ambivalent or ignorant in their attitude to intellectual property. The survey acted as a catalyst to precipitate changes in intellectual property law within both the domestic and global spheres.

The pharmaceutical industry was foremost among those high-tech information-based producers that called for changes in intellectual property rules. The ITC study stated that the cost of piracy to ten major US drug manufacturers was almost $US2 billion per annum. The Merck Corporation estimated the annual losses to the US pharmaceutical industry overall at $US6 billion.[21] Global piracy of pharmaceutical products was estimated to reduce annual R&D investment by US firms by between $US720 million and $US900 million a year.[22]

Bringing new drugs to market requires vast research and development resources. Imitating these products once they are in the marketplace by a process of reverse engineering is eminently easy. Reverse engineering is the process of taking a product apart in order to analyse its workings and then constructing a new product based on that knowledge. According to a much-cited 1991 study, a pharmaceutical product that can cost on average $US231 million to bring to market can be copied for virtually nothing.[23] The Pharmaceutical Research and Manufacturers of America (PhRMA)[24] claimed in 1999 that it costs at least half a billion US dollars to bring a new chemical entity to market.[25] A study conducted by Arnold Relman and Marcia Angell,[26] however, is sceptical of PhRMA's claim. The authors contend that:

> The average out-of pocket, after-tax R&D cost of most of the drugs upon which the [pharmaceutical] industry's revenue now depends was probably much lower than $266 million (in year 2000 dollars). Tax credits for certain types of R&D would probably reduce that estimate even more.[27]

PhRMA's view was that only a stringent legal agreement such as TRIPs would obviate rampant intellectual property piracy and allow its members to plough back profits into R&D. In return for intellectual property protection, the pharmaceutical industry would bring investment and technology transfer to developing countries.[28] PhRMA is one of the world's most politically influential and well-financed industrial lobbies. The organisation employs 297 full-time lobbyists on Capitol Hill – one for every two congressional representatives.[29] One of the primary sources of PhRMA's power is its influence over the Office of the United States Trade Representative (USTR), which has consistently backed PhRMA's claims with the threat of trade sanctions.[30]

Throughout the 1980s, the veracity of the claim that intellectual piracy was undermining profits and R&D sat uneasily with the pharmaceutical industry's phenomenal performance. The dominance by pharmaceutical corporations of the Fortune 500 was reflected in the fact that Pfizer's return on investment was almost double the median return for Fortune 500 companies, while the group's net income rose from $US103.4 million in 1972 to $US800 million by 1990.[31] Nevertheless, policy-makers in Washington were loath to contradict the industry's claims.

In response to the aforementioned ITC study, the US Congress passed the Omnibus Trade and Competitive Act in 1988. This act contained 'Special 301' legislation requiring trading partners of the United States to extend intellectual property protection to US companies. Failure to comply with the Act would render countries subject to tariff retaliation for 'unreasonable' practices.[32] However, the country-by-country approach inherent in 'Special 301' actions was highly inefficient. Firstly, there were too many countries with lucrative pharmaceutical markets to approach individually.[33] Bringing a 'Special 301' action against each recalcitrant state would therefore prove unwieldy. Also, trying to impose economic or trade sanctions on powerful economies such as China for infringements of US intellectual property was especially problematic in the face of trenchant opposition to such sanctions from the US automobile and other exporting industries.[34] If pharmaceutical companies' intellectual property rights were going to be protected on a global basis, 'some kind of comprehensive agreement would be necessary'.[35] TRIPs fulfilled all the criteria of such a comprehensive agreement.

Creating new norms in intellectual property

PhRMA saw the globalisation of US intellectual property protection standards as the requisite panacea to intellectual property piracy.[36] In order for its argument to sway policy-makers in the US Congress, PhRMA had to formulate a new normative framework on intellectual property rights (IPRs). One of the strategies undertaken in constructing new norms in the area of IPRs was to link the perceived decline in US competitiveness throughout the 1980s with weakly enforced intellectual property rights in developing countries, and especially in the 'dragon economies' of east and south-east Asia.[37]

The expansion of these Asian economies, and that of Japan in particular, during the 1980s began to erode the industrial foundations of the United States and was seen as a portent of US decline.[38] Public myths were constructed in the US about the provenance of Japan's phenomenal growth. According to one commentator, 'American ideas, American know-how were being stolen by the Japanese, it was widely believed. The trade surplus that Japan had with the US became a rallying cry for protectionist elements within the United States.'[39] When representatives of US intellectual property interests arrived on Capitol Hill in the mid-1980s to relate their grievances, they not only encountered bipartisan congressional sympathy, but also a hardened resolve among policy-makers to stymie America's economic decline by placing the issue of intellectual property rights within a multilateral body with a powerful enforcement mechanism.[40]

Placing intangible intellectual property rights, a concept synonymous with monopoly privileges, within an organisation committed to trade liberalisation, such as the WTO, would require turning this maxim on its head and instead equating the protection of intellectual property with the precepts of the free market. As Edwin J. Prindle of the US Patent Office stated, 'patents represent the best and most effective means of controlling competition. They occasionally give absolute command of the market, enabling their owners to name the price without regard to the cost of production.'[41] Edmund Pratt of Pfizer continuously stressed that it was necessary to demonstrate to governments abroad that protecting foreign intellectual property was in their enlightened self-interest. The framework successfully promoted by the pharmaceutical industry, that patent protection would lead to greater free trade, economic growth, investment and technology transfer to developing countries, became 'the normative building block of the TRIPs Agreement'.[42] The fundamental reason for embracing intellectual property rights, according to Pratt, was not simply to comply with GATT or WTO rules or avoid trade sanctions, 'but to provide a base for the extension of liberal democratic principles that can lift economies and better lives'.[43]

The formation of two business groupings, the International Intellectual Property Alliance (IIPA) in 1984 and the Intellectual Property Committee (IPC) in 1986, was critical in ensuring that the outcome of the Uruguay Round of trade talks was satisfactory to corporate interests. The IPC, which consisted of thirteen large US corporations such as Pfizer, Merck, Johnson & Johnson, Bristol-Myers and Dupont, set about establishing a global private sector/government network that would lay the ground for what became TRIPs.[44] The IPC's primary achievement was convincing US government officials to take a tough stance on intellectual property issues in trade negotiations. This led to the issue of trade-related intellectual property rights being included on the GATT agenda when negotiations began in Punta del Este, Uruguay, in 1986.[45]

In order to secure a deal on intellectual property in the Uruguay Round, negotiators from the US, European Community and Japan had to make certain trade-offs, but even these reflected the great asymmetries of power in the global political economy. Conditions that exist in order for democratic bargaining to take place, namely full representation, full information and non-coercion, were excluded from the TRIPs negotiations and resistance within the GATT to the agreement becoming part of the new WTO was eradicated.[46] The so-called 'Green Room' procedure was often invoked during TRIPs deliberations, whereby the GATT director-general consulted in confidential surroundings primarily with the major trading powers of the 'Quad', namely the USA, Canada, Japan and the European Community. The findings of this group were then presented to the more formal GATT meetings, effectively as a *fait accompli*.[47]

While the TRIPs deliberations were taking place, PhRMA lobbied policy-makers in Washington to ensure that the North American Free

Trade Agreement (NAFTA) between the USA, Canada and Mexico contained stringent intellectual property provisions. Mike Privatera, public affairs director of Pfizer Inc., stated at the conclusion of the talks: 'The Mexicans gave us everything we wanted.'[48] The TRIPs agreement represented a failure of democratic processes, both nationally and internationally, as a tiny clique of knowledge-based companies was able to capture the US trade agenda-setting process and draft intellectual property principles that were to become the template for TRIPs.[49] Curiously, as Susan Sell writes, 'despite the fact that the TRIPs deliberations focussed on policies that affect virtually everyone on the planet, the GATT Secretariat received no complaints from consumer groups at the time of the negotiations'.[50] The TRIPs agreement came into being on 1 January 1995 with a virtual whimper. Reaction to the agreement only began after its implementation, when the profound implications of TRIPs for public health were assessed. TRIPs moved from being purely a 'trade-related' issue to one of access to life-saving medicines.[51]

Implications of TRIPs

Price is not the only determinant of access to essential medicines. Other vital factors which need to be addressed by policy-makers include providing a well-functioning and efficient healthcare infrastructure, comprehensive reach, adequate medical supplies and the presence of well-trained medical personnel.[52] Nevertheless, price remains a primary component in determining whether people live or die. For this reason, the Indian Drug Manufacturers Association (IDMA) predicts that a 'national health disaster' is imminent with the introduction of the TRIPs agreement.[53] Under TRIPs it is inevitable that twenty-year patents will lead to either monopolistic or oligopolistic practices, with only a tiny coterie of firms controlling the supply and market prices of drugs. As a result, competition will be stymied and prices of medicines will inevitably increase.

A critical examination of the retail prices of drugs in thirty-nine countries around the world by William Pretorius suggests that the guiding principle which the pharmaceutical industry adopts when fixing prices is 'to charge what the market can bear'.[54] In most countries of the South, this may result in companies adopting a high-price, low-volume strategy aimed only at those with the ability to pay (as was the case in India prior to the introduction of its 1970 Patents Act). Elsewhere, charging what the market can bear entails a low-price, high-volume strategy aimed at the bulk of the population. The Delhi-based National Working Group on Patent Laws undertook a comparative study in 1993 which contrasted the price of drugs in India with countries that have patent protection for pharmaceuticals. The findings of the group showed that in several cases drug prices in India were forty-one times lower than those in countries that provided patent protection. Since TRIPs provisions relating to the patenting of pharmaceutical products and processes were implemented in India in 2005, generic pharmaceutical manufacturers are restricted from reverse engineering patented drugs until the twenty-year patents on such drugs expire.

The pharmaceutical industry lobbied successfully for the uniform patent period of twenty years before and during the Uruguay Round. This duration is highly contentious. An optimal patent period should always reflect a balance between the rules of appropriation and the rules of diffusion by providing an incentive to innovate on the one hand and an opportunity to capture benefits on the other. One eminent economist describes the twenty-year patent duration as 'a period so long that few economists of repute can be found who would call it efficient in terms of balancing the two opposing forces [of appropriation and diffusion]'.[55]

Jayashree Watal, Counsellor in the Intellectual Property Division of the WTO, in a study undertaken in 2000, demonstrated how prices of generic medicines in India would rise by at least 26 per cent after the full implementation of TRIPs in 2005. In her study, Watal also verified that the price of patented drugs would rise by between 200 and 300 per cent from 2005 in India.[56] An International Monetary Fund (IMF) survey on the possible consequences of TRIPs highlighted that annual welfare losses to India could range from $US162 million to $US1.26 billion, while the annual profit transfer to foreign firms based in India would be between $US101 million and $US839 million.[57]

The groundbreaking 1970 Indian Patents Act, which did not allow the patenting of pharmaceutical products, was emasculated in order to conform to TRIPs. Indian negotiators to the GATT, who viewed TRIPs as a process befitting the country's programme of economic liberalisation that was initiated in 1991, cannot be exonerated from blame. S. P. Shukla, Indian ambassador to the GATT from March 1984 to February 1989, characterised the Indian capitulation on TRIPs as 'The Geneva Surrender'.[58] India provides a salutary example of how even a powerful developing country can cede sovereignty over its laws governing property rights in pharmaceuticals. The multilateral framework embodied in the

WTO, while allowing for bargaining between members, has, on the issue of TRIPs, disproportionately favoured exporters of intellectual property, with potentially calamitous consequences.

TRIPs-related cases

The TRIPs agreement is liable to have profound implications for national sovereignty, particularly in the area of health policy. While the Doha Declaration on Public Health of 2001[59] allows for the issuing of a compulsory licence in the case of a national medical emergency or threat to public health, test cases illustrate that the issue is laden with complexity and ambiguity. The remaining options for WTO members to circumvent the stringencies of TRIPs include compulsory licensing and/or parallel importation. Although the option of compulsory licensing is permitted under TRIPs, only a few technologically advanced developing countries, such as India and Brazil, have the necessary facilities to undertake the production of generic pharmaceuticals.

Countries without manufacturing facilities for pharmaceutical products can gain access to lower-priced drugs produced in other developing countries, or by generic manufacturers in some developed countries, by using parallel importation. This tactic allows a government to sanction the importation of pharmaceutical products when the price being charged by the patent holder in that jurisdiction is higher than the price being charged elsewhere.[60] Balasubramaniam[61] states that the analysis of empirical data 'supports the position that compulsory licensing and parallel imports are two regulatory tools that should be included in the national legislation of all developing countries'.[62] The cases documented below highlight how the use of parallel imports and compulsory licensing, despite their legality under TRIPs, are still liable to opprobrium.

The cases of South Africa, Brazil and the anthrax crisis of 2001 in the USA highlight how flexibilities within TRIPs can be utilised to implement public health policy in those respective countries, but also serve to illustrate that concessions in the arena of intellectual property rights must be fought for assiduously.

In November 1997, the government of South Africa amended its Medicines Act to allow it to undertake parallel importing and compulsory licensing in order to help it combat the country's burgeoning HIV/AIDS crisis. This would allow the South African government to purchase antiretroviral drugs from a third country instead of buying them from pharmaceutical firms within South Africa. Under TRIPs, this provision applies only to patented drugs and not to generics. The South African government's amendment was immediately subject to a lawsuit by thirty-nine pharmaceutical firms on the grounds that it breached the obligations South Africa had agreed to under TRIPs. In April 2001, the case was withdrawn in Pretoria by the pharmaceutical companies primarily on account of the bad publicity concerning the case that was generated by groupings such as Treatment Action Campaign, Medicins Sans Frontières and Oxfam.[63] The South African case elucidated how, even when a country adheres to the provisions of TRIPs, it can still become subject to a legal challenge citing a breach of WTO rules. This also proved to be the case with the Brazilian government.

In March 2001, the Brazilian Health Ministry announced that it would issue compulsory licences to local producers in order to manufacture generic copies of two antiretroviral drugs used in the treatment of HIV/AIDS unless Merck and Roche – the patent holders of both drugs – agreed to substantial price decreases. The cost of purchasing both drugs was absorbing half the Brazilian government's AIDS budget. Local producers estimated that they could produce both drugs at half the import price.[64] International pharmaceutical companies had threatened to withdraw investment if the Brazilian government did not remove its threat to use compulsory licensing in order to alleviate the crisis.[65] Under direction from PhRMA, the USA brought a WTO case against the Brazilian government. The suit challenged the latter's attempt to issue a compulsory licence in order to help counter a public health crisis. The case generated such negative publicity that Merck and Roche agreed to drop the prices of their patented antiretrovirals and the United States Trade Representative (USTR) withdrew the complaint against Brazil. Nevertheless, the US government did not concede on the substance of the issue and stressed that it would deal with the issue bilaterally, while Brazil agreed to consult with the USTR over possible future use of its compulsory licensing laws.

The South African and Brazilian cases illustrate the pressures that countries can be subjected to even when their legislation is in compliance with TRIPs. As Brazil and South Africa are advanced developing countries and, to a certain extent, regional powers, the cases against them generated levels of publicity that helped them overcome their respective TRIPs-related crises. Countries lacking the financial resources and political influence of both Brazil and South Africa may incur greater problems in resisting coercion.

The TRIPs agreement contains provisions in Article 31 which allow WTO members to use the subject matter of a patent without the authorisation of the rights holder in certain cases, such as a national emergency or 'other circumstances of extreme urgency or in cases of public non-commercial use'.[66] The USA found itself facing such an emergency in October 2001 when anthrax spores dispatched by post killed a number of its citizens and threatened to cause a major health crisis among a public still convulsed by the 9/11 terrorist attacks. For USA trade officials, the anthrax crisis provoked a dilemma. With a WTO Ministerial Conference due to be held in Doha, Qatar, in November 2001, the USA did not wish to be perceived as malleable regarding patent rules.

Nevertheless, the anthrax deaths provoked the US Secretary of Health and Human Services, Tommy Thompson, to threaten Bayer AG, the producer and patent holder of the anti-anthrax antibiotic ciprofloxacin (Cipro), that if the corporation did not lower its price significantly he would disregard its patent and issue a compulsory licence to domestic manufacturers.[67] Under a 1918 national security law, Thompson had the power to grant a compulsory licence to allow domestic manufacturers to produce generic Cipro to increase the government's dwindling back-up supply of the drug. In response to this threat, Bayer rescinded and dropped the price of Cipro that it had hitherto supplied to the US government by half. Bayer agreed to supply 300 million ciprofloxacin tablets to the US government at the drastically reduced price of 95 cents per tablet, a move which effectively averted the anthrax crisis. This gesture by Bayer served to undermine the US government's position on the sanctity of patents in the lead up to the crucial WTO Ministerial Conference which took place in November 2001 in Doha, Qatar.

The stance taken by the US on the anthrax crisis stressed not only the flexibilities of the TRIPs agreement, but how the US was willing to jettison its standpoint at international level on intellectual property to cope with a domestic crisis.

The US government can be readily eulogised for acting in the public interest when its population was under threat from bio-terrorism. Nevertheless, when Brazil sought to ameliorate its devastating HIV/AIDS crisis utilising the same tactics – i.e. the use of a compulsory licence – it was excoriated by the USTR and threatened with a case against it at the WTO. In the run-up to the Doha WTO Ministerial Conference, and with the anthrax crisis ongoing, the USTR sought to block proposals that would clarify rules to allow developing countries to issue compulsory licences during a public health crisis.[68] The reach of the USTR's power is highly extensive, not only in developing countries. It was also seen to great effect in dealings with the Irish government throughout the late 1990s.

Ireland and TRIPs

The threat of taking a fellow member before the WTO's dispute settlement panel has proven to be a highly effective means of enforcing TRIPs. Despite the often supine stance taken by successive Irish governments in relation to United States' foreign policy, Ireland was the subject of a TRIPs-infringement case brought against it by President Clinton's United States Trade Representative, Charlene Barshefsky, in 1998. The case related to the Irish government's failure to enforce TRIPs provisions, which allowed the copyright of US software producers and filmmakers to be violated with virtual impunity.

With trade sanctions a very realistic possibility, the Irish government committed itself in February 1998 to adopting a bill that would ameliorate the most apparent TRIPs deficiencies in Irish law by July 1998. As a consequence, the USTR decided to withdraw its case against Ireland. The case did highlight, however, that the US government is capable of enforcing its power by the threat of coercion and is symptomatic of how TRIPs can be used as an effective means of enforcing what John Ikenberry and Charles Kupchan have termed 'socialisation through external inducement'.[69] It was somewhat ironic that Ireland was cited for copyright infringement in a global forum, as the first recorded instance of a judgement on copyright can be traced back to sixth-century Celtic Ireland, when An Breitheamh Diarmuid ruled that Saint Columba had infringed Brehon law by plagiarising the Latin Psalter of Saint Finian of Clonard. Diarmuid's decree that 'as to every cow its calf, so to every book its copy', set the precedent for copyright law worldwide.[70]

Present-day Ireland deposited its ratification of the WTO agreement, together with the annexes thereto, on 30 December 1994 and became an original member of the WTO on 1 January 1995, the date on which the TRIPs Agreement entered into force. Generally, ratification of a treaty or convention or agreement by a state constitutes the consent of that state to be bound by their respective provisions. While it had been deemed flagrant in its stance on software and video piracy, successive Irish governments have been loath to take any standpoint inimical to the interests of the pharmaceutical industry in the area of intellectual property rights. This perspective is perhaps reflective of the fact that sixteen of the top twenty pharmaceutical companies in the world have established facilities in Ireland and that the Irish pharmaceutical industry consists of 120 companies, which employ more than 24,000 people.[71]

As intellectual property rights are regarded as fundamental to the development and progress of the pharmaceutical industry, Ireland is considered a safe location for investment, not least due to its TRIPs-compliant patent laws. Indeed, when TRIPs came into force in Ireland in January 1995, Irish patent law was already compatible with the agreement: Dáil Éireann had passed the Irish Patents Act on 27 February 1992 and Ireland was a signatory to the European Patent Convention of 1973, both of which rigorously protect the intellectual property of innovators. Provision is made for compulsory licensing in the 1992 Act that allows a government minister to use 'Inventions for the Service of the State'.[72]

The Irish government can issue a compulsory licence to a domestic manufacturer in the case of a national health emergency or 'for the maintenance of supplies and services essential to the life of the community'. However, Article 31(c) of TRIPs prevents the commercial use of a drug for which a compulsory licence has been issued and stipulates that products made under compulsory licensing must be 'predominantly for the supply of the domestic market of the Member authorising such use'.[73] This provision has profound implications for countries that do not have manufacturing capacity and need to import generic drugs, and for WTO members such as Brazil that export generics to other developing countries. Due to the opprobrium generated by Article 31(f) of TRIPs, the WTO agreed to relax this provision in August 2003. Countries that are unable to manufacture medicines required in an emergency or other circumstances of extreme urgency may now import generic copies made under compulsory licence subject to certain conditions. Consequently, any WTO Member may export generic medicines made under compulsory licences to meet the requirements of importing countries.

While all WTO members may import generic medicines *in extremis,* twenty-three 'developed' countries within the WTO, including Ireland, voluntarily declared that they would not avail of this new, relaxed provision. Fifteen of the twenty-three countries are European Union (EU) members. The EU has consistently adopted the US stance on intellectual property, never better exemplified than when the European Commission recommended in September 2002 that it saw 'no reason' to amend the highly contentious Article 27.3(b) of TRIPs, despite the vociferous objections of many developing country representatives.[74]

Ireland's ability to influence EU policy in the area of intellectual property rights was further eroded with the passing of the second Nice Treaty referendum by the Irish electorate in October 2002. Article 133 of Nice transfers competence for the negotiation of issues pertaining to intellectual property to the European Commission. National ratification of intellectual property agreements is no longer required as the EU Council of Ministers will in future decide whether the EU enters a final agreement on the issue. Prior to Nice, voting on intellectual property agreements was subject to unanimity within the EU, which meant that a single EU Member State had the power to block any agreement. Since the ratification of Nice, the issue of intellectual property is decided by qualified majority voting.[75] This aspect of Article 133 of the Nice Treaty severely limits the competence of national governments with regard to intellectual property negotiations and hands enormous powers to the EU Trade Commissioner in WTO negotiations.

Conclusion

Perhaps the most curious aspect of the TRIPs agreement is that it has transformed intellectual property from an area of esoteric analysis by trade lawyers into an issue of pivotal importance in both the global knowledge economy and the developmental strategy of individual nation states. Nowhere is this highlighted more than in the issue of access to essential medicines.

The pharmaceutical industry achieved a remarkable feat by creating new norms in a form of monopoly privileges (i.e. intellectual property) that were inserted into an organisation (the WTO) whose primary aim is the liberalisation of trade. A small coterie of knowledge-based companies was effectively able to enact public law for the rest of the world by linking transgressions of intellectual property rights around the globe with declining US competitiveness and inducing policy-makers and the office of the United States Trade Representative to accept this normative frame.

Nevertheless, the victory of the pharmaceutical industry in bringing TRIPs within the WTO has since been undermined by the global HIV/AIDS crisis, which has provoked a backlash against the industry's stance on intellectual property rights. TRIPs does contain flexibilities such as compulsory licensing and parallel importation to help counter public health emergencies. However, attempts by two powerful developing countries, South Africa and Brazil, to avail of these provisions have been greeted with reproach by PhRMA. The continued use of unilateral

'Special 301' legislation by the United States to counteract piracy acts as a huge disincentive to countries to avail of TRIPs' flexibilities.

The use of so-called 'TRIPs-plus' measures have also undermined the public health safeguards permitted to WTO members in TRIPs. Since the adoption of the TRIPs Agreement, the Clinton and Bush administrations have negotiated numerous bilateral and regional trade agreements that have imposed such 'TRIPs-plus' intellectual property rules on other WTO members. As a result, patented medicines have even higher levels of intellectual property protection than required in TRIPs, a tactic which has delayed the availability of affordable generic medicines. This trend is symptomatic of the Bush administration's tendency to use bilateral and regional agreements to enforce TRIPs rather than utilising the multilateral trade mechanisms in the WTO. For example, while the Clinton administration filed fifteen cases with the WTO from 1996 to 2000 charging other WTO members with violations of US intellectual property, the Bush administration had filed only one intellectual-property-related case with the WTO between 2001 and September 2004.[76]

The ability of WTO member states to avail of the flexibilities within TRIPs will determine if the agreement is to achieve a balance whereby innovators can be rewarded without diminishing accessibility to essential medicines. If the TRIPs agreement fails to achieve this balance, and the WTO ignores the varying exigencies of its member states, the provisions within TRIPs pertaining to public health are likely to provoke even greater opprobrium and discord in the future.

CHAPTER 3

Bias and Science in Knowledge Production:
Implications for the Politics of Drug Regulation

John Abraham

Introduction

The regulation of pharmaceuticals is often referred to as science-based regulation.[1] This is not only because the product research and development of the pharmaceutical industry involves the work of many scientists, but also because industry data on the quality, safety and efficacy of new drugs is reviewed by scientists working for government regulatory agencies before approval for marketing. It is often inferred from this that pharmaceutical regulation is a scientific process, but the meaning of this is rarely explored.

Philosophers, sociologists and other political thinkers have long pondered on the conditions for effective science and hence the production of scientific knowledge. Writing at the time of Nazism and its purge of 'Jewish science', Merton was particularly concerned about how science could be protected from political interference.[2] With this in mind he proposed a set of norms and values for the proper functioning of scientific activity:

- the open and free exchange of scientific ideas and findings ('communalism')
- the treatment of knowledge claims on their merits, irrespective of the social background of the scientists making the claims ('universalism')
- freedom from economic or political motivations ('disinterestedness') and
- the tendency to treat any knowledge claim with caution and subject it to close scrutiny ('organised scepticism').

Thirty years later, Popper looked more closely at the process of knowledge production.[3] He contended that, in order to establish knowledge, scientists endeavoured to falsify hypotheses about the world. The hypotheses that withstood attempts to falsify them were the ones closest to the truth and contributed to knowledge.

In these landmark treatises on science we see a number of ideals for science that are intended to achieve the goal of objectivity, and to distinguish it from prejudice or biased beliefs. In particular, there is an assumption that bias enters into science as a result of economic and socio-political interests. In this view, science needs to be 'disinterested' or 'neutral'. However, this conflates and confuses neutrality with objectivity. While the pursuit of truth and objectivity are essential prerequisites for coherent scientific activity, these are not the same as value-freedom or neutrality, because the discovery of truths is not necessarily best achieved from an ostensible position of value-neutrality or social indifference. Indeed, the commitment to truth in science is itself a value.

Moreover, in modern science it is hard to imagine that choices in research questions could be entirely devoid of social values and interests, because they reflect not only matters of internal logic, but also social priorities. This is especially so in the case of science in the pharmaceutical sector, where most of the scientists either work for industry or government or are funded by them. Objectivity in science, therefore, is best achieved not by striving for an illusionary neutrality, but rather by enhanced consciousness of the interests and values inherent in science and how they influence scientists' questions, hypotheses and analyses. This is important because it emphasises that bias in science should not be regarded as non-neutrality or confused with the intrusion of interests *per se*.

Values and interests are endemic to, though not exhaustive or determinative of, science. The issue of bias, therefore, is not about whether or not science can be free from values and interests, but rather about the relationship between values, interests and scientific activity. In the case of science-based pharmaceutical regulation, the publicly declared goal of the scientific activity is to produce new drugs that are beneficial to public health, and to protect the public from unsafe drugs. The pharmaceutical industry also has commercial interests in the maximisation of markets and profits, but the rationale for having an industry that produces medicines must be that the commercial interests are subordinate to the interests of public health if the existence of the industry is to be intelligible.

Consequently, the science of drug testing and regulation has developed standards which are *supposed* to be consistent with the interests of public health. Such scientific activity operates at a number of complex levels, but basically bias is likely when scientists act in contradiction to the standards of their own science or in the development of scientific standards that are not in the interests of public health. It is the contention of this chapter that bias towards the commercial interests of the pharmaceutical industry is a problem in the science of drug testing and regulation. Three cases of 'science' are discussed to illustrate how this bias has operated and persisted for decades. In discussing such bias, I am not suggesting 'bad faith' on the part of individuals involved. Indeed, these individuals may have begun their work with the best of motives, but the outcomes are a product of institutional cultures and social interests larger than any individual scientist.

Industry testing and reception of scientific papers

Under current arrangements, and since drug regulation began in the West, drug testing is conducted and co-ordinated by the pharmaceutical manufacturer, while the regulatory agencies' role is limited to review of the data submitted to them by companies or occasionally other sources, such as doctors. By analysing benoxaprofen, a drug better known as Opren, in this section I shall focus on the relationship between the pharmaceutical company and the production of scientific papers – a crucial part of knowledge production in medical and pharmaceutical science. Benoxaprofen, a propionic acid derivative, now withdrawn from the market, was a non-steroidal anti-inflammatory drug (NSAID) available in the 1980s. NSAIDs are used to treat arthritis. The NSAIDs generally do not suppress the progression of the disease; they treat only the symptoms. Drugs such as gold salts and penicillamine are capable of retarding the progression of arthritic disease, but they are much more toxic than NSAIDs.[4] Consequently, any NSAID capable of suppressing the progression of arthritis would be of tremendous medical and commercial value, assuming it exhibited typical low toxicity compared with gold or penicillamine.

It was in this context that Dr Gilbert Bluhm, employed by a hospital in Detroit, received a grant from the pharmaceutical company Eli Lilly (Lilly) on behalf of the hospital, to conduct a clinical study of the efficacy of benoxaprofen in arresting and retarding rheumatoid arthritis in the early 1980s.[5] After presenting his results at a symposium in Paris, he submitted it for publication in the *European Journal of Rheumatology and Inflammation,* which was edited by Edward Huskisson, who was an established expert on NSAIDs and was also involved as a consultant trialist in the clinical testing of benoxaprofen in the UK.[6] The paper was accepted for publication by Huskisson.

The scientific standard for the assessment of efficacy was (and remains) the double-blind controlled clinical trial, where patients take either the test drug or placebo under various controlled conditions (such as exclusion of some types of patients or parallel medication), but neither the patients nor the clinical investigators administering treatment know who is receiving the test drug and who placebo.[7] Moreover, at a symposium on 'The Principles and Practice of Clinical Trials' organised by the Association of Medical Advisers in the Pharmaceutical Industry in 1976, Huskisson commented:

> Experience suggests that 12 to 18 patients with active disease [rheumatic] are sufficient to show that a drug like aspirin is superior to placebo, but this is only a crude screening test of effectiveness. Much larger numbers of patients are required to obtain information about variability and frequency of response . . . any comparison between one propionic acid derivative and another using anything less than about 60 patients would be meaningless.[8]

In the Bluhm et al. study, thirty-nine patients with rheumatoid arthritis were given the high dose of 600–1,000 mg of benoxaprofen per day for a mean duration of twenty-one months. X-rays of the joints of the patients were taken before and after this period in order to assess radiologically the progression of osseous defects (OD) and joint space narrowing (JSN). There were no control patients and the effects of benoxaprofen using this method were not compared with other NSAIDs. Thus, the study was not a controlled clinical trial. As Bluhm characterised it, 'each patient served as their own control'.[9] Nor did the study meet Huskisson's quantitative criterion of sixty patients for a sufficient test of efficacy.

Bluhm et al. acknowledged that their results showed no statistically significant retardation of rheumatoid arthritis. However, they concluded:

> Our study of 39 patients with rheumatoid arthritis suggests a trend for benoxaprofen therapy given over a prolonged period to retard the rheumatologic process when measured radiologically by both OD and JSN rates . . . Because there is also a trend for this drug to retard or arrest radiological progression, it becomes a promising agent for the long-term treatment of rheumatoid arthritis.[10]

According to Bluhm et al., 'a patient's improvement was determined by a decreased OD and JSN rate during therapy when compared to the pre-treatment rate for the same patient'.[11] However, not only were the results not statistically significant, but the JSN rate on average *increased* during benoxaprofen therapy and the mean OD rate decreased more during pre-treatment observation than during benoxaprofen therapy. Hence, on average, mere observation of the patient was associated with more effect than administration of benoxaprofen. As William O'Brien, Professor of Rheumatology at the University of Virginia Hospital, concluded, the data could not correctly be interpreted as suggesting that benoxaprofen retarded the progression of rheumatoid arthritis and should have been interpreted as suggesting that the drug had no such effect.[12]

Even Huskisson, who accepted the paper for publication in his journal, stated that the mathematical interpretation of the study was 'extremely suspect' and that 'the whole design of the study was suspect'.[13] Yet, in the published journal the challenges to this study made at the symposium are conspicuous by their absence. Nor did Huskisson express grave reservations about the study in his editorial.[14] Little evidence in this case, then, of the Mertonian ideal that scientists should treat any knowledge claim with caution and subject it to close scrutiny.

Furthermore, the Bluhm et al. paper received an enthusiastic welcome from Lilly. Rather than trying to falsify Bluhm's hypothesis in the Popperian mould of scientific progress, Lilly scientists felt able to cite it to uphold the statement that 'a number of findings support the hypothesis that benoxaprofen has a disease modifying effect in man, at least in rheumatoid arthritis'.[15] At a press conference in Lilly's UK headquarters in February 1981, Bluhm gave a BBC television interview, filmed by the company for public relations purposes, with the following message:

> BBC INTERVIEWER: Would you go as far as to say that in your opinion, at this point in time, on the basis of what you've done, you are actually talking about the possibility of modifying disease?
> BLUHM: That's it precisely, what I've tried to tell you.[16]

Similarly, in the US, Congress heard how in 1982 one of Lilly's public relations firms made available to media professionals tape recordings over the telephone of Bluhm stating that 'there is preliminary clinical data that suggests that it [benoxaprofen] may have this [arthritis] disease modifying potential'.[17]

This case not only illustrates an example of commercial bias, but also demonstrates the importance of the concept of bias in analysing science and knowledge production in the pharmaceutical sector. Had Bluhm's research been technically consistent and scientifically valid, then his findings would not have been biased and could have been in the interests of public health as well as in the commercial interest of Lilly. However, it is the technical inconsistencies of his claims with standards of testing in this field, and with his own evidence, that reveals the fundamental bias. The reception given to his claims reveals a weakness in the ability of the scientific community in the pharmaceutical sector to 'falsify' or treat with sufficient scepticism such bias.

Interpretation of evidence in regulatory science

One of the most crucial types of judgements that drug regulators have to make is balancing risks against benefits. Integral to that process is the interpretation of drug safety and efficacy by scientists employed by and/or advising the regulatory authorities. One of the expert committees that advise the US drug regulatory agency, the Food and Drug Administration (FDA), about psycho-active drugs is the Psychopharmacological Drugs Advisory Committee (PDAC). In this section I examine the PDAC's assessment of safety and efficacy evidence regarding the drug triazolam.

Triazolam (also known as Halcion), a benzodiazepine, is one of the most controversial hypnotics (sleeping pills) ever marketed. It was manufactured and first marketed by Upjohn in the 1970s. In 1991, the British regulatory agency suspended its licence because they believed that its risks outweighed its benefits. Since then it has been banned in the UK, Norway and Denmark and was once banned in the Netherlands as early as 1979. However, triazolam remains on the market in the US and many other countries, including Ireland. The FDA is one of the most influential drug regulatory agencies in the world. It reviewed the safety and effectiveness of triazolam in 1992, drawing on the expertise of its specialist committee, the PDAC. These expert assessments concluded that triazolam was safe and effective enough to remain on the US market. Undoubtedly many other countries felt reassured by this.

From a public health perspective, the safety of any drug can only be sensibly considered in relation to its effectiveness to treat illness. Notably, there is no known population for which triazolam is uniquely effective compared with other hypnotics. In 1988, the manufacturers, Upjohn, reduced the recommended starting dose for American adults from 0.5 mg/day to 0.25 mg/day due to safety concerns. Accordingly, the recommended starting dose for the elderly was reduced to about half this, 0.125 mg/day. However, the FDA did not require the company to prove the efficacy of the lower dosages at that time. Almost four years later the FDA sought to do this by convening its expert science advisers on the PDAC to examine the drug's safety and efficacy.[18]

On 18 May 1992, the FDA presented two of a number of placebo-controlled clinical trials showing efficacy of the 0.25 mg dose for insomniacs.[19] There were just two studies of the efficacy of the 0.125 mg dose for the elderly – both seventeen-day placebo-controlled with geriatric insomniacs. In one, triazolam was found to have no significant therapeutic effect, while, in the other, it was effective in increasing total sleep time and in shortening sleep onset, but did not help in reducing patients' number of awakenings.[20] One member of the PDAC, Regina Casper, Professor of Psychiatry at the University of Chicago, was 'not convinced' that sufficient data had been presented to address the effectiveness of the 0.125 mg dose in the elderly.[21] Another, Dr Larry Ereshefsky, Director of Psychiatric Pharmacy at the University of Texas Health Centre, concluded that the sample sizes (of four and forty-four patients) were too small to meet the scientific standards of a New Drug Application (NDA).[22]

Despite these limitations, most members of the PDAC were willing to conclude that the 0.125 mg dose was effective *by extrapolating beyond the controlled clinical trial data to experience of use of the drug in clinical practice.*[23] For example, David Dunner, Professor of Psychiatry at the University of Washington Medical Centre, reasoned: 'I think that if these were a new NDA, looking at the dose ranges being described, I think there would be an inadequate number of patients to support efficacy. But I think that, given the clinical use of this drug, the efficacy is supported.'[24]

Similarly, Ereshefsky surmised:

> I think many of us have the *sense* that we are dealing with an effective drug, but the data that we are looking at isn't satisfying . . . I think there's enough data to at least begin to address that issue . . . my sense is that there's enough data out there to suggest that the blood levels achieved in most people at the doses being used is sufficient for sedation.[25]

In addition, the PDAC considered two main types of safety data: controlled clinical trials and post-marketing spontaneous reports of adverse drug reactions (ADRs) in clinical practice, which the FDA stores in its Spontaneous Reporting System (SRS) database. The latter demonstrated that triazolam was associated with far more reports of adverse central nervous system (CNS) effects per prescription than another benzodiazepine hypnotic, temazepam (Restoril) – about forty times as many seizures, twenty-six times as many cases of amnesia, twenty-three times as many cases of hostility, thirteen times as many cases of dependence and over ten times as many cases of psychosis, even after adjusting for secular trends in reporting. Robert Temple, the FDA's Director of New Drug Evaluation, characterised some of these adverse events as 'scary'.[26] As the incidence of triazolam ADR reports increased with dosage and the *large risk ratios remained*, despite adjusting for many factors, including publicity, time of entry into the market, manufacturers' reporting practices and secular trends in overall reporting rates,[27] among others,[28] FDA's epidemiologists concluded that triazolam's high reporting rate ratios for amnesia, dependence, hostility, psychosis and seizures appeared to 'reflect actual differences in risk of neuropsychiatric adverse effect causation', and that triazolam appeared to 'have *greater intrinsic capacity* to provoke these adverse effects'.[29]

The FDA's presentation of safety data from controlled clinical trials analysed twenty-five Upjohn-sponsored studies with insomniacs of at least

Table 3.1. Drop-out analysis sorted by dose[30]

Patient Groups	Per Cent Drop-out/Risk Ratio		
	Triazolam	Flurazepam	Tr/Fl
Any Adverse Event			
Low dose	19/272 (7.0%)	3/71 (4.2%)	1.7
High dose	126/896 (14.1%)	55/536 (10.3%)	1.4*
Anxiety			
Low dose	8/272 (2.9%)	0/71 (0.0%)	>>
High dose	36/896 (4.0%)	9/536 (1.7%)	2.4*
Memory Impairment			
Low dose	0/272 (0.0%)	0/71 (0.0%)	—
High dose	8/896 (0.9%)	0/536 (0.0%)	>>
All Psychiatric Adverse Events			
Low dose	9/272 (3.3%)	0/71 (0.0%)	>>
High dose	54/896 (6.0%)	15/536 (2.8%)	2.1*

Note: * = statistically significant (p<0.05, 1-sided p-value, Fisher's exact test)
>> = 'infinitely large' and hence 'significant'
Low dose = 0.125, 0.125–0.25, 0.25 mg Halcion; 15 mg Dalmane
High dose = 0.25–0.5, 0.5, 0.6 mg Halcion; 15–30, 30 mg Dalmane

one week duration, comparing triazolam with flurazepam (Dalmane) or placebo. These twenty-five studies involved 1,168 patients on triazolam, 607 on flurazepam and 566 on placebo, comparing 0.5 mg triazolam with 30 mg of flurazepam ('high' doses) and/or 0.125/0.25 mg of triazolam with 15 mg of flurazepam ('low' doses). That is, they assumed that 30 mg of flurazepam was 'equipotent' to 0.5 mg of triazolam and 15 mg of flurazepam was 'equipotent' to 0.25 mg of triazolam. There was a statistically significantly higher risk of patients dropping out of trials due to adverse reactions when taking 0.5 mg triazolam than when on 30 mg flurazepam, and that relative risk increased when considering solely 'psychiatric' adverse effects (Table 3.1). These differences were not statistically significant at the lower doses.

The findings in Table 3.1 supported the trends identified in the SRS data, albeit at much lower levels. However, FDA scientists also presented an alternative analysis in which they accepted Upjohn's argument that 30 mg of flurazepam was equipotent to just 0.25 mg of triazolam, even though the trials themselves were based on protocols defining 30 mg of flurazepam as equipotent to 0.5 mg of triazolam.[31] Given that the adverse effects of triazolam were generally dose-related, an acceptance that 30 mg of flurazepam was equipotent with just 0.25 mg of Halcion was guaranteed to lower the recorded risk of triazolam relative to flurazepam.

FDA scientists constructed 'appropriately dosed' patient groups in which 'low'-dose triazolam was compared with 'high'-dose flurazepam. As the clinical trials were not designed in this way, the length of time for which 'appropriately dosed' patients had taken the two drugs was very different and the sample dropped to about a quarter of its original size (Table 3.2). Specifically, the relatively small sample ensured that the analysis lacked the power to translate differences into statistical significance, and secondly, patients were dosed for much longer on flurazepam, thus skewing analysis in favour of triazolam.[33] Taking all the adverse effects together, the 'appropriately dosed' analysis implied a

Table 3.2. Sample size and duration of use features for 'appropriately dosed' subgroups[32]

Subgroup Features	Triazolam	Flurazepam
Sample size	285 patients	423 patients
Median duration	7 days	14 days

disappearance of any difference in risk in clinical trials for drop-out between triazolam and flurazepam,[34] but a greater risk remained for triazolam psychiatric adverse effects, albeit without statistical significance (Table 3.3).

Seven out of eight PDAC members voted that triazolam was safe and effective at the doses of 0.125 mg and 0.25 mg as recommended in the labelling.[36] They *prioritised the safety data from controlled clinical trials in spite of the robustness of the SRS data,* as Ereshefsky noted: 'The spontaneous reporting data was the most bothersome of all the data, this apparently large signal sticking out there, and the agency has done a good job of trying to explain it away and control for variables, and it's still there.'[37] Even in the closing minutes of the meeting, another of these seven members said: 'I don't believe that there is not safety – I fail to believe that there is safety.'[38]

The triazolam case illustrates just how complex bias in regulatory science can become. A great deal of technical manipulation may be involved, including interpretative frameworks of the manufacturer. Nevertheless, these complexities do not detract from the evident bias in favour of the commercial interests of the company over and above the interests of public health. The fundamental bias is reflected in the inconsistency of interpretation of types of data. The PDAC gave priority to anecdotal evidence about triazolam in use instead of controlled trial evidence when assessing *efficacy,* but gave priority to controlled clinical trial evidence instead of ancedotal evidence when assessing *safety.* This is technically contradictory, but it is consistent with the commercial goal

Table 3.3. Summary drop-out analysis for 'appropriately dosed' patients[35]

	Number of Drop-out Events Risk Ratio		
Adverse Event Term	Triazolam (N=285)	Flurazepam (N=423)	Tr/Fl
Any adverse event	20 (7.0%)	31 (7.3%)	1.0
All 'psychiatric'	8 (2.8%)	7 (1.7%)	1.7
Anxiety	8 (2.8%)	4 (0.9%)	3.0
Memory impairment	0	0	—

Note: * = statistically significant (p<0.05, 1-sided p-value, Fisher's exact test) >> = 'infinitely large' and hence 'significant'.

of maintaining the drug on the market, irrespective of the scientific evidence. Furthermore, this bias was supported by a secondary bias in favouring Upjohn's interpretation of the controlled trial safety data over the initial analysis by FDA scientists because that decision was without technical basis.

The production of 'scientific' standards

One of the most influential bodies in establishing international scientific standards in recent times is the International Conference on Harmonisation of Technical Requirements for Registration of Pharmaceuticals for Human Use (ICH). The key participants are scientists from the three pharmaceutical industry associations and three government drug regulatory agencies of the EU, Japan and the US – the three largest pharmaceutical markets in the world. Since 1991 the ICH has developed 'science-based' guidelines on drug quality, safety and efficacy for new drug approval, which the regulatory agencies of the EU, Japan and the US invariably adopt. Furthermore, ICH guidelines may go beyond the EU, Japan and the US. For example, the drug regulatory authorities of Australia, Canada and the European Free Trade Association (EFTA) have already adopted some ICH guidelines, and WHO officials have indicated that, in the long term, the results of ICH may provide a basis for the revision of WHO guidelines on clinical evaluation of new drugs.[39] While all ICH standards require the agreement of the EU, Japanese and US regulatory agencies, the ICH process is industry-led, as indicated by the fact that the International Federation of Pharmaceutical Manufacturers' Associations (IFPMA) is its secretariat.

Specifically, the origins of ICH are in the industry's decline in productivity in terms of the number of new chemical and biological entities launched on the market between 1975 and 1990.[40] In response, the industry strove to decrease the cost and duration of R&D by reducing regulatory requirements, and to reach larger markets more effectively. Such transnational firms could get better returns on R&D investments if they could access international markets more or less simultaneously, but faced increased costs if they had to cope with separate, and sometimes divergent, national regulatory regimes.[41]

While these industrial and trade interests have motivated pharmaceutical harmonisation, the ICH process is often presented by its proponents as a scientific endeavour in the interests of patients and public health. At the opening session of the first ICH conference in Belgium in

1991, it was argued that the savings made by companies from harmonised regulations would further the delivery of innovative research yielding therapeutic benefit to patients.[42] Four years later, at the opening of the third ICH conference in Yokohama, the Director-General of the Japanese drug regulatory authorities declared that 'patients should be given the highest priority', and that 'the judgement criteria for any discussions in ICH are – is this for the benefit of patients?'[43] The secretariat of the ICH contended that 'the urgent need' for harmonisation was 'impelled' by 'the need to meet the public expectation that there should be a minimum of delay in making safe and efficacious treatments available to patients in need'.[44]

In this section, I shall examine only the ICH's safety standards that have a bearing on the exposure of patients on drug trials for non-life-threatening diseases to drugs before completion of carcinogenicity testing. The purpose of carcinogenicity testing is to determine whether a drug causes cancer in the experimental animals and, therefore, poses a carcinogenic risk to humans. Animal carcinogenicity testing is important because cancers in humans and other mammals are often induced over long periods of the life-span and may manifest themselves some time after the carcinogenic exposure. Testing on rodents permits lifespan exposure (usually for eighteen to thirty months), which is *not duplicated* in the clinical sphere, because it is impractical and self-defeating to test a drug in patients over their lifespan of about seventy years.

According to the FDA, pharmaceuticals generally used for three months or more require carcinogenicity testing, while under the drug regulations of the EU and Japan such studies are required if patients take the drug continuously for at least six months or frequently in an intermittent manner so that the total exposure is similar to continual exposure of six months or more. Furthermore, it is expected that most pharmaceuticals indicated for three months treatment would also be likely to be used for six months.[45] The clear implication of this is that exposure to a drug for more than three or six months presents a potential carcinogenic risk, which needs to be screened for by long-term animal testing.

This is relevant to the exposure of patients in clinical trials because, in order for potential ADRs to be detected during clinical drug evaluation, the trials need to last for up to a year, as recommended by ICH scientists themselves:

> There is concern that, although they are likely to be uncommon, some adverse drug events (ADEs) may increase in frequency or severity with time

or that some serious ADEs may occur only after drug treatment for more than 6 months. Therefore, some patients should be treated with the drug for 12 months.[46]

In other words, when conducting clinical trials with new drugs intended to be used long-term to treat non-life-threatening illnesses, some serious and non-serious ADRs might not be detected properly, or at all, without trials of up to one year's duration – and some trials last for more than one year.[47] For such drugs, clinical trial data on patients treated for twelve months must be submitted to the regulatory agencies prior to marketing approval in the US and Japan.[48]

Yet ICH scientists also recommended that 'completed rodent carcinogenicity studies are not needed in advance of the conduct of large scale clinical trials, unless there is special concern for the patient population'.[49] Given that the US and Japanese regulatory agencies acknowledge that there must be some clinical trial data of twelve months prior to marketing approval, then this is entirely inconsistent with the FDA's technical requirement of carcinogenicity testing for drugs to be used for more than three months. In effect, the ICH recommended that no carcinogenicity testing needs to be completed prior to exposing patients to new drugs for more than three months or even six months *during clinical trials.* The ICH process did not even consider the possibility of the international harmonisation of regulations so that the completion of carcinogenicity testing in rodents is required prior to exposing patients to long-term clinical trials of over three or six months.

Clearly the construction of these 'technical' standards involved the interests of the pharmaceutical industry and regulatory agencies. While this may be suggestive of bias towards commercial interests, it does not itself constitute bias because it is theoretically possible for these institutions to produce coherent regulatory science in the interests of public health. The bias, however, is evident from the inconsistencies in the 'technical' standards, which reflect the prioritisation of commercial interests over public health. Unfortunately, such bias in ICH's 'scientific' standards is not unusual.

Discussion and conclusion

Science cannot be understood as entirely divorced from its social context. Nor can it be value-free or disinterested, as some conventional sociologists and philosophers have supposed. On the other hand, science is not merely politics by another name as some modern relativists would have us believe.[50] The systematic pursuit of knowledge does matter, not least in medicine and in the endeavour to improve public health. The declared goal of drug testing and regulatory science is to produce knowledge underpinning the supply of safe and effective medicines beneficial to health.

The problem is that institutions employing scientists do not necessarily produce this declared scientific outcome. Instead, bias towards commercial interests that diverge from, or are in conflict with, the interests of public health may enter 'scientific' activity, and has done so for decades. This occurs within both the science of industrial testing and the relatively unaccountable regulatory science of government agencies.

The implication for drug regulation is that a new institutional framework for scientific work in this sector is needed. Above all, such a framework should be better at producing scientific research and knowledge consistent with the declared goals of drug testing and regulation. That is, it should maximise the interests of public health and, by implication, minimise bias towards commercial interests. Such an institutional framework requires scientists to be working in a culture dominated by concern to protect and promote public health. This demands two simultaneous transformations: the conduct of some key tests of new drugs by government scientists in regulatory agencies; and full public accountability of the testing and reviewing conducted by the regulatory agencies.

Judgement would have to be applied for each drug, but generally the government scientists would aim to conduct one high-quality controlled clinical trial. At least for this trial, the government scientists would be working directly with patients and raw data, which could allow a much more rigorous, insightful and independent analysis. All scientific reviews and data underpinning regulatory decisions would be placed in the public domain immediately upon completion and government scientists would be required to justify their regulatory analyses and decisions before a public investigation at the end of each year.

This framework has the additional advantage of building up a major body of scientific expertise in drug testing outside the pharmaceutical industry. The new testing responsibilities of the regulatory agencies need not cost the taxpayer, because the pharmaceutical companies could be charged the cost of the mandated tests. Nor would it produce duplication of tests by different national agencies because, as ICH has demonstrated, regulatory agencies can easily share their regulatory science internationally.

Nevertheless, it is unlikely that science-based pharmaceutical regulation in the interests of public health can be achieved without some support from public finances. The current situation in which some drug regulatory agencies, such as the Irish Medicines Board and the UK Medicines and Healthcare Products Regulatory Agency, are entirely funded by fees from pharmaceutical companies is not conducive to independent regulatory science, especially when regulatory agencies are competing with each other for such fees in exchange for rapid drug approvals.[51] Governments need to provide core funding for regulatory agencies so that their scientific reviewing can maintain public health priorities irrespective of pressure from pharmaceutical companies for rapid approval of their products.

PART TWO

Medicines Regulation in Ireland:
Health and Democracy at Risk?

CHAPTER 4

The Emergence of Pharmaceutical Industry Regulation for Competition (aka Profit) in Ireland

Orla O'Donovan

Introduction

'Silent watchdogs' and 'servants of industry' are some of the metaphors used by critics in their analysis of what certain state drug regulation authorities have become. An article posted in July 2005 on Depressiondialogues.ie, a website established by Irish mental health movement activists, led with the heading 'IMB: watchdog that failed to bark'.[1] The article discussed the inaction of the Irish medicines regulatory authority, the Irish Medicines Board (IMB), following the issuing of a statement by its US counterpart, the Food and Drug Administration (FDA), to alert people to the possible increased risks of suicidality in adults taking certain antidepressants. While the Depressiondialogues article suggests the US system of regulation is more stringent than the Irish one in protecting the public from unsafe drugs, scathing criticisms have also been levelled against the FDA. Marcia Angell, former editor-in-chief of *The New England Journal of Medicine,* argues that changes in the US regulatory system since the 1980s, particularly legislation that made the FDA dependent for its income on fees paid by industry, resulted in the regulatory authority becoming 'big pharma's handmaiden'.[2]

In academic speak, assessments in this vein of changes in drug regulation talk about 'regulatory capture' and see it as a feature of neo-liberal capitalism, the phase of capitalism that emerged in the 1980s. Angell's commentary on the recent history of the FDA supports the argument that regulatory authorities can be 'captured', so that their role is changed and they serve the interests of the very industry they are supposed to regulate. In a similar vein, as will be elaborated below, research undertaken by John Abraham on several drug regulatory regimes has prompted him to conclude that they have become highly susceptible to pharmaceutical industrial capture.[3] He argues that many European countries have witnessed the emergence of 'neo-liberal regulatory states' that privilege commercial interests over the interests of public health and democracy.[4] There are strong parallels between the regulatory capture thesis and a broader argument that a consequence of capitalist globalisation is that many Western countries have shifted from being ostensible 'welfare states' to 'competition states', evident in the prioritisation of economic competitiveness over public welfare.[5] In this chapter, I present a short history of medicines regulation in Ireland in light of these ideas.

There has been a double redefining of the role of the Irish state in protecting the public from unsafe and ineffective medicines. First, the state shifted from a Pontius Pilate 'it's nothing to do with us' official attitude at the time of the thalidomide drug disaster in the 1960s to the establishment of a severely under-resourced and consequently largely ineffective regulatory system. This initial regulatory system was primarily concerned with pharmacovigilance; i.e. promoting drug safety by monitoring reports of suspected negative side effects of medicines, or adverse drug reactions (ADRs). Second, the establishment of the Irish Medicines Board in 1995 constituted a move to a commodified and industry-funded drug regulation system principally concerned with the industry's priority of speedy drug licensing, which enables the marketing of pharmaceuticals as quickly as possible. I argue that this second resituating of the state involved a new mode of capitalist regulation, a shift from 'hands-off' regulation to regulation for 'competition'.

It is a story of a realm of policy-making that is intensely secretive and scientised, and one where the limitations of parliamentary politics in contributing to public debate about issues that are literally of vital importance to citizens are laid bare.[6] Despite the growing importance of drug regulation for public health due to the dramatic escalation in the consumption of pharmaceutical industry products and messages, there has been scarcely any public debate about the significant changes that have occurred. It is a sphere in which scientific expertise, which is officially constructed as neutral and immune from the social milieu in which it is produced, allegedly drives the regulatory process and where the scope for public participation in decision-making and scientific knowledge production is severely constrained. While official discourses increasingly proclaim that regulatory policy is the outcome of 'evidence-based policy-making', this short history highlights the significance of a number of aspects of the political and ideological context that have shaped the Irish medicines regulatory regime, not least of which is the Irish state's eager embracing of neo-liberalism and its logic of economic competitiveness. Neo-liberalism is often associated with calls for reduced state intervention, policies that *deregulate* the private sector. For example, the president of Merck Sharpe & Dohme's Europe, Middle East and Africa division has argued that the EU has failed to create the right environment for pharmaceutical innovation and the pharmaceutical industry in Europe is disadvantaged compared to its US counterpart 'as a function of over-regulation'.[7] Against this, I argue that neo-liberalism is better characterised as involving *reregulation,* a new mode of state and supranational authority intervention that prioritises the facilitation of corporate profit-making, now euphemistically referred to as 'competitiveness'.

Regulatory capture and the competition state

The regulatory capture thesis was developed by political economists in the 1970s in response to what were perceived as the naiveties of 'public interest' approaches to state regulation, which maintained that regulation is generated by governments to protect the interests of the public from abuses of the regulated industries.[8] The regulatory capture thesis argues that state regulation can develop in such a way that it exists primarily to benefit those who are subject to the regulation, as argued by Angell in her analysis of the FDA. State institutions are understood to be shaped by, rather than insulated from, the political context in which they function and powerful interest groups are thought to have the capacity to capture governments (and supranational authorities) to promote their own interests. The diffusion of private-sector values and *modus operandi*, enabled by the 'revolving door' that allows the easy movement of personnel between industry and the state, is a central theme in much of the literature on regulatory capture.[9] In some formulations of this approach, 'capture' refers to a historical process whereby regulatory regimes with public interest origins come to be dominated by powerful interests. Other formulations question the assumption that regulatory authorities are established to serve the public interest in the first place and assert that the main emphasis has always been on risk management and damage limitation aimed at protecting the commercial interests of industry.

While recognising that the notion of regulatory capture can lead to oversimplified accounts of regulatory regimes that fail to acknowledge the complex and sometimes contradictory nature of the state, John Abraham nevertheless uses the term in his analysis of international drug regulation trends over the past fifty years.[10] In explaining the concept he says: 'The more the pharmaceutical industry influences the perspective of the regulatory agency – so it comes to adopt their interests over and above those of patients – the more the agency could be said to be captured.'[11] Here the 'perspective' of the regulatory agency refers to its institutional culture, underlying policy paradigm, logic and common sense knowledge, manifested in its interpretations of the role and priorities of drug regulation, the contribution of drugs to promoting health, the kinds of knowledge that it validates and the actors it deems to have a legitimate role in the regulatory process. By way of example, Abraham points to research that shows how some senior European regulatory officials have come to believe the industry 'truth' that speedy regulatory processes are desirable because they ensure that patients have access to drugs in the fastest time possible. Abraham identifies a series of trends that reflect and enable regulatory authorities' increasing vulnerability to capture by the pharmaceutical industry: the industry is succeeding in assuming a major role in shaping the regulatory science and safety standards used in drug testing and risk-benefit assessment; drug regulation agencies have become increasingly reliant on industry fees for their operating costs; the marketing approval process whereby regulatory authorities assess the safety and efficacy of drugs is being accelerated, not least because EU policy now encourages the drug agencies of member states to compete with each other for business by selling their speedy approval processes for new drugs; the ongoing failure to seriously address conflicts of interest, particularly in respect of the scientific experts who act as advisers to regulatory authorities; the continuing secrecy and lack of public accountability of drug regulation authorities; and regulatory bodies' dogged reluctance to develop rigorous systems of pharmacovigilance.

Specifically in relation to the history of drug regulation in Germany, Sweden and Britain, John Abraham and Graham Lewis argue that some of the trends listed above amount to the emergence of neo-liberal regulation.[12] These three national governments, they argue, moved from being regulatory states significantly concerned with re-establishing public trust in the safety of drugs to being neo-liberal regulatory states that are highly sensitised to responding to the pharmaceutical industry's demands for extended private property rights and profits from investments in research and development. According to Abraham and Lewis, the initial emergence of the regulatory state created a new form of citizenship, as it extended the responsibilities of the state into the realm of protecting citizens from unsafe medicines and curtailed the pharmaceutical industry's private property rights to sell medicines that did not have official authorisation. This new form of citizenship, however, has tended to be passive, as regulatory systems generally operate in a highly secretive manner (thus protecting the private property rights of industry) and in a way that constructs drug regulation as a purely technical matter, best left to scientific experts. In recent years, this secrecy and exclusion has been increasingly challenged by patients' organisations, especially those mobilised in the aftermath of drug disasters. However, Abraham and Lewis argue that, in the face of these challenges, regulatory authorities have been seen to form alliances with the manufacturers of drugs, resulting in situations where citizens have had to look to the courts rather than the regulatory state to redress their grievances with drug companies.

There is significant resonance between these arguments about captured neo-liberal medicines regulation and the claim that in recent years many 'welfare states' have been transformed into 'competition states', although the former approach emphasises changes in institutional cultures and the latter places the emphasis on changing global economic relations. The competition state thesis, as expounded by Peadar Kirby and Mary Murphy, is that capitalist globalisation has eroded the conditions that are conducive to strong welfare states, as states fear being bypassed by footloose international investors if they have domestic policies that hamper profit accumulation.[13] The increased mobility of international investment due to new information and communications technologies is regarded as a key feature of this new phase of capitalism in which nation states compete with each other for transnational corporation investment. In contrast to the argument that capitalist globalisation has resulted in the eclipsing of the nation state, rendering it irrelevant, they argue that changed global economic conditions have created pressures on Western states to redefine their core activities and change the nature of governance. This argument challenges the frequent association of neo-liberalism with deregulation and the withdrawal of the state, but instead suggests that we are witnessing reregulation, a transformation in state regulatory discourses and practices. Increasingly, the logic of economic competitiveness informs state interpretations of regulation: the shift from a welfare to a competition state involves a move 'from a regulation that sought to harness market forces for the welfare of society to one that seeks to impose competitive disciplines on society for the good of the market'.[14] This resituating of the state is evident in a de-emphasising of (albeit limited) redistributive discourses and measures and a prioritisation of promoting profitable entrepreneurialism, and amounts to the state prioritising 'the well-being of market actors over the well-being of citizens'.[15] It entails a redefining of the relationship between the state and the citizenry, an undermining of the power of nation states, and a consolidation of the power of transnational market actors, namely transnational corporations and their owners. While global economic transformations in capitalism impel this change in the state, competition state theorists emphasise that the emergence of the competition state is by no means inevitable and that it manifests itself differently in different national contexts.

Kirby and Murphy note that a significant shortcoming of competition state theory is its limited empirical application. However, the conclusion that emerges from their initial research into Ireland's social security regime is that the Irish state is an exemplar of a competition state, a state that has wholeheartedly embraced global market actors and forces. Furthermore, in contrast to countries such as France and Germany, Kirby bemoans the absence of widespread public resistance to this prioritisation by the state of enabling corporate profits over promoting citizen's welfare.[16] The analysis of the history of the Irish drug regulation system presented here provides a further example of an empirical analysis using the analytical frame of the competition state. In keeping with the argument that the emergence of the competition state plays out differently in different contexts, it is worth noting a number of significant aspects of the context in which the Irish system of drug regulation developed. These are the approach to economic development of consecutive Irish governments since the late 1950s that prioritised making Ireland an attractive location for transnational corporate investment, a tradition of a secretive and centralised system of government, a weak welfare state with a healthcare system that facilitates market-based medicine, a deepening denial of conflicts of interest evident in the dominance of the ideology of consensualist 'partnership' governance and, in recent years, an official framing of state policy that prioritises the so-called Lisbon objectives to make the European economy the most competitive economy in the world.

The emergence of the regulatory state in Ireland

While the welfare state in some countries such as Sweden extended into the realm of drug regulation as early as the 1930s, it was not until the

1960s that this happened in Ireland. In 1962, when the thalidomide drug disaster (that resulted in an estimated 8,000 deaths at birth and 10,000 people being born with disabilities worldwide) became apparent, the initial response of the Irish government was that it had no responsibility in regard to harm caused by the drug and that compensation was a private matter between the individuals affected and the German-based manufacturers of the drug. Thalidomide sold very well in Ireland between 1959 and 1961 as an 'over-the-counter' drug, but the extent of harm it caused is difficult to determine. In 1970, when the Department of Health placed an advertisement in the press inviting people who were affected to come forward, eighty-four responses were received. However, when compensation was eventually paid in the mid-1970s, only thirty-three people were deemed to be 'thalidomide children'.

For the period immediately following this drug disaster, the position of the Irish government was that it had no role in ensuring the safety of medicines and in compensating people harmed by them. In 1968, when the Minister for Health (Seán Flanagan) was asked in the Dáil if the Department of Health had taken any initiative on behalf of the victims, he replied: 'My Department would have no standing in relation to civil claims in respect of deformity alleged to have been caused by this drug.'[17] This initial reluctance on the part of the state to accept any culpability for the disaster was also reflected in its refusal to provide healthcare free of charge to the victims. When free medical care was called for over and over again in the Dáil between 1968 and 1972, it was repeatedly refused. Then, as now, the limited public system of healthcare entitled only those on low incomes (and, since 2001, older people) to medical cards, which allowed them to access general practitioner and hospital services free of charge. In the history of Irish healthcare, struggles to introduce even modest measures in socialised healthcare have been thwarted, producing a system in which lucrative market-based medicine is publicly subsidised and leeches off the public system.[18]

It was not until 1972 that the first allegation of state neglect was made in the Dáil in respect of the thalidomide disaster. The then Labour Party Deputy, John O'Connell TD, stated that: 'The tragedy in Ireland can be attributed in no small measure to the negligence of the Department of Health who allowed, under our laws, the dispensing of this drug over the counter.'[19] His and others' repeated questions in the Dáil during this period can be regarded as calls for a resituating of the state in respect of drug safety. It is likely that the Association for Justice for Thalidomide

Children, formed by parents of children who were affected, also played an important role in challenging the interpretation of the role of the state at the time, which saw it as having no responsibility in protecting citizens from unsafe medicines. Gradually, the position of the state changed. In 1973, it was announced that as a matter of social justice the government was establishing a fund to augment the compensation paid to the victims by the manufacturers of the drug. Around this time too it was decided that medical cards should be given to all of the victims. This period also saw the emergence of a drug regulation system.

The state doggedly refused to disclose information about the extent of the harm caused by thalidomide. In 1962, the Minister for Health requested the Medical Research Council of Ireland to include babies born with deformities caused by thalidomide in its survey of congenital disabilities. However, in 1964 the Minister reported that the study was unable to determine those cases where deformities were caused by the drug. A further study was initiated to see if there was a reduction in the number of babies born with disabilities following withdrawal of the drug. In 1968, the Minister reported that this subsequent study suggested that fifty-three children had deformities that were possibly caused by thalidomide. The government repeatedly refused to publish this report. Following a request in 1968 to make the report available to the public, the Minister said that it was not in the public interest to do so.[20] The refusal to publish the report was raised again in the Dáil in 1972, when it was noted that the author of the report had been forbidden by the Department of Health to make it publicly available. This refusal to disclose information about the harm caused by thalidomide is consistent with many historians' commentaries on the Irish state's obsessional concern with secrecy. Dermot Keogh attributes the tradition of secretive democratic centralism to a number of factors.[21] These include the colonial inheritance of the closed and secretive Westminster model of governance, the emergence of a system of 'strong' government in the face of the perceived threat of subversion of the state by the Irish Republican Army (IRA), the legacy of the post-civil-war distrust between government and opposition and a civic culture in which literary censorship was normalised. Keogh asserts that between 1922 and 1960 Irish government and ministerial attitudes and behaviour were characterised by 'an obsessional concern with secrecy' and 'at worst outright hostility for the citizen's right to know'.[22] Such secrecy and the official expectation of passive citizenship were to become par for the course in the newly emerging regulatory state.

The transition from 'hands-off' regulation to regulation for 'competition'

In an account of the historical relationship between the pharmaceutical industry and the state, the Irish Pharmaceutical Healthcare Association (IPHA), the body that represents the interests of the globalised pharmaceutical industry in Ireland, notes that in the late 1960s the Irish state identified the pharmaceutical industry as one that it wanted to attract to Ireland. It sought to entice this transnational investment through its education, taxation, labour and health policies. Furthermore, it is noted that 'A crucial element in that success story was the State's willingness to engage in a dialogue with the pharmaceutical sector, to seek mutually beneficial solutions to any difficulties which arose . . .'.[23] However, it was not until the 1990s that corporatist dialogue came to characterise state/pharmaceutical industry regulatory relations. Fundamental to corporatism is the belief that state-coordinated dialogue between diverse 'stakeholders' can resolve conflicts of interest and produce win-win consensualist policy-making. This approach has become a defining feature of Irish governance since the era of social partnership began in 1987 with the first so-called 'national agreement'. Obfuscation of conflicts of interest is similarly a feature of Irish state regulatory discourses. The Taoiseach's foreword to the 2004 White Paper *Regulating Better* spells out the official interpretation of what constitutes good regulation; it ensures that Ireland continues to be a competitive and open economy and promotes the Lisbon objectives of making the EU the most competitive economic bloc in the world.[24] While emphasis is placed on 'simpler' regulation that provides 'predictability and certainty in the business world', the White Paper suggests that such corporate-friendly regulation can coincide with regulation that protects citizens' rights. In other words, pharma-friendly regulation is win-win regulation that benefits pharmaceutical corporations and citizens alike.

Corporatist 'partnership' structures are just one of many significant differences between the National Drugs Advisory Board (NDAB), established in 1966, and the body that replaced it in 1995, the Irish Medicines Board (IMB). The NDAB was entirely funded by the state and all of the members of the board were clinicians or civil servants. In contrast, the IMB receives scarcely any funding from the exchequer, as most of its income is derived from fees paid by industry, reflecting the commodification of its activities. Furthermore, membership of the second board of the IMB appointed by the Minister for Health and Children included the Chief Executive Officer of the Irish Pharmaceutical

Healthcare Association. While the first chairman of the NDAB was a professor of therapeutics, the first chairman of the IMB was a former general manager of the Allied Irish Banks Group. These differences reflect a resituating of the regulatory state and a granting of a new role to the industry in funding the key regulatory authority and to private sector actors in key decision-making arenas. As I explain below, these two regulatory bodies are significantly different in their interpretations of the priorities of medicines regulation.

The National Drugs Advisory Board

The National Drugs Advisory Board was established in 1966 and its functions were to gather information about drug safety and to advise the Minister about drugs that could be marketed in the state. This initial licensing scheme was a voluntary one. It was not until 1975, prompted by a series of EU Directives, that licences or product authorisations became compulsory. The NDAB then became responsible for processing product authorisation applications, but responsibility for issuing licences rested with the Minister for Health. By 1987, the responsibilities of the NDAB had been extended to advising the Minister about the mandatory licences that were, by then, required for blood products and clinical trials.

The superiority of post-marketing pharmacovigilance over pre-marketing clinical trials as a source of drug safety information is widely recognised. Clinical trials tend to involve relatively small numbers of people and homogeneous populations. Some adverse reactions only come to light when a drug is used in the wider community and over long periods of time. The pharmacovigilance work of the NDAB was, however, seriously stymied by the lack of reporting of adverse drug reactions (ADRs) by health professionals. Then, as now, direct reporting of ADRs by patients suffering the ill effects of drugs was not allowed and patients had to rely on health professionals doing so on their behalf. In recent years a number of countries have piloted or initiated systems that allow direct reporting by patients in recognition of their valuable contribution to knowledge production concerning drug safety.[25] In 1981, the NDAB estimated that only about 5 per cent of ADRs occurring in general hospitals were being reported, and almost none from maternity and psychiatric hospitals.[26] In 1995, during a debate in the Seanad about the IMB Bill, one senator (Mary Henry) addressed the gross under-reporting of ADRs and expressed hope that the establishment of the IMB would contribute towards rectifying this.[27]

While pharmacovigilance never rose to the top of the drug regulation policy agenda, the industry priority of accelerating the product authorisation process did. Similar to the criticisms made of regulatory authorities in other countries, during the 1980s the NDAB was accused of being tardy in processing licence applications and was criticised because of its mounting backlog. By 1986, a backlog of 2,097 applications had accumulated.[28] By the mid-1990s, official documents indicate that there was widespread frustration with the regulatory system operated jointly by the NDAB and the Department of Health. In 1995, the Minister of State at the Department of Health (Brian O'Shea) stated that it was 'cumbersome and unsatisfactory'.[29]

What is remarkable about the prioritisation of the backlog issue is the virtual absence of evidence of critical questioning amongst policy-makers about its causes and consequences for public health. In fact, reading the parliamentary 'debates' about the establishment of the IMB suggests that this is a misnomer, as striking features of these discussions are the absence of any real debate and the repetition *ad nauseam* of similar positions. With a few exceptions, the explosion in the number of drugs queuing up to go on the Irish market and the pharmaceutical invasion of public spending on health were not questioned. By and large, the equation of more drugs with better health was accepted. An examination of the parliamentary debates reveals that the backlog was almost invariably discussed with reference to the importance of the pharmaceutical industry to the Irish economy and the industry's disquiet about the delays in getting its products onto the Irish market. A further factor that is likely to have contributed to the prioritisation of speedy processing of product authorisation applications is the introduction of the mutual recognition procedure in the EU that coincided with the establishment of the IMB in 1995. Under this new system drug companies choose the regulatory authority they want to undertake the product authorisation assessment and, therefore, the IMB has to compete with other regulatory authorities for business in this newly commodified European regulatory system in which the industry rather than the public are the 'customers'.

It would be inaccurate, however, to suggest that the prioritisation of the backlog of licences resulted solely from responsiveness to industry pressure. A consequence of the backlog was the unsafe practice of issuing product authorisation renewals on a retrospective basis, as revealed in public inquiries into the mass infection of women with hepatitis C. The hepatitis C affair, which is widely regarded as the biggest public health scandal in the history of the state, played a significant role in highlighting the failings of the regulatory system operated by the NDAB. However, only for the protests of Positive Action, an organisation of women infected with hepatitis C by contaminated blood products produced by the state's Blood Transfusion Service Board, these regulatory failings would never have been named and made public.

Over the past decade, a series of tribunals of enquiry prompted by other health scandals made public by recently mobilised patients' organisations have also shown the NDAB in a poor light and provide evidence that it facilitated the pharmaceutical industry while compromising the well-being of citizens. For example, in 1973 the NDAB gave approval for a trial of a Wellcome-manufactured vaccine to be conducted in so-called 'mother and baby homes', institutions to which unmarried mothers were secreted away. These women exercised little control over the welfare of either themselves or their babies and the issue of consent to the trial did not even arise.[30] The Lindsay Tribunal into the infection of haemophiliacs with HIV and hepatitis C provided further evidence of the NDAB's failure to contribute to the protection of the consumers of blood products. The Senior Counsel who represented the Irish Medicines Board at the tribunal stated that the board had never been sufficiently resourced to carry out its functions properly. In addition to being extremely under funded, he described the licensing scheme adopted in Ireland in the late 1970s as a 'hands-off approach'.[31] Further evidence of the disorder within and lack of transparency of the NDAB is the fact that, by 1995, it had yet to publish its annual report for 1991. In sum, the drug regulation system that emerged in the aftermath of the thalidomide disaster bore the hallmarks of a feeble welfare state.

The Irish Medicines Board

In 1995, the National Drugs Advisory Board was replaced by a new industry-funded body, the Irish Medicines Board. While the NDAB was an advisory body, the IMB is a licensing authority, and therefore it assumed responsibility for functions previously performed by the Department of Health. There was unanimous support from the major political parties for the establishment of the IMB. Furthermore, its establishment was enthusiastically welcomed by the pharmaceutical industry. The importance of close and co-operative relations between the state and the industry was emphasised by most contributors to the Oireachtas discussions about the establishment of the IMB; it was repeated mantra-like when the IMB Bill was discussed. This desire for close links with the industry was reflected in the Minister for Health and Children's appointment of the Chief Executive Officer of the industry body IPHA to the IMB in 2001. A representative of the industry's interests, therefore, was given a key decision-making position in the Irish regulatory system.

The legislation under which the IMB was established placed an obligation on the board to be self-financing. There was broad support among politicians for this funding arrangement. Where concern was expressed, it tended to stem from a fear that it would be contrary to the policy of enticing the industry to locate in Ireland. It should be remembered that by the mid-1990s the pharmaceutical industry accounted for almost a quarter of Irish exports and was widely regarded as playing a central role in the achievement of the so-called Celtic Tiger economy. Prior to the 1960s, the pharmaceutical industry had virtually no presence in Ireland, but government policies such as a low corporate tax rate and ensuring the availability of industrial sites that met the locational requirements of the pharmaceutical industry (including access to high volumes of water and effluent disposal facilities) had successfully attracted footloose transnational pharmaceutical corporation investment.[32]

While within parliamentary arenas the industry-financing arrangement was generally perceived to be laudable, the Fianna Fáil senator Marian McGennis was amongst the small number of dissenters. In a speech in Seanad Éireann, she asked if the IMB 'is to be self-financing, is it possible its work might be compromised if it has to seek funding for its costs and cost structure?'[33] McGennis went on to point out what she regarded as a worrying reorientation in the regulatory system evident in the replacement of the NDAB with the IMB. Despite its shortcomings, the NDAB's first function had been concerned with obtaining and assessing information regarding the safety of drugs. In contrast, she noted that the first function of the IMB is 'the licensing of the manufacture, preparation, importation, distribution and sale of medicinal products', the pre-marketing assessments of drugs required to get them on the market. McGennis's concerns had no impact on the course of the legislation. The IMB was established in early 1996 and in the second annual report the chairman of the board stated that he was pleased to declare that the new regulatory authority had operated with no cost to the taxpayer.[34] Since then, the IMB has operated without state subsidy.

The IMB successfully tackled the backlog issue and reduced the duration of the product authorisation process. By January 2002, the backlog had been reduced to 327 licence applications, down from 2,097 in 1986. In 1999, the median time for new product authorisations was 73 weeks; one year later, it had been reduced to 45 weeks.[35] By 2004, it was down to 34 weeks.[36] IMB reports represent this acceleration of the product authorisation process as a regulatory success, but some of the European drug regulation agency personnel interviewed by John Abraham and Graham Lewis had a different view of speedier licensing. They argued that the increased pressure on regulators to approve drugs could threaten public health, because regulators have to place greater trust in industry drug-testing data that they have less time to validate.[37] As a result of the IMB's increased efficiency, by March 2007 there were 7,915 authorised medical products for human use on the Irish market. Critics of the proliferation of drugs licensed for sale in Western countries highlight that many supposedly new medicines are simply 'me too' drugs, copies of drugs already on the market, and many others, especially so-called lifestyle drugs used in the treatment of recently medicalised conditions, are of dubious benefit.[38] In 2005, there were 306 drugs on the World Health Organisation's Model List of Essential Medicines.[39]

There is little evidence that the gross under-reporting of ADRs was similarly redressed by the IMB. The number of ADRs reported to the IMB decreased between 2001 and 2002, and again between 2002 and 2003. In 2004, the IMB received 1,727 ADR reports, which is very small considering that somewhere between 1 per cent and 10 per cent of administrations of medicines are thought to result in an ADR and that there are over 2,500 general practitioners prescribing to at least 100 people per week and many of these are receiving more than one medicine. The largest number of ADR reports came from marketing authorisation holders, or drug companies, the only group who are required to report ADRs. Only 277 reports were submitted by general practitioners in 2004, indicating that one in ten general practitioners on average submit one ADR report per annum. Hospital doctors, of whom there are approximately 4,000, made even fewer reports; assuming that every report comes from a different doctor, it would appear that fewer than 4 per cent of these doctors make one report per year.[40] These figures suggest that the rate of reporting ADRs may now be even worse than in the days of the NDAB. However, following resolute campaigns by aggrieved citizens and particularly mental health movement activists, official recognition has recently been given to criticisms of the ADR reporting system and a subcommittee of the Joint Oireachtas Committee on Health and Children was established in 2006 to consider the adverse side effects of pharmaceuticals. Having received extensive correspondence, particularly concerning the adverse effects of antidepressants on adults and children, a politician on this committee stated: 'If people feel there are unscrupulous practices in the supply of medication to the general public, the health committee would have an obligation to inquire into it.'[41]

The endurance of the obsession with state secrecy was evident in discussions about the establishment of the IMB. In outlining the IMB legislation in a speech in Seanad Éireann, the Minister of State at the Department of Health noted that the IMB would be required to present an annual report within six months of the end of the financial year. However, he went on to say: 'I must sound a note of caution in this context. A report might contain sensitive material and the Minister of the day might be advised that the report in its entirety at that particular time should not be laid before the Houses of the Oireachtas for legal reasons.'[42] Clearly, the days of secretive governance and passive citizenship were not over. In April 1998, the IMB became subject to the 1997 Freedom of Information Act. While the introduction of this legislation was hugely significant, the exemption of 'commercially sensitive' information, which prioritises private property rights over democratic rights, is a serious limitation. IMB strategic plans have identified better communication with 'stakeholders' as a priority and, when stakeholders are listed, members of the public are always mentioned first. However, the IMB's commitment to better communication with its stakeholders has primarily involved measures for better communication with the pharmaceutical industry, particularly in the case of its newsletters. One of two IMB initiatives that could be regarded as efforts to promote greater communication with the public was the appointment in 2001 of a 'consumer representative' to the board. A member of the Consumers for Health Choice Ireland, an organisation that opposed the move to make Saint John's wort a prescription drug, was amongst the ministerial appointees. However, similar to the representatives of citizens on many other corporatist structures, it was an extremely limited measure in public participation due to the secrecy rules that apply to members of the board and because there were no mechanisms of mandating or accountability in place for the consumer representative. Secondly, the IMB claims that its Herbal Medicines Project involved a process of open and transparent public consultation.[43] However, members of the Irish Association of Health Stores, key 'stakeholders' with a commercial interest in increased regulation of herbal medicines and who actively participated in the consultation process, contest this depiction of the consultation process.[44]

Overall, the new mode of regulation that emerged in the 1990s is one that commodified drug regulation and made the pharmaceutical industry the fee-paying customer, responded to industry pressure to accelerate the product authorisation process while failing to redress the gross shortcomings of the pharmacovigilance system, and continued to promote a passive form of citizenship.

The 'fruitful partnership' between the pharmaceutical industry and the Department of Health?

While much of the responsibility for drug regulation shifted to the industry-funded IMB in 1995, the Department of Health retained a role in respect of some matters, such as the pricing and advertising of drugs. Furthermore, for a number of decades, the Department of Health has been the site of ongoing discussions, albeit with little action, concerning the need to control public expenditure on medicines.

Since its establishment in 1998 with financial support from the Department of Health, the National Centre of Pharmacoeconomics has played an important role in questioning the driving forces behind the exponential growth in public expenditure on medicines, and the high rate of prescribing of patented medicines where equally effective generics are available. However, there is evidence of this kind of questioning dating back over at least two decades. In the early 1980s, one proposed solution to the problem of the mounting public drugs bill was the establishment of a publicly owned drug company. A centrepiece of the 1982 Fine Gael/Labour programme for government was the establishment of a National Development Corporation. This National Development Corporation was to be given responsibility for establishing a national drug company to manufacture and supply the public healthcare system with drugs and thereby make substantial savings.[45] This venture in welfare state socialised medicine never came to fruition and seems preposterous in the current neo-liberal climate in which the privatisation of the few remaining public companies is widely viewed as inevitable.

In 1985, the Secretary of the General Medical Scheme Payments Board (the statutory body with responsibility for the administration of public expenditure on medicines) wrote to the Secretary of the Department of Health to express the 'deep disquiet and dissatisfaction' of the board at 'the absence of adequate means to control the growth of expenditure' by the state on medicines.[46] He pointed out that 'Every other area of the health services has had to bear substantial cutbacks and be subjected to stringent control'. This was the bleak period in recent Irish history when unemployment soared and drastic cuts in public expenditure on social welfare were introduced. The Secretary of the GMS Payments Board went on to point out the wide scope for savings through greater use of generic drugs. However, generic substitution did not become a priority in Irish drug policy and the situation as described in the early 1980s remained much the same two decades later. Similar concerns were raised by the Brennan Report, published in 2003.[47] This report recommended that the remit of the IMB should be extended to include a role in identifying drugs that are cheaper but equally effective to other similar drugs on the market and delisting those deemed not to be clinically cost-effective. Recent research undertaken in the National Centre of Pharmacoeconomics has highlighted the considerable savings that could be made through generic substitution; based on 2003 data, generic substitution of thirty frequently prescribed drugs could reduce public expenditure on medicines by an estimated €21.8 million per year.[48]

In the 1985 letter from the Secretary of the GMS Payments Board to the Secretary of the Department of Health, he noted that the board considered the difference between the prices it paid for drugs and those paid in Britain was too high. Here, reference was being made to the agreement about drug prices between the pharmaceutical industry and the state. In 1983, the first of these agreements was negotiated and provided for a direct relationship between trade prices in Ireland and in Britain; companies could charge up to 15 per cent in excess of the British price and the average industry-wide differential could be as high as 7.5 per cent over British trade prices.[49] A comment made in the Dáil that same year by the Minister of Health (Barry Desmond) suggests that he viewed the terms of the original agreement as favouring the industry and that the state could do better. Speaking about the plans for the renegotiation of the agreement, he said: 'I think we can do an even tougher deal in the months ahead.'[50] However, tougher deals were not brokered by the Department of Health. Up to 2006, the price control formula resulted in Ireland having 'Northern European' drug prices, higher than most of the rest of the world. The pricing agreement has been singled out as an example of the 'fruitful partnership' between the pharmaceutical industry and the Department of Health by IPHA.[51] The industry body notes that the 2001 report *Value for Money Audit of the Irish Health System*, commissioned by the Department of Health and Children, found that the pricing agreements 'provided good value for money for the State and has provided the industry with a stable framework within which it has become a leading contributor to the economic success of the country in recent years'. While the agreements have been fruitful from the point of view of the industry, they have been costly to the Irish taxpayer. In 2004, researchers in the National Centre for Pharmacoeconomics highlighted the potential savings that could be made by altering the pricing system; for example, they noted that the adoption of Danish prices for 39 commonly prescribed drugs could potentially save the General Medical Service alone in excess of €20.7 million.[52] In 2006, the terms of the pricing agreement between the state and the pharmaceutical industry were renegotiated in a manner that gave recognition to the unduly high prices being paid by the state for drugs. Notwithstanding acclamations that the new terms could result in savings to the state of over €250 million per year, investigative journalistic accounts involving interviews with 'industry whistle blowers' have argued that the revised pricing agreement continues to be excessively generous to pharmaceutical companies and pharmacists selling their products.[53]

Regulation of the advertising of drugs is a further site of interaction between the pharmaceutical industry and the Department of Health, and this too involves 'partnership' structures. The advertising of medicines is regulated by the Medical Preparations (Advertising) Regulations 1993, which enact in Irish law EU Directives on advertising, including a ban on direct-to-consumer advertising of prescription medicines. These regulations allow the pharmaceutical industry to be largely self-regulating in respect of its marketing practices. IPHA has two voluntary codes of practice, one of which relates to the promotion of prescription medicines and the other to 'over-the-counter' drugs. The Code of Marketing Practice for the Pharmaceutical Industry focuses on pharmaceutical company marketing directed at health professionals, a form of marketing that has become intensive and sometimes lavish.[54] The code is administered by a panel of mainly industry representatives, but also a nominee of the Minister for Health. According to the code, IPHA submits an annual report to all its members, the Minister and the IMB on complaints that were upheld. The industry favours this arrangement and claims that: 'This transparent system has worked well and shows that in certain circumstances self-regulation can provide an effective and efficient form of regulation.'[55] When I interviewed the Minister for Health's nominee to the panel, he informed me that in the ten years he served on the panel it had dealt with no more than twelve complaints.[56] The panel met more frequently when he was first nominated, but in recent years, due to the low volume of complaints, which are 'few and far between', it has become very inactive. Complaints are typically submitted by companies against bigger rival companies who manufacture similar products but who have greater marketing power. Despite the claim that this is a transparent regulatory arrangement, annual reports on complaints about breaches of the code that are upheld are not circulated and the Minister's nominee reported that he has never seen a copy of these annual reports. This evidence suggests that industry self-regulation in respect of advertising amounts to lax regulation.

In 2003, EU health ministers rejected proposals from the pharmaceutical industry to allow drug companies to advertise their drugs directly to particular groups of patients. In New Zealand, one of the two countries in the world where direct-to-consumer advertising (DTCA) is permitted, medical professionals have called for it to be banned, because it serves the profit-making interests of industry and not the health interests of the public.[57] An industry strategy that has been identified as a means of bypassing the ban on DTCA is 'disease awareness raising', or what some critics refer to as 'disease mongering', whereby the industry not only promotes consumption of its products but also pharmacocentric conceptions of health and well-being.[58] Pharmaceutical industry-funded disease awareness campaigns, which are frequently conducted in association with patients' organisations, have proliferated in Ireland in recent years.[59] The industry is generally self-regulating in respect of its marketing activities, including its sponsorship of patients' organisations, but there are also indications of the erosion of the ban on DTCA. In April 2004, GlaxoSmithKline (GSK) was given permission by the Department of Health and Children for the first ever television advertising campaign for a prescription drug in Ireland. The advert was for Twinrix, a combined vaccine for hepatitis A and B. Newspaper articles reported that 'GlaxoSmithKline persuaded the Department of Health and the TV stations that the vaccine would be "in the interest of public health"'.[60] In an effort to investigate this process of persuasion, I submitted a Freedom of Information request to the department for all files relating to the GSK advertising campaign. While I was denied access to GSK's formal submission on the grounds that it constituted information provided in confidence to a public body and commercially sensitive information, the documents to which I was granted access provided some insights into the nature of the relationship between the Department of Health and the pharmaceutical industry giant GSK. They revealed how the department treated the GSK request with tremendous urgency; there was an interval of less than two months between when GSK first wrote to the department about the proposal and when permission was granted, even though the advertisement was at odds with national regulations. They also reveal that, while permission was sought through the formal channels of the department, representatives of GSK had informal discussions with the Minister in advance of this. The uniformity of support for the so-called 'health awareness campaign' amongst departmental officials was also striking. The only evidence of questioning of the appropriateness and implications of the advertisement for further prescription drug advertising was in a letter to the Minister submitted by the Irish Patients' Association. This is a final example of questions about changes in regulatory policy coming from actors outside of the realm of the state.

Conclusion

The historical evidence presented here traces two shifts in the definition of the role of the Irish state in protecting the public from unsafe medicines. Firstly, it was not until the mid-1960s that the remit of the welfare state extended into the realm of medicines regulation, and secondly, the 1990s witnessed a transformation in the official logic underpinning its regulatory approach. Similar to what has been concluded in respect of regulatory policy in many other countries, medicines regulation in Ireland has followed a neo-liberal pharma-friendly course and emerges as a clear illustration of the transformation of the welfare state into a competition state. The dramatically altered relationship between the pharmaceutical industry and the state evident in the differences between the National Drugs Advisory Board (NDAB) and the Irish Medicines Board (IMB) has enabled the industry to exert greater influence over drug regulation policy and consequently can be regarded as being indicative of regulatory capture, as defined by John Abraham. However, this short history of drug regulation in Ireland highlights the importance of a nuance in both the regulatory capture thesis and competition state theory. The rhetoric of the regulatory regime that pre-dated the rise of neo-liberalism and the hegemonisation of the logic of market competition prioritised public health over commercial imperatives but in practice was lax regulation. It is not that we have seen a move from stringent regulation for public health to lax pharma-friendly regulation, as the initial mode of medicines regulation reflected the residual character of the welfare state and was 'hands-off'.

Since the 1960s, policy issues in which the pharmaceutical industry has a direct commercial interest have become policy priorities in a way that issues that are of significant importance to public health, but which can undermine the industry's profit-making, do not. The prioritisation of accelerating the marketing authorisation process for drugs, or 'speed to market', stands in sharp contrast to the failure to seriously address the gross under-reporting of adverse drug reactions. Efforts to promote pharma-unfriendly policies foundered, such as control of public expenditure on medicines through generic substitution and effective price controls, not to mention the nationalisation of drug manufacturing. What has emerged is a regulatory regime favoured by the industry, particularly in respect of its corporatist, industry-funded and self-regulatory aspects.

Despite positive developments such as the introduction of freedom of information legislation, this short history points to the endurance of the official expectation of passive citizenship. The system of medicines regulation that emerged has consistently displayed an official hostility to citizens' right to know. The poverty of debate in parliamentary arenas about changes in medicines regulation is a further striking theme in the story, especially in regard to the new mode of regulation that emerged in the 1990s. By and large, fundamental questioning of the regulatory regime has not occurred, despite the fact that Irish people consume more and more drugs for an expanding range of health conditions. One possible explanation for such widespread passivity in the face of the emergence of 'regulation for competition' is the myth that the promotion of corporate profits and citizens' welfare are one and the same thing has been successfully promulgated. In so far as the failings of the regulatory system have been made public concerns, this has largely occurred due to the actions of actors in arenas outside of the state, such as the campaigns of patients' organisations and tribunals of enquiry. Perhaps it is from these actors and arenas that we will hear a critical questioning of the supposedly win-win regulation for competitiveness?

CHAPTER 5

Alliance for Progress or Unholy Alliance?
The Transnational Pharmaceutical Industry, the State and the University in Ireland

Kathy Glavanis-Grantham

Introduction

Undertaking research on the transnational pharmaceutical industry is both a challenging and difficult task. It requires not only a grasp of global processes, but likewise requires an intimate and detailed knowledge of how these socio-economic and political processes are articulated and experienced at the local level. The task at hand, namely a study of the transnational pharmaceutical industry in Ireland with a particular focus on the Cork region as the key geographical site[1] for its development in the country, is made more difficult given the dearth of previous studies on this topic.[2] This is compounded by the lack of disaggregated data on the sector, particularly at the regional level, in addition to the high level of secrecy that characterises how this economic sector does its business.[3] This thus suggests that undertaking an adequate analysis of the pharmaceutical industry in Ireland is an extremely difficult task for any one researcher. But in this task I have not been alone. Here, I would like to acknowledge that the following chapter emerges out of and builds upon previous research carried out by Orla O'Donovan and myself on the political and cultural influence of the transnational pharmaceutical industry in Ireland.[4] To a large extent, this line of research was initially inspired by the work of Health Action International,[5] an organisation that we joined in 2002. Thus, this work must be seen as the fruit of a more collective network of relations and has been enriched by the research and advocacy of many others who are part of a loose collective of those working to challenge the dominance of the transnational pharmaceutical industry within the domain of health.

The analysis that follows is underpinned by the fundamental question: who benefits from an economic policy that is based upon privileging the transnational pharmaceutical industry? This challenges the dominant neo-liberal ideology in Ireland that this type of development is good for the country and its citizens in general that is often expressed in the Irish context by the common phrase, 'rising tides lift all boats'. On the contrary, this chapter will argue that economic development underpinned by transnational capital in the form of the pharmaceutical industry chiefly benefits the industry. In spite of this, the Irish state through its policies, legislation and institutions will be shown to have actively advanced and chosen this type of development. Here, particular attention will be given to the important change in the role of the university in these development processes. A major dimension of this policy trajectory in Ireland must be located at the ideological and cultural level in the form of modernisation and neo-liberal principles which underpin and help explain the extent to which this type of development is dominant and to a large extent goes unquestioned. In fact, it is argued in this chapter that the scope for debate about these issues is restricted by the dominance of this ideology. However, scope for resistance is always possible, and this too will be explored in the following analysis as it pertains to the domain of health under the impact of the transnational pharmaceutical industry.

Therefore, in this chapter I will first sketch out the context within which the pharmaceutical industry in Ireland, and more specifically in Cork, has come to play such a prominent role in the economy and in the wider society. Second, I will delineate the major characteristics of this sector of corporate capitalism in Ireland. Third, I will examine the Cork region, and specifically the Cork harbour area, or, as Barry Roche has called it, 'pharmachem city',[6] in order to study at a micro level the nature of the dynamics in this industry. Fourth, I will examine the planning process as a key instrument for the implementation of the Irish government's neo-liberal agenda. Fifth, I will examine the educational sector's role in this agenda and will demonstrate that universities through 'partnerships' with transnational capital in general and more specifically with the transnational pharmaceutical industry are being increasingly transformed into institutions oriented towards market-driven capitalist development. Finally, I will look at how the power of this industry has been challenged and resisted in Ireland through a brief examination of one group in particular, Medicines for All, in their campaign against Pfizer.

Situating the transnational pharmaceutical industry in Ireland

During the 1950s an important shift occurred in the orientation and ethos of Irish economic policy: development aimed at providing self-sufficiency gave way to one focused on foreign investment. Likewise, there was a shift in orientation away from Britain and towards the USA. A number of salient features of this development since the 1970s that are relevant to our understanding of the place of the pharmaceutical industry in Ireland today can be identified.

First, the Irish state has played a central role in pro-actively shaping economic development and monetary policies that are pro-capitalist and, more importantly, pro-transnational and more specifically pro-US capital. Perhaps the most important of these policies has been the tax regime. First, a dual tax regime was implemented, giving mainly foreign investors zero rates. This was challenged by the EU as discriminatory against indigenous capital. As a result, the state imposed a rate of 10 per cent on all manufacturers. Again, in the 1990s the EU found this discriminatory against other economic sectors, so the Irish state introduced in 2003 a new rate of 12.5 per cent for all corporations.[7] This rate was and is still extremely favourable *vis-à-vis* other European tax regimes, which are typically between 30 and 35 per cent.[8] However, existing overseas operations, which were eligible for a 10 per cent rate, will be entitled to this rate until the end of 2010.[9]

A key mechanism for this development policy has been the IDA (Industrial Development Authority), the handmaiden of contemporary Irish economic policy. This authority was first established in 1950 as a state-sponsored body charged with the promotion of industrial development in Ireland and specifically foreign investment. Part of this policy has been grants-in-aid and establishing business parks for foreign investors. Most new industries coming to Ireland receive some kind of IDA economic aid.[10]

A third key component has been an educational policy that was and has become increasingly oriented towards the market. The White Paper of 1980 stated that public higher education must match market needs. In July 2004, the Enterprise Strategy Group Report, *Ahead of the Curve: Ireland's Place in the Global Economy*,[11] stressed that technological development and business processes and systems now demand greater links between the education sector and enterprise. Governance of higher education is seen to need to be flexible in order to increase the application of knowledge in enterprise. The Higher Education Authority and governing bodies of the higher education institutions should include individuals from the corporate (enterprise) sector.[12] The report goes on to emphasise the importance of developing 'entrepreneurial' skills through the syllabus for the senior cycle and curricular changes at the primary and junior cycle level to inculcate the entrepreneurial spirit and skills.[13]

Fourth, economic development in Ireland has been dominated by transnational corporations (TNCs), and especially US-based corporations, in the areas of computers, electronics and pharmaceuticals. In 2004, there were 1,025 foreign companies operating in Ireland, 48 per cent of them from the US, with the next largest figure for German companies, which amounted only to 14 per cent. However, the gap was even wider in terms of employment. Of the 127,578 who were employed in foreign companies, 70 per cent worked for US companies, while only 9 per cent worked for German companies.[14]

This dramatic dependence on foreign capital, and specifically US capital, as shown in the above figures can be partially explained by an important shift in US corporate strategy during the 1990s, which coincides with the decade of Irish history now widely known as Celtic Tiger Ireland. After a downturn in the US economy in the 1980s, US corporate strategy in the 1990s moved towards flexible production, which was based on two elements: decentralisation of production and foreign investment complexes in a few key locations. (Cork became one of these locations for the pharmaceutical industry in Ireland.) In order to be closer to European markets, especially with the coming of the 1993 Single Market Act, and in line with the above two principles, US TNCs moved into Ireland in increasing numbers and firms already here expanded significantly, while both other TNCs and Irish corporations declined in importance. This is clearly demonstrated by the data on fixed industrial investments in Ireland between 1983 and 1998. In 1983, US TNCs' share of the total was 35.7 per cent, while the Irish share was 34.5 per cent. However, by 1998, US TNCs' share of the total had become 65.7 per cent, while the Irish share was 16 per cent.[15]

Over the decade of the 1990s, both gross domestic product (GDP) and gross national product (GNP) in Ireland increased dramatically, with GDP higher than GNP.[16] As O'Hearn states, 'in the second half of the 1990s, TNCs accounted for 85 per cent of economic growth in terms of their value-added, and their profits alone accounted for 53 per cent of economic growth'.[17] This growth can be predominately attributed to exports from US firms in three manufacturing sectors: chemicals, computers and electrical engineering.[18]

Two related and startling types of data that are important to an understanding of the transnational pharmaceutical industry (TPI) in Ireland, and more specifically US pharmaceutical companies, is the rate of profit attained by these firms and the extent of the repatriation of profits. According to O'Hearn, US firms in Ireland maintained profit rates as a percentage of sales of 35 to 70 per cent. Profit rates of US companies were three times higher than the average of other TNCs and up to ten times higher than the average among Irish-owned firms. US TNCs maintained profit rates during the 1990s were five times greater than elsewhere in the world.[19] In terms of the repatriation of profits, the amount of profits removed by the TNCs from Ireland grew. In 1983, foreign profit repatriations amounted to 3 per cent of GDP, while by 1995 they were nearly 19 per cent and by 1999 they had risen to 40 per cent of GDP.[20] O'Hearn emphasises that these figures indicate the extent to which economic growth in the Irish economy was dependent on foreign profits, which were mainly repatriated. He calculates that, in 1998, growth of foreign profits was equivalent to 80 per cent of economic growth.[21]

Two other key characteristics of this TNC and US-led dependent development were and continue to be little research and development (R&D) carried out by these firms and poor linkages between the TNC sector and indigenous firms. Contrary to common belief, data collected by Forfás[22] showed that very little R&D was carried out by TNCs in Ireland. Expenditure analysis over the decade of the 1990s showed that only 1.25 per cent of total TNC expenditures in Ireland were on R&D, compared with 1.1 per cent for indigenous industry and 2.4 per cent which was the OECD average.[23] In July 2003, Barry O'Leary of IDA Ireland admitted that 'most R&D by pharmaceutical companies have been a small "r" and a big "D". Many of them have focused on developing manufacturing processes rather than drugs.'[24] As O'Leary pointed out, fully-fledged R&D facilities tend to remain close to an individual group's headquarters, i.e. not in Ireland, but in the US or Germany, for instance. Contrary also to common belief, there are poor linkages between the TNC sector and indigenous firms. According to O'Hearn, in 1996, out of 2,667 indigenous firms with ten people or more, only 174, or 6.5 per cent, were sub-suppliers to TNCs, and only three of these were in the chemical sector.[25]

Another key element of the foregoing developments has been the policy of partnership. Partnership agreements between employees, employers and government began in 1987 with the Programme for National Recovery (PNR).[26] According to the IDA, these agreements 'have played a central role in helping monetary policy keep inflation under control by promoting wage moderation'.[27] The IDA proudly claims that 'Ireland's hourly compensation cost for production workers in manufacturing has increased only moderately from $14.13 in 1996 to $15.55 in 2003'.[28] O'Hearn's analysis corroborates the declining share of wages relative to the profit share of Irish income over 1985–1999.[29] In spite of this disparity, social partnership has done what the state had hoped it would. These agreements have acted as 'golden handcuffs' on workers during their negotiations over pay rates. As the Labour Relations Commission stated on 3 September 2004, the year 2003 was the best ever for industrial peace, with fewer disputes taking place than in any year since records began in 1923.[30] According to Kieran Mulvey, chief executive of the commission at the time, the dispute resolution institutions were a 'beacon of stability' and an opportunity for foreign companies considering investing in Ireland.

The transnational pharmaceutical industry in Ireland and the Cork region

The foregoing has attempted to identify the salient features of Irish economic development since the 1950s, but has also highlighted the intensification of these trends during the 1990s. During this period, pharmaceuticals were a key sector of TNC activity.

Geographical distribution

According to IDA statistics,[31] there are seventy-two pharmaceutical plants operating in Ireland. Of these, nineteen are located in the Cork harbour region, if you include the Schering-Plough plant at Brinny, Inishannon. That is, 26 per cent of the total pharmaceutical plants are located in Cork. It is significant that twenty-nine of these pharmaceutical plants are FDA approved, according to the IDA. However, it would be wrong to suggest that the concentration of the TPI in Cork harbour and its environs was externally driven by the TPI. The IDA in the 1970s adopted a strategic plan of zoning Cork harbour for pharmaceutical and chemical investment. Land was bought for business parks and infrastructure was developed.[32]

National origins

Foreign direct investment in the pharmaceutical sector has a long history in Ireland. The first company to locate in Ireland in 1964 was Squibb (now Bristol-Myers Squibb). The first pharmaceutical company to locate in Cork at Ringaskiddy was Pfizer, in 1969. GlaxoSmithKline, the second largest pharmaceutical company after Pfizer, set up a plant in 1975 in Ringaskiddy. Currently, thirteen out of the top fifteen companies in the world have substantial operations in Ireland.[33]

Twelve countries operate pharmaceutical plants in Ireland, but the distribution amongst these twelve countries is unequal. US plants number 32, or 44 per cent of the total. The second largest number, ten, are German-based, or 14 per cent, followed by the UK with seven plants, or 9 per cent of the total. Both France and Switzerland have five each, or 7 per cent. Japan follows with three plants. Italy and Denmark have two each. Finally, Canada, India, the Netherlands and Israel each have one plant.

In Cork, seven countries operate pharmaceutical plants. Here, the pattern at the national level is duplicated, though there is an even greater concentration of US foreign investment at the local level. US firms number eleven out of the nineteen, or 58 per cent. Germany has three, or 16 per cent, while the UK and Switzerland each have two, or 10.5 per cent. France, Italy and Denmark each has one plant. An even more striking feature of this concentration is the fact that out of the nineteen plants, five are owned by Pfizer, the world's largest pharmaceutical company. Thus, Pfizer plants in Cork harbour constitute 26 per cent of the total number of plants in the area.[34] The other large US pharmaceutical companies operating in Cork harbour and environs include Janssen, Schering-Plough, GlaxoSmithKline and Eli Lilly. Amongst the other bigger plants are Altana, which is German, and Novartis (formerly Sandoz), which is Swiss. The Italians are represented by Recordati, a smaller plant in comparison to the others. The concentration of US pharmaceutical companies in Cork harbour will be further increased by the new plant of Johnson & Johnson subsidiary Centocor, which is to be built in Ringaskiddy over the next five years.[35]

Employment

Relative to the total workforce in Ireland, a small percentage work in the pharmaceutical industry. In 2004, the IDA estimated that there were more than 17,000 people working in this sector. Likewise, if those employed in the chemical industry are included, direct employment is more in the range of 24,000. This small number reflects the tendency for the use of advanced technology in this sector. Nevertheless, this number is a massive increase when compared to the 1988 figure of just 5,200. Therefore, there was an increase of over 200 per cent over the fifteen-year period. This is indicative of the massive expansion of the TPI in Ireland during the Celtic Tiger decade. However, this does not mean that the TPI is invulnerable to market forces. In spite of their economies of scale and the facilitating policies of low taxes and large grant aid from the IDA in Ireland, patent expiry, research setbacks, increased competition from generic products, declining sales, excess manufacturing capacity, and pressure from health authorities to reduce drug prices can contribute to plant closures and redundancies. In 2004, 150 workers were made redundant at the Schering-Plough plant in Brinny, Inishannon.[36] More recently, Pfizer's decision to make 545 staff redundant at its Ringaskiddy, Loughbeg and Little Island plants in Cork[37] and Sanofi-Aventis's announcement that it would close its Waterford plant with 200 redundancies[38] reveal the insecurity of those employed in the sector.

Another point often made by those supporting TPI development is the claim that the industry provides employment for supporting businesses and services. According to the then IBEC[39] director, Matt Moran, another 24,000 jobs result from the TPI that include engineering, maintenance, catering and transport.[40] In July 2004, the headlines of an article in the *Irish Examiner* announced '1,000 jobs bonanza as drugs giant expands', in reference to the agreement between the Irish government and Johnson & Johnson.[41] However, the article goes on to detail that only 330 jobs will be located in the plant and that the other 660 will be ancillary jobs in the service and construction industries. However, these types of figures might be somewhat of an exaggeration. An informed source suggested that, from his experience, it would be closer to the figure that for every ten workers in the plant another one was employed in a supporting sector.[42] In addition, an important point to remember is that the foregoing does not necessarily indicate that the TPI is well integrated and linked to Irish indigenous business, a tendency identified by O'Hearn,[43] as mentioned earlier. In the Cork County Development Board's report, *Integrated Strategy for the Economic, Social and Cultural Development of County Cork 2002–2011*, it is stated that 'pharmaceutical companies remain poorly integrated with few spin-off businesses emerging'.[44] In spite of this rather negative evaluation of the TPI in terms of integration and links to the local economy, the more recent draft of the south west regional authority's *Regional Planning Guidelines*[45] sees the pharmaceutical concentration in Cork harbour as a role model for building up clusters of similar types of jobs in Tralee and Killarney.

If we look in more detail at the employment figures for the twelve major plants in Cork harbour and its environs, we can see that the TPI plants are large in comparison to most other industries, both TNCs and indigenous. The average number employed in these plants is 325, but if we subtract those employed by Recordati, the smallest of the twelve, then we arrive at an average of nearly 350. What is again striking is that 83 per cent of the jobs are with US-based companies, and Pfizer alone employs nearly 1,500 people, which accounts for 38 per cent of those employed directly in the pharmaceutical industry of the twelve plants in Cork harbour and its environs. These figures indicate the extent to which the welfare of the workers in the pharmaceutical industry in Cork is tied to the fortunes of the US-based TPI, and more specifically to one company, namely Pfizer.

Job creation and employment have been key elements in state economic and development policy, especially over the decade of the Celtic Tiger. Likewise, jobs have been a central concern for Irish citizens in general and for those living in the communities where the TPI has located. The importance of the 'jobs' dimension needs to be seen in light of the high unemployment of the 1980s and the high rate of emigration which this necessitated. The 1980s were very bleak times for the vast majority of working-class people, as well as many with third-level qualifications. Most young people emigrated in search of work to Britain or the US. This has now changed, and rates of unemployment have dropped to around 4.4 per cent for 2004/05.[46] It is important to point out that there is much argument about the exact number of unemployed and especially the long-term unemployed and the type of jobs being created during the decade of the Celtic Tiger, with critical commentators emphasising that many of the jobs are part-time and poorly paid service-sector jobs. Nevertheless, there are now more people in employment than the 1980s.

It is against this background and in the context of the Irish state policy of social partnership, which has tied employees, employers and the state together in a series of pay deals, that we can understand the quiescence of the working class. As an informed source[47] has told me, there is a culture of silence amongst the workers about the industry and that they would be very conscious of 'saying nothing'. At the lower end of the job spectrum, a certain percentage are drawn from the local population. Some companies have a definite policy of trying to hire a certain percentage from the local area, such as Novartis. Schering-Plough's workers are almost exclusively from the Inishannon area. This source characterised these communities as close-knit, where it is hard to criticise. He also mentioned the informal policy of vetting workers, where known 'troublemakers' would not be hired or moved to another location, though the Construction Industry Federation (CIF) would deny that this happens. However, not everyone in the area would agree that the pharmaceutical companies employ local people. According to the chairman of the Ringaskiddy and District Residents' Association, Braham Brennan, the sector does not employ any Ringaskiddy people, as most employees seem to come from Carrigaline, Cork city or farther afield.[48] Another mechanism for bringing the local community on board is that many of the pharmaceutical companies sponsor community activities as part of Corporate Social Responsibility. In Little Island, Cognis Ireland sponsors the local GAA club, while Janssen Pharmaceuticals runs projects in Glanmire Community College and supports the Glounthaune scout troop.[49] Pfizer announced in May 2006 that it will be donating €100,000 to the Cobh Community Centre Complex over the following three years.[50]

In addition to the above, wages in TNCs in general are higher than the average wage rate, but wages in the pharmaceutical and chemical industry are the highest. This partially reflects the fact that in Ireland, according to the IDA, 'there has been consistent evidence of a strong correlation between company size and the level of remuneration for a particular job'.[51] According to CSO figures for December 2003, average gross earnings for this sector were €16.10 per hour, while average gross earnings for food and beverages were €13.81 per hour, €12.76 for metals and engineering, and €10.42 in textiles. This means that TPI workers receive on average wages that are 17 per cent higher than those in the food and beverage industry and 55 per cent higher than those working in the textile industry. These wage differentials are also present in terms of clerical staff, with the TPI paying the highest. However, at the managerial level, the TPI salaries are the third highest, coming after the food and beverage sector and manufacturing. It is also interesting to look at the disaggregated data for the pharma/healthcare sector in comparison to the UK, Germany and the Netherlands. Here we see that, out of the eleven types of employees listed, Irish labour is the cheapest in six of the categories, is cheaper bar one of the other countries in three of the categories, and in only two of the categories is more costly than two of the countries.[52] This means that the TPI in Ireland is paying less for its staff than in some European countries. While acknowledging that wage levels have not been the main consideration in the location of the TPI in Ireland nor in determining its profits, it is nevertheless appropriate to consider the possible future implications of the 2004 accession of eight Eastern European low-wage economies to the EU on the TPI in Ireland. If the infrastructural and tax requirements can be replicated in these countries, then it is possible to imagine a movement of the TPI away from Ireland and towards these new locations with much more sizeable markets and lower costs of production.[53]

Another factor possibly contributing to the quiescence of the workforce is the move towards more flexible and less demarcated work patterns in some of the factories. In Pfizer, for instance, work is carried out in teams, where, according to an informed source,[54] it is hard to distinguish between an operative and a chemical engineer on the factory floor. All of the team members would 'get stuck into' the work and often a graduate of Cork Institute of Technology would begin as an operative and work his/her way up the employment ladder. That is not to say that there is no vertical segregation of jobs in the TPI, but the emphasis on teamwork would seem to contribute to an ethos of camaraderie which cuts across the job description divide.

Profits and profitability

According to CSO figures for 2004, Ireland is now the biggest net exporter of pharmaceuticals in the world.[55] This is an incredible economic feat, given that Ireland is such a small country with a relatively small industrial base. In 2002, the Irish net trade in pharmaceuticals (exports less imports) amounted to more than €13.7 billion. Switzerland came second with a net trade balance of €10.4 billion. Between January 2003 and November 2003, medical and pharmaceutical products accounted for over €1 in every €6 of exports.[56] In terms of export earnings, according to IDA figures for 2003, Ireland's TPI exported $33 billion per annum, which represented 36 per cent of the total exports from the country.[57] The gigantic leap in the production and exportation of pharmaceutical products by the TPI in Ireland over the decade from 1994 to 2004, and in particular in the five years between 1999 and 2004, is captured by the fact that, in 1980, Ireland exported only $10 million worth of drugs. By 1996, the figure had risen to $2,045 million.[58] This means that from 1980 to 2003, Ireland's exports of pharmaceuticals increased by an incredible 330,000 per cent. Between 1996 and 2003 the Celtic Tiger era, Ireland's exports of pharmaceuticals increased by 1,514 per cent. These almost unbelievable figures reflect the meaning of the Celtic Tiger and the role of the TPI in this period of economic growth.

According to the IDA, the replacement value of the investment by the pharmaceutical sector in Ireland is estimated at €40 billion.[59] However, considering that they exported pharmaceuticals in 2003 worth $33 billion, we can see the extent of the high returns on investment in Ireland by the TPI. The sector is diversified, according to the IDA. Plants producing bulk active materials have been followed by finished product pharmaceutical operations. Forty finished pharmaceutical plants are in operation in Ireland.[60] Many plants are now engaged in product development.

The pharmaceutical industry in Ireland produces many of the top-selling drugs in the world, or 'blockbusters'. According to the IDA, six out of the ten top-selling drugs globally, including Lipitor and Zocor, are made in Ireland. In Cork harbour and environs, many of the leading drugs are made by the ten largest pharmaceutical operations in the area. For example, Janssen, the US company, produces the anti-psychotic drug, Risperidone, and the gastrointestinal treatments, Motillium and Imodium. Pfizer Ringaskiddy, the US company, makes sildenafil citrate for Viagra, while Novartis, the Swiss company, makes the anti-cancer drug, Glivec. Schering-Plough in Brinny, Inishannon, produces the anti-cancer drug, Interferon. Pfizer, Loughbeg, produces the world's leading cholesterol treatment, Lipitor, while GlaxoSmithKline (GSK), the UK company, in Curraghbinny, produces the anti-depressant, Seroxat. Finally, Eli Lilly in Dunderrow, Kinsale, the US company, makes the active pharmaceutical ingredients for the anti-depressant, Prozac.[61] Many of these drug products are household names, recognised around the world, and earn their companies millions and billions of euros.

The planning process and the pharmaceutical industry in Ireland

It is abundantly clear from the discourse of the official documents of the Irish state, from statements made by political parties in power and from the controversies which have regularly erupted into the public domain that planning is a key instrument for the implementation of the state's neo-liberal economic agenda and has been an important site for struggle by community groups. In the IDA's industry profile of the pharmaceutical industry, it proudly claims that 'an efficient planning permission process exists in Ireland to enable rapid and trouble-free start-up'.[62] It is interesting to note the use of the words 'rapid' and 'trouble-free'. Focus is on speed and on a process that occurs smoothly, i.e. without opposition. However, the government embarked in 2003 on introducing legislation that would make the planning process even easier and faster by fast-tracking the planning process for major infrastructure projects. Despite opposition from some departments and ministers who opposed the inclusion of dumps and incinerators in the new process,[63] the Planning and Development (Strategic Infrastructure) Bill was passed by the Dáil on 4 July 2006.[64] This legislation has established a new Strategic Infrastructure Board within An Bord Pleanála[65] to consider major projects from the start. This is a significant departure from the previous system, where planning proposals first went to the local authority and then to An Bord Pleanála. This new law also 'prevents an application for Judicial Review to be taken by an organisation which has not pursued the same objectives during the last twelve months . . . preventing a newly formed community-concern group from applying for Judicial Review'.[66]

Nevertheless, the pharmaceutical industry has faced much opposition in the past from community groups that have utilised the planning process as a site of struggle. The campaigns against Merrell Dow in 1988, when Cork County Council granted planning permission to establish a pharmaceutical plant in Killeagh, east Cork, and in 1989, when again Cork County Council gave permission to Sandoz (currently Novartis) to construct a pharmaceutical plant on 90 acres of the IDA-owned site at Ringaskiddy, which represented the largest single investment in the sector, are two important examples, which have been documented by Mullally[67] and more recently by Allen in *No Global: The People of Ireland versus the Multinationals*.[68] The major thrust of the campaigns focused on the potential environmental damage that these proposed plants would cause. These concerns have emerged once again in the context of the state's policy of establishing a toxic waste incinerator in Cork harbour at Ringaskiddy. As the then Minister of the Environment, Martin Cullen, continually reiterated while in office in 2002–04, 'waste infrastructure, including modern landfills and incinerators . . . [are] of national importance'.[69] Though the campaign mounted by Cork Harbour Alliance for a Safe Environment (CHASE)[70] against Indaver Ireland is not directly aimed at the pharmaceutical industry, the two are inextricably linked. As the draft regional plan for the South West uncategorically states, incineration is a 'necessary technology to support the continued growth of the pharmachem sector'.[71] The struggle around the proposed toxic waste incinerator has exposed to an unbelievable extent the lack of democracy and the inadequacy of environmental protection in Ireland. Even though Cork County Council voted against the proposal in June 2003, Indaver

Ireland lodged an appeal to An Bord Pleanála and won the appeal, in spite of the head planner arguing against granting the permission on fourteen points. Members of An Bord Pleanála justified their decision based on the fact that incineration was the government's policy. When the government subsequently appointed Laura Burke, formerly project manager for Indaver Ireland's two incineration projects, as the new director of the EPA (Environmental Protection Agency),[72] no one could doubt the thrust of the government's policy, which seems to contravene the spirit of the Code of Standards and Behaviour for Civil Servants announced in September 2004.[73]

An unholy alliance? Universities, industry and the state in Ireland

The increasing importance of the links between the university sector and industry is not particular to Ireland. In 1998, Mayoshi wrote with alarm about the growing corporate ethos in US universities. As he states, '[o]nce professors presumably professed; they are now merely professionals, entrepreneurs, careerists, and opportunists, as in the corporate world. We may be in a far worse situation than we like to imagine – unless we seriously tackle what we should think, teach, and do.'[74] More recently, Krimsky[75] has examined the nature of the relationship between universities and industry in relation to science, and more specifically biomedical research. In his book, *Science in the Private Interest: Has the Lure of Profits Corrupted Biomedical Research?*, he documents how corporate interests have had a worrying influence over what research is done, how it is done and how and when the results are disseminated. He provides overwhelming evidence to substantiate his claims. One such case cited is the Nancy Olivieri case. Olivieri worked at the University of Toronto and its associated teaching hospital, the Hospital for Sick Children, where she was engaged in research on thalassaemia, a hereditary blood disease. Krimsky documents how the clinical trials funded by the pharmaceutical company Apotex to develop a tablet in the treatment of thalassaemia were stopped and how Olivieri was threatened by the company if she published the results, which showed that liver damage was a side effect of the drug in some cases. Olivieri was removed from her post by the university, but three years later a committee of three professors ruled that she had behaved ethically and professionally and she was subsequently reappointed. One of the missing pieces of these events and key to our analysis, is that at that time, the University of Toronto was in negotiations with Apotex for a multimillion dollar gift ($20 million, to be exact).[76] It is within such a context that Krimsky advocates what he calls 'public-interest' science, which 'includes the academic researcher's role as an independent voice of critical analysis on contested public issues involving his or her expertise'.[77] He categorically challenges those who believe that disclosure, 'the presumed universal antidote to conflicts of interest',[78] solves the problems identified above.

In Ireland, these issues have yet to be seriously considered and discussed. The hegemony of neo-liberalism and the promotion of partnerships between the state, universities and industry are pervasive and taken for granted as the obvious way forward to make Ireland 'a knowledge society', a common phrase, reiterated within official documents, by politicians and by university administrations. As was pointed out earlier, research and development has been generally underdeveloped in Ireland as well as within the TNCs resident in Ireland, the pharmaceutical industry included. Increasingly, the Irish state has advocated research and development as the key mechanism for continued growth and development, with a specific focus on biotechnology and ICT. This is to be carried out through partnerships between the universities, the state and industry and, in terms of biotechnology, in partnership with the pharmaceutical industry. In order to facilitate this process, the state set up Science Foundation Ireland in 2000 with a commitment of an investment of €646 million over six years. This foundation is part of the National Development Plan 2000–2006. Mary Harney, as Tánaiste (deputy prime minister) and Minister for Enterprise, Trade and Employment in Ireland at the time, stated that:

> This policy aims to generate clusters of world-class technology-based companies, both Irish and foreign-owned, that work in new knowledge areas in collaboration with university researchers. Together, they will advance scientific knowledge, commercialise research output, create high-level jobs, and build an entrepreneurial environment in which new technology-based businesses will prosper.[79]

According to the then Science Foundation Director General, William Harris, biotechnology and information and communications technology have been selected for initial investment because 'Ireland has a huge industrial presence' in them. He went on to say that '[i]f we didn't provide an intellectual foundation for these activities, the country might have a difficult time retaining a lot of these companies in the future'.[80] The low level of research and development in TNCs in Ireland is perhaps reflected by the fact that, in the Department of Enterprise, Trade and Employment's document, *Building Ireland's Knowledge Economy: The Irish Action Plan for Promoting Investment in Research and Development to 2010,* there is an admission that a 'key challenge for Ireland is increasing research and development performance in the enterprise sector'.[81] This helps us to understand why the state has stipulated 'that industry in Science Foundation Ireland partnerships add a minimum of 20% to each award in the form of funding, personnel, or equipment'.[82] In other words, it is predominantly the state, and this means the tax payers, who are footing the Science Foundation Ireland bill.

In both of the documents, the Department of Enterprise, Trade and Employment's *Building Ireland's Knowledge Economy*[83] and the Enterprise Strategy Report Group's *Ahead of the Curve: Ireland's Place in the Global Economy,*[84] emphasis is given to the need for 'a new and less bureaucratic approach' and the continuation of an 'effective and agile government' which has been responsive to the needs of enterprise.[85] This would suggest that the state is set to deregulate further the rules by which industry operates in Ireland. This is reflected in the new Planning and Development (Strategic Infrastructure) Bill, passed in July 2006, mentioned previously. The 2004 Finance Act further illustrates the manner in which the Irish state is facilitating this new focus on research and development in biotechnology and ICT. According to the Act, the 9 per cent tax charged on the transfers of Intellectual Property (IP) has been abolished. It also provides for an exemption from stamp duty on the sale, transfer or other disposition of IP, which includes any patent, trademark, copyright, registered design, design right, invention, domain name, supplementary protection certificate or plant breeders' rights. This was effective from 1 April 2004.[86] On top of that, a research and development tax credit for incremental expenditure by companies was introduced, which gave a tax credit of 20 per cent in addition to a tax deduction at 10/12.5 per cent for research and development expenditure in Ireland from 1 January 2004.[87] Finally, the Act gave an exemption from Capital Gains Tax for Irish-resident companies which make tax disposals from substantial shareholdings in trading subsidiaries tax resident in an EU or tax treaty country.[88] All of the foregoing are indicative of a state facilitating corporate interests to a high level.

The third partner in this 'alliance for progress' is the higher educational sector. Again, throughout government documents, constant reference is made to the importance of the educational system as a producer of graduates for the market and as research partners with industry. According to the Enterprise Strategy Report Group's *Ahead of the Curve,* governance of higher education must likewise be flexible.[89] It explicitly states that the Higher Educational Authority board and the governing bodies of higher education institutions should include individuals from the 'enterprise sector'.[90] Such an orientation reflects the trends identified by Mayoshi[91] and Krimsky[92] in US and Canadian higher educational institutions.

In this context, University College Cork in particular and Cork Institute of Technology are seen to be the key players in the Cork region for the establishment of industry, and state and university partnerships. Already, University College Cork has received considerable Science Foundation Ireland funding. One of the CSET awards (Centres for Science, Engineering and Technology) on alimentary pharmabiotics was established at University College Cork in 2003,[93] while another such award for $12 million (€10 million) funded the Centre for Research on Adaptive Nanostructures and Nanodevices (CRANN) at Trinity College, with University College Cork and University College Dublin as partners. Science Foundation Ireland also operates a variety of other funding programmes, among them its investigator programme, which provides grants for researchers in Ireland of up to $300,000 per year for up to four years. One of the recipients is Damien Arrigan, a senior research scientist in the transducers group at the National Microelectronics Research Centre (incorporated into the Tyndall National Institute, which was founded in July 2004) at University College Cork. As he has stated, 'As chemists we are extremely lucky that our research can underpin both biotechnology and ICT . . . Chemists can contribute enormously to the future technologies that the Irish government has decided will be important in the development of our knowledge-based economy.'[94] He went on to point out that his research 'could even result in new biotech start-up companies'.[95]

In a 2003 document, *Growing Excellence,*[96] Gerard Wrixon, as the then president of University College Cork, emphasised the importance of partnership links with industry, and among the success stories according to this document is University College Cork's links with the pharmaceutical industry. University College Cork's Development Office/Cork University Foundation is oriented to establishing partnerships with industry and many of these are with the pharmaceutical industry, according to the current Director, Jean van Sinderen-Law.[97] For many years, University College Cork science, engineering and other graduates have found work placements in the pharmaceutical industry.

The Careers Service office has a designated employee for placements in the pharmaceutical and computer science sectors. Many science and engineering graduates go on to work in the pharmachem industry, according to the records of the Careers Service *Annual Report 2003*,[98] which lists first-destination jobs of those who respond to their questionnaire a year after graduation. The new School of Pharmacy at University College Cork will obviously strengthen and deepen these relationships, which have a long history in the university. The intended links and benefits to the pharmaceutical industry in the area are clearly spelled out by the Development Office, University College Cork, on its website, which states that the School of Pharmacy 'will encourage collaboration with the large number of Pharmaceutical companies based around the Southwest of Ireland', that '[t]he region will become a hub for the pharmaceutical sector' and that '[t]he pharmaceutical industry, drug distribution companies and pharmacy chains all stand to benefit by the introduction of a pharmacy degree programme and associated post-graduate and research training at UCC'.[99]

University College Cork as an institution is characterised by a corporate ethos to a high degree. In official documents, students have become customers, the application process is the purchasing process, and teaching has become a product that we sell to students. Business interests are well represented on the governing body of University College Cork and during 2001–2004 the pharmaceutical industry was represented by the Managing Director of Schering-Plough. Corporate sponsorship for conferences, prizes and other events is widespread. In this context, the pharmaceutical industry has been prominent. In November 2005, AstraZeneca sponsored the 1st Interdisciplinary Conference of the College of Medicine and Health. In September 2004, Eli Lilly sponsored the Postgraduate Research 2nd Annual Symposium. In September 2003, BioResearch Day was sponsored by Taro Pharmaceuticals Ireland and Novartis. A similar event organised by the medical school in May 2002 was sponsored by Pfizer. Pfizer Ireland is likewise co-funding a new postgraduate researcher in the Department of Chemistry in conjunction with the Embark initiative.[100] Even more significant is Pfizer's €100,000 commitment to the Orphan Drug Contract Research Organisation in 2006.[101] Given the prominence of Pfizer in the Cork region, it is not surprising that the university conferred an honorary degree of Doctor of Laws on John Mitchell, Senior Vice President of Pfizer Inc. and President of

Pfizer Global Manufacturing, in September 2004. As Conor Healy of the IDA stated at the time, the clustering of the pharmachem industries in Cork harbour and environs has created a comfort zone for these companies[102] and the long historical relationships with the university have created a strong sense of mutuality and trust. I would argue that, within this context, it is extremely difficult to criticise these policies. Critics are seen as 'not buying into the vision', and ultimately are seen to be against progress and development. However, it is my contention that we are in urgent need of debate about these issues, about the nature of the university, and in particular about the increasing corporate ethos that has come to dominate higher educational institutions in Ireland. Finally, I would argue that the place of the pharmaceutical industry in particular needs examination in light of what we know about the ways in which the pharmaceutical industry has come to influence health priorities and scientific research in other countries, as indicated earlier.[103]

Resisting the transnational pharmaceutical industry in Ireland

In spite of the economic and cultural dominance of the TPI in Ireland, as I have pointed out previously, community groups over the years have led campaigns against the establishment of new plants because of environmental issues. In 2003, a small group of Irish professionals working mainly in veterinary services formed an organisation called Medicines for All, which advocates 'that health is the right of every individual, and that affordable medicines for serious illness should be available to all in our world'.[104] It was the Channel Four documentary, *Dying for Drugs*,[105] produced by Brian Woods, that alerted them to 'the unethical practices by the world's major pharmaceutical companies, resulting in the abuse of health rights of poor people especially in the developing world'.[106] Their campaign has focused on Pfizer, as the industry's largest company, whose market value of $266 billion is larger than the combined GDP of the eighteen biggest economies in sub-Saharan Africa.[107] They point out that what it does and says is highly influential both within the industry and beyond. In particular, the campaign against Pfizer emerged in the context of Pfizer using a new drug, Trovan, during an outbreak of meningitis in Kano, Nigeria, in 1996. Eleven children died during the trials and others were left with swollen joints, a well-known side effect of the drug. It is important to note that clinical trials of this drug were refused in the US. There are thirty families who are trying to take Pfizer to court because they claim that they did not give informed consent. Importantly, according to Woods,[108] when Pfizer's own childhood diseases specialist, Juan Walterspiel, wrote to the company's chairperson protesting that Trovan had never before been tested for the strain of meningitis found in Kano, he was sacked shortly afterwards.[109] This incident certainly raises questions about Pfizer's understanding of its 'social corporate responsibility' and its claim that they make 'every country and community in which . . . [they] . . . operate a better place to live and work'.[110]

Another reason for targeting Pfizer is the company's record on access to medicines for countries in the South. Pfizer is the sole owner of three important drugs for infectious diseases, namely the antifungal Diflucan, the antibiotic Zithromax and the antiretroviral Viracept. As Medicines for All point out, Pfizer 'has shown little flexibility on pricing and patent enforcement in poor countries'.[111] As demonstrated by Downes in this chapter, Pfizer was at the forefront of the campaign to have Intellectual Property Rights included in the remit of the World Trade Organisation. Therefore, many of the poor in the world, especially in sub-Saharan Africa, where the pandemic of HIV/AIDS rages, are being denied access to life-saving and life-extending medicines because of the corporate policies of this pharmaceutical giant.

In Ireland, Medicines for All have focused their work on convincing veterinarians not to use Pfizer products, the largest provider in Ireland of veterinary products such as vaccinations, antibiotics and antifungals, when there is a cheaper alternative. According to Lilian Collier, the group found that Pfizer drugs are more expensive than similar products produced by other pharmaceutical companies. By the autumn of 2004, six Dublin veterinary clinics had agreed not to buy Pfizer products. While Medicines for All as an organisation remains small and its impact on Pfizer has been minimal, it has sought out alliances with other groups, such as Physicians for Social Reform, as a means of widening the campaign.[112] They organised a discussion session at the Irish gathering of the Social Forum in Dublin in the winter of 2004. They have also tried to convince RTÉ to broadcast *Dying for Drugs*,[113] so that a wider Irish audience will be exposed to the issues underpinning their campaign.[114] Thus, Medicines for All have demonstrated how resistance to the hegemony and practices of the transnational pharmaceutical industry can be ignited by a small event such as the viewing of a critical documentary such as *Dying for Drugs* and how resistance to such practices is possible, while circumscribed by the many intersecting and powerful interests discussed in this chapter.

Conclusion

The foregoing data and analysis provide strong evidence for the argument that there is a web of intersecting and mutually supporting interests between transnational capital, the state and the educational sector in Ireland. These interests underpin what I have called 'an unholy alliance'. Transnational corporations have dominated economic development in Ireland since the 1970s, with the transnational pharmaceutical industry being one of the key players, especially in the Cork region, where the highest concentration of its plants and workforce are located. I have demonstrated that the Irish state has actively encouraged and facilitated these processes through its development policies. And though it can be argued that it is an unequal partner in the alliance *vis-à-vis* the transnational pharmaceutical industry, nevertheless it needs to be stressed that the Irish state has *chosen* to develop policies that support a neo-liberal agenda where the private property rights of capital and, specifically, the TNCs, are given precedence over other interests.[115] This is in spite of the high rate of the repatriation of profits by these corporations, including the pharmaceutical industry, and the relatively small percentage employed by this sector, contrary to the emphasis by the Irish government at the rhetorical level on the necessity to expand employment opportunities for Irish citizens.

The third arm of the alliance, the educational sector and in particular institutions of higher education, has become increasingly important and more deliberately incorporated into the state's drive for the expansion of TNC investment in Ireland. These institutions of 'learning' have become more and more characterised by a corporate ethos, with 'partnership' with industry identified as the key mechanism for this development. I have highlighted these trends at the local level in which I am situated, namely Cork city and University College Cork. In this context, the dominance of the TPI is palpably felt and experienced. However, it is important to remember that, even in the new drive by the Irish state to garner further TNC investment, it nevertheless is the state, through organisations such as Science Foundation Ireland, which is primarily footing the bill. Hence, it can be argued that, when answering the question 'who benefits?', it is primarily transnational capital and a small but significant sector of the middle and working classes of Ireland.

As the neo-liberal agenda has been more actively pursued and its logic deepened in Irish society, there has been less and less space for debate about socio-economic and political issues in the country. This focus upon consensus politics has a long history in Ireland, but its new version is particularly strong in excluding dissent, critique and debate. No where has this phenomenon been more clearly expressed than at the Fianna Fáil parliamentary party meeting in Inchydoney, County Cork, in September 2004. On this occasion, Mary Harney, the then Tánaiste and Minister for Enterprise, Trade and Employment, stated that:

> [w]e need to focus on and address the problems that we all know are there, rather than *wasting valuable time engaging in ideological soul-searching* . . . The last thing we need to do is increase taxation . . . Raising taxes would be like deconstructing our prosperity. It would *drive investment out of Ireland, return unemployment to the dismal levels of the 1980s and 1990s and create even greater social injustice.*[116] [my emphasis]

Here we see encapsulated the trivialisation and marginalisation of debate about fundamental socio-economic issues. Likewise, we see the Irish state through its second most powerful leader espouse the neo-liberal agenda, tapping into a deep-seated fear and not too distant memory of an Ireland which experienced its own 'lost decade' in the 1980s.[117] This is in spite of the fact that the *UN Human Development Report 2003*,[118] published just two months prior to the Inchydoney meeting, documented 'the darker side' of the Irish success story. Elaborating on this 'dark side', Paul Cullen stated that 'Once again, we emerge as one of the most unequal societies in the West. Once again, our figures for adult illiteracy and concentrations of poverty are appalling and our figures for life expectancy and health and education spending little better.'[119] Thus, it is clear that there are those in Irish society who are having their boats raised more than others from the 'unholy alliance' of the transnational pharmaceutical industry, the state and the higher educational institutions in Ireland in its neo-liberal agenda. While oppositional groups such as CHASE and Medicines for All challenge the domination of the transnational pharmaceutical industry and its negative implications for the health of citizens, both local and global, these sites of resistance are vigorously contested by the pharmaceutical industry, and TNCs in general, and the Irish government and are able to bring to bear tremendous financial and political pressure to influence the policy process in their favour. Nevertheless, both CHASE and Medicines for All demonstrate the extent to which a small group of informed, dedicated and active citizens acting collectively can challenge the status quo.

CHAPTER 6

Drug Expenditure in Ireland:

Explaining Recent Trends

Michael Barry, Lesley Tilson and Máirín Ryan

Introduction

In Ireland, healthcare policy and expenditure is governed by the Department of Health and Children (DoHC) and administered through the Health Service Executive (HSE), which replaced the ten regional health boards in January 2005 as part of the health service reform programme. Funding is mainly derived from taxation (75 per cent), with private funding via insurance agents accounting for 11 per cent and patient co-payment the remainder. In recent years, coincident with increased economic prosperity, expenditure on healthcare in Ireland has increased considerably, from €3.5 billion in 1997 to an estimated €11.5 billion in 2005. Expenditure on pharmaceuticals under the Community Drugs Schemes in Ireland was estimated to be in the region of €1,198 million, exceeding 15 per cent of total public expenditure on healthcare in 2005. Funding of pharmaceutical expenditure occurs via three channels: (a) as part of the overall funding of public hospitals, (b) funding for community clinics, e.g. methadone maintenance, childhood immunisation and sexually transmitted infection services, including payment of outpatient HIV medicines dispensed by specialist hospitals, and (c) through the HSE–Shared Services–Primary Care Reimbursement Service (formerly the General Medical Services Payments Board), which accounts for the majority of total public expenditure on the acquisition cost of pharmaceuticals prescribed by general practitioners. As is the case for many European countries, more detailed and accurate information is available for community as opposed to hospital prescribing.

The HSE–Shared Services–Primary Care Reimbursement Service provides capitation funding to general practitioners, direct funding to pharmaceutical wholesalers for high-cost medicines dispensed under the High Tech Drugs Scheme and payment to pharmacists for drug acquisition cost and dispensing fees for medicines dispensed under the various Community Drugs Schemes. Drugs supplied under the Community Drugs Schemes are provided through retail pharmacies on the production of a completed prescription form. As of March 2002 there were 3,155 pharmacists and a total of 1,258 pharmacies registered with the Pharmaceutical Society of Ireland. Of these, 1,222 were classified as community pharmacies.

Pricing

The agreement between the Irish Pharmaceutical Healthcare Association (IPHA) and the DoHC outlines the supply terms, conditions and pricing of medicines supplied to the health service in Ireland. The current agreement commenced in September 2006. The agreement covers all medicines prescribable and reimbursable in the Community Drugs Schemes and all medicines supplied to hospitals. Under the current agreement, Ireland links its drugs price by formula to those of nine other Member States. The price to the wholesaler of any medication will not exceed the currency-adjusted wholesale price in Belgium, Denmark, France, Germany, the Netherlands, Spain, the United Kingdom, Finland and Austria (Figure 6.1).[1]

Figure 6.1. Ireland links its drug price by formula to those of nine other Member States

Prior to the current agreement the pricing mechanism reflected a northern European price, which was higher than the European average. An international price comparison study determined the potential cost savings should the previous pharmaceutical pricing mechanism be changed.[2] The analysis covered a sample of thirty-nine drugs (44.8 per cent of the total ingredient cost) selected from the top seventy drugs in order of ingredient cost under the General Medical Services scheme. Potential cost savings ranged from €20.73 million if a Danish price were adopted, to €16.23 million for the average European price. Therefore, the new pricing mechanism should result in lower drug prices in Ireland. A pharmaceutical company wishing to launch a new prescription product must submit an application to the DoHC with the wholesale prices in each of the reference states where it is available. If a product is not available in any of the reference countries, the Irish wholesale price is agreed between the DoHC and the manufacturer or importer. A price freeze at the introduction price has been in existence since 1993. It is noted that many European countries, including Belgium, France, Italy, Spain and Sweden, have had price reductions in recent years. At the end of 2004, the UK Pharmaceutical Price Regulation Scheme (PPRS) was renegotiated and a 7 per cent price cut for branded prescription medicines was agreed with the Association of the British Pharmaceutical Industry (ABPI). It is estimated that the price cut will deliver savings of £1.8 billion to the National Health Service over the next five years.

Reimbursement

Following the receipt of market authorisation, there is a short time delay to reimbursement. Prior to reimbursement under the Community Drugs Schemes, a medicine must be included in the GMS code book or positive list. The new IPHA/HSE agreement confirms that new medicines granted a marketing authorisation by the Irish Medicines Board or the European Commission will become reimbursable under the Community Drugs Schemes within sixty days of the date of the reimbursement application. This is an important component of the agreement for the pharmaceutical industry, where the single pricing and reimbursement step should maintain speed to market. However, the HSE reserves the right to assess new and existing technologies (pharmaceuticals, diagnostics and devices) that may be high cost or have a significant budget impact. Where such a review is requested, the sixty-day rule for reimbursement will not apply. Where a new medicine is subjected to pharmacoeconomic assessment, the

Table 6.1. Number of prescription items, cost, eligibility criteria and patient co-payment for each of the Community Drugs Schemes in 2005

Community Drug Scheme	No. of prescription items (millions)	Payment to pharmacies: drug cost + dispensing fee € million	Eligibility	Patient co-payment†
GMS	37.4	831.44	All below income threshold & all over 70 years	None
DP	10.5	246.68	All who are not eligible for GMS or LTI schemes	€85 per month
LTI	1.9	100.55	Fifteen specific chronic conditions (see text)	None
HTDS	0.2	8.73*	All patients for selected high-cost drugs	None if GMS eligible; otherwise €85 per month
EEA	0.08	1.88	EC nationals from other Members States	None
Other	0.3	8.86		
Total	50.38	1,198.14		

GMS = General Medical Services, DP = Drugs Payment, LTI =Long Term Illness, HTD = High-Tech Drugs Scheme, EEA = European Economic Area, Other = Methadone Treatment Scheme & Dental Treatment Services.
* Payment to wholesalers under the HTDS = €168.76 million.
† Patient co-payment increased to €85 per month on 1/1/2005

reimbursement decision will be notified within ninety days of receipt of the reimbursement application. Assessments will be conducted in accordance with the existing agreed Irish Health Technology Assessment guidelines. Products subjected to an assessment will be reimbursable under the scheme within forty days of a positive reimbursement decision. There is an increasing trend in European Member States to request cost-effectiveness data when considering reimbursement of pharmaceutical products. In Finland, pharmacoeconomic evidence is mandatory for evaluating new therapies and may also be requested for existing therapies. Pharmacoeconomic evidence is explicitly required in the Netherlands for reimbursement decisions of new products. Cost-effectiveness data will also be considered during the reimbursement process in countries such as

Belgium, Denmark, Italy, Norway, Portugal and Sweden. In England and Wales, the National Institute for Health and Clinical Excellence (NICE) evaluates the cost-effectiveness of medicines.

Community Drugs Schemes

The majority of drug expenditure under the Community Drugs Schemes (€1,198 million in 2005) related to claims processed under the General Medical Services (GMS) scheme, the Drugs Payment (DP) scheme, Long-Term Illness (LTI) scheme, European Economics Area (EEA) and the High-Tech Drugs Scheme (HTDS). The number of prescription items, cost, eligibility criteria and patient co-payment for each of these schemes is shown in Table 6.1.

General Medical Service (GMS) scheme

Those who are unable without undue hardship to arrange general practitioner medical and surgical services for themselves and their dependants are eligible to receive a free general practitioner service under the GMS scheme and are issued with medical cards. Medical card holders are entitled to free GP medical and surgical services and free prescription drugs, medicines and appliances through their local participating pharmacist. The issuing of medical cards is means tested and dependent upon factors such as age, marital status, living alone or with family, and allowances (e.g. for children under sixteen years). Since October 2005, the weekly rate income guidelines for a medical card for persons under 65 years of age are €184 for a single person living alone, €164 for a single person living with family and €266.50 for a married couple. For those between the ages of sixty-six and sixty-nine years the thresholds for a medical card are €201.50, €173.50 and €298 respectively. Since July 2001, all residents over the age of seventy years are entitled to a medical card regardless of means. The number of eligible persons under the GMS scheme at the end of the year 2005 was 1,155,727 (i.e. 29.5 per cent of the population). Over 95 per cent of eligible persons availed of the scheme in 2004.[3]

Long-Term Illness (LTI) scheme

The Long-Term Illness (LTI) scheme entitles patients suffering from any one of fifteen specified chronic conditions to full drug reimbursement, irrespective of income. At the end of December 2005 there were 99,280 persons registered under the LTI scheme (2.46 per cent of the population) and expenditure on medicines under this scheme was €100.55 million for

LTI scheme for patients with the following medical conditions			
Mental Illness for persons <16 yrs	Cystic Fibrosis	Cerebral Palsy	Multiple Sclerosis
	Spina Bifida	Epilepsy	Acute Leukaemia
Mental Handicap	Hydrocephalus	Diabetes Mellitus	Parkinsonism
Phenylketonuria	Haemophilia	Diabetes Insipidus	Muscular Dystrophies

that year.[4] Therefore, approximately one-third (31.96 per cent) of the population of Ireland is eligible to receive free medication under the GMS and LTI schemes. This one-third of the population accounts for approximately two-thirds of total drug expenditure. The remaining two-thirds of the population have to pay towards the cost of their medication.

Drugs Payment (DP) scheme
The DP scheme, introduced in July 1999, applies to Irish residents who do not have a medical card. Under the DP scheme, no individual or family will be required to pay more than €85 in any calendar month for approved prescribed medicines for use by that person or his/her family in that month. Family expenditure covers the nominated adult, his/her spouse and children under eighteen years – persons over eighteen years and under twenty-three years who are in full-time education may be included as dependants. The number of persons registered under the DP scheme at the end of the year 2005 was 1,478,650 (i.e. 36.57 per cent of the population) and the cost of medication under the DP scheme was €246.68 million that year.[5] None of the private health insurance companies in the state provides cover for the DP scheme co-payment. Patient co-payment under this scheme was €143.6 million in 2005.

European Economic Area (EEA) scheme and High-Tech Drugs Scheme (HTDS)
The European Economic Area (EEA) scheme provides visitors from other Member States, with established eligibility, emergency general practitioner services while on a temporary visit. In 2005, prescription items dispensed under the EEA scheme cost €1.88 million. The High-Tech Drugs (HTD) scheme, introduced in November 1996, facilitated the supply by community pharmacies of certain high-cost medicines (e.g. those used in conjunction with chemotherapy, beta-interferon, etc.), which had

previously been supplied primarily in the hospital setting. The cost of medicines dispensed under the HTD scheme is paid directly to the wholesalers and pharmacists are paid a standard patient care fee of €54.82 per month to cover dispensing. In 2005, payment to wholesalers under the HTD scheme was €168.76 million and payment to pharmacies to cover dispensing fees was €8.73 million.

Drug expenditure under the Community Drugs Schemes 1993–2005

Total pharmaceutical expenditure under the community drugs schemes (i.e. payment to pharmacies for cost of medicines and dispensing fees plus payments to wholesalers under the High-Tech Drugs scheme) has increased from €211 million in 1993 to €1,367 million in 2005 (Figure 6.2).

Prior to 1997, the annual increase in payments ranged between 8 per cent and 11 per cent. In recent years this has increased significantly, from approximately 15 per cent in 1997–1998 to over 27 per cent in 2000–2001, 22 per cent in 2001–2002, 16.6 per cent in 2002–2003, 18 per cent in 2003–2004 and 10.8 per cent in 2004–2005.[6]

Factors contributing to increased drug expenditure

The two main factors contributing to the increased expenditure on medicines include 'product mix', the prescribing of new and more

Figure 6.2. Public expenditure on medicines in Ireland (Community Drug Schemes 1993–2005)

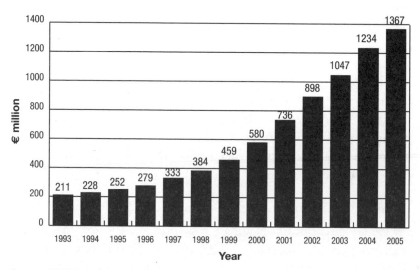

Source: GMS Payments Board Reports 1993–2005.

expensive medication, and 'volume effect', comprising growth in the number of prescription items. This is demonstrated by analysis of the GMS scheme, where the number of eligible patients has fallen by 9.5 per cent, from 1,277,055 persons in 1995 to 1,155,727 persons in 2005. However, the 37.4 million items prescribed in 2005 represents an approximate twofold increase over the ten years. When compared with 1995, there was a 3.9-fold increase in the number of forms with six items per prescription and a 7.8-fold increase in the number of forms with seven or more items per prescription in 2005. Despite the price freeze on medications since 1993, the influence of product mix is seen as the cost per item prescribed increased over twofold. Consequently, the cost of medications per patient in the GMS scheme increased by a factor of 4.5 during the decade.

The products of highest cost to the GMS in 2005 are shown in Figure 6.3. It is notable that the five proton pump inhibitors (used for conditions such as peptic ulcer disease), omeprazole, lansoprazole, esomeprazole, pantoprazole and rabeprazole, accounted for approximately 10 per cent of the total ingredient drug cost for the GMS scheme in 2005. Similarly, the three cholesterol-lowering 'statins', pravastatin, atorvastatin and simvastatin, accounted for 10 per cent of total ingredient cost in 2005. Clinical nutritional products were the second most expensive item reimbursed under the GMS scheme in 2005, with expenditure exceeding €28.7 million. This represents a greater than sixfold increase since 1995. A recent review (July 2004) of oral supplements in primary care conducted by the National Medicines Information Centre (NMIC) concluded that, whilst the clinical use of these preparations had greatly increased in recent years, particularly in elderly patients, the evidence base supporting their use was poor.

The ageing of the Irish population combined with an extension of the GMS scheme to all over the age of 70 years has also contributed to increased pharmaceutical expenditure. The observed increase in pharmaceutical expenditure occurs against a background of low pharmaceutical consumption per capita when compared with other Western European countries.[7]

Pharmacy retail prices under the Community Drugs Schemes

For the GMS scheme, the pharmacy retail price is calculated from the ex-wholesale price plus dispensing fee (€3.26). The DP/LTI price comprises the ex-wholesale price plus 50 per cent mark-up plus dispensing fee (€2.86). Therefore, payment to pharmacists is much greater under the DP

Figure 6.3. Top ten products of highest cost in order of their ingredient cost in the GMS scheme 2005

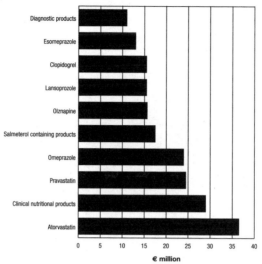

€ million

Source: GMS Payments Board Report 2005.

scheme compared to the GMS scheme. High-Tech Drugs Scheme prices include payment by health board to wholesaler direct = ex-wholesale price minus 5 per cent. Set patient care fees of €54.82 per patient per month are paid by the HSE–Shared Services–Primary Care Reimbursement Service to the pharmacy to cover dispensing costs. A rate of VAT at 21 per cent is charged on non-oral formulations, including inhalers, topical preparations and injections.

Generic medicines

A generic medicine may be defined as a medicinal product which has the same qualitative and quantitative composition in active substances and the same pharmaceutical form as the reference medicinal product, and whose bioequivalence with the reference medicinal product has been demonstrated by appropriate bioavailability studies. Ireland has traditionally had a low rate of generic prescribing, despite the fact that the DoHC has a policy of encouraging generic prescribing. Payments to pharmacies for the GMS scheme totalled €650.66 million, representing 69 per cent of the total payment to pharmacies, for the year 2003. Approximately 19 per cent of prescription items were dispensed generically: branded generics 15.2 per cent and non-branded generics 3.9 per cent for the year 2003 (Figure 6.4). Over 21 per cent of prescription

Figure 6.4. The percentage of prescription items that were dispensed generically on the GMS for the year 2003

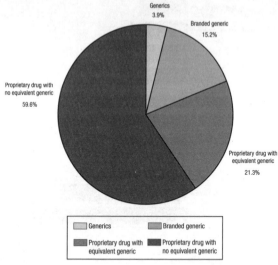

Source: Tilson, Bennett and Barry 2005.

items were dispensed as proprietary preparations when a generic equivalent was available.[8]

Only 7 per cent of the total ingredient cost of drugs dispensed in 2003 was spent on generic drugs. Just over 16 per cent (€75.03 million) of the total ingredient cost of medications was spent on proprietary drugs where there was an equivalent generic product available. In many European Union Member States, incentives and regulations to encourage prescription and/or substitution of cheaper generic drugs for the more expensive original branded products have been introduced. Generic substitution is the process whereby pharmacists are authorised to dispense a generic product regardless of whether the prescription is written generically or for a branded product. European countries that have implemented generic substitution policies include Denmark, Finland, France, Germany, Norway, Spain, Sweden and the Netherlands. The introduction in April 2003 of generic substitution in Finland resulted in savings on reimbursement payments in the region of €49 million.[9] Both the prescribing physician and the purchasing individual had the power to forbid the substitution. However, during the first twelve months of implementation, physicians forbade the substitution on only 0.4 per cent of prescriptions, whilst patients refused it in 10.7 per cent of cases. There are also examples of substitution schemes which have had a low impact, for a variety of reasons including a lack of incentives for physicians/pharmacists to substitute a generic drug (e.g. Germany). An assessment of the generic substitution scheme in Sweden during the first year of its implementation (2002) demonstrated that the actual savings achieved were on average 60 per cent of the maximum potential savings. In a recent study, Tilson, Bennett and Barry investigated the potential impact of implementing a system of generic substitution on the two main community drugs schemes (GMS and DP) in Ireland.[10] Using 2003 prescribing data, substitution of the cheapest generic equivalent preparations of the top thirty drugs by expenditure in each scheme would result in estimated annual savings of €12.7 million on the GMS and €9.1 million on the DP scheme. Potential savings if the most expensive generic drugs were dispensed would result in estimated savings of €9 million on the GMS and €6.4 million on the DP scheme. Interestingly, a comparison with a similar analysis of 2001 data illustrated the potential for an increase in savings over time.

An important component of the new 2006 IPHA/HSE agreement is the 35 per cent, two-stepped price reduction for off-patent substitutable products.[11] This ensures that the HSE no longer pays a price premium for many medications that are off patent. This move will obviate the need for strategies such as pharmacist-led generic substitution, which could have been difficult to implement in practice. It will also be welcome news for

Figure 6.5. Leading self-medication markets in Ireland in 2003

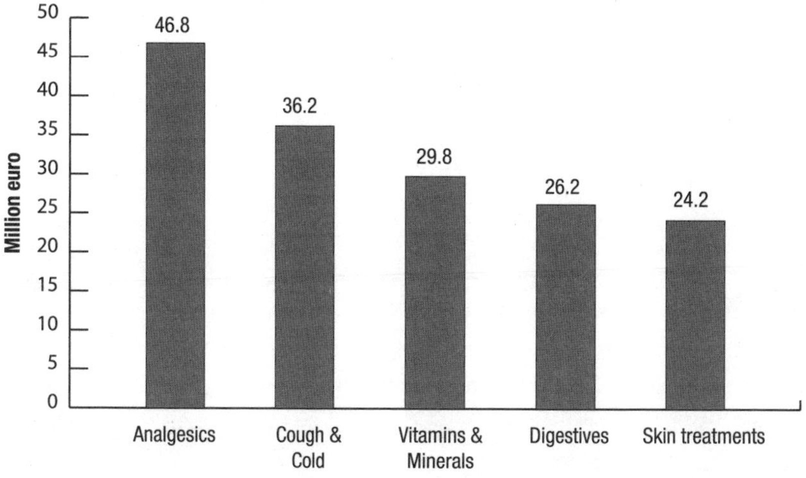

Source: Association of the European Self Medication Industry 2003.

consumers who contribute towards medication costs, as the co-payment for off-patent medicines will fall.

Over-the-counter medicines

Sales of all medicines legally available without a prescription for 2003 were €2,19.2 million (16.6 per cent of the total pharmaceutical market).[12] Over-the-counter (OTC) medicines can be priced freely and traditionally pharmacists charge a 50 per cent mark-up on their own purchase price (Figure 6.5).

Conclusion

There is little doubt that the 2006 IPHA/HSE agreement is a significant development in the pricing and reimbursement of medicines in Ireland with the HSE announcing savings of up to €300 million over the next four years as a result. For the pharmaceutical industry it should ensure that innovative products will continue to be reimbursed at a satisfactory price whilst maintaining speed to market. For the HSE it provides a mechanism for determining the value-for-money associated with new pharmaceutical products in addition to ensuring that it no longer pays a price premium for many off-patent products.

CHAPTER 7

The Medical Profession and the Pharmaceutical Industry:

Entwined, Entangled or Ensnared?

Colin Bradley

Introduction

Imagine you went to a restaurant but instead of ordering your meal someone else, whom you trust to know more about the food on the menu than you, came in and ordered your food for you and then another person came in and paid on your behalf. A pretty satisfactory situation you might think. A situation analogous to this may arise in relation to prescription medicines, whereby a doctor decides on your behalf which medicines you need to take and the state or some other third party pays for them. In Ireland, GMS (General Medical Service) patients are provided with prescribed medicines for free. Patients not eligible for GMS may avail of the Drug Payment Scheme, under which the costs of a family's medicine in excess of €85 per month (as of February 2007) are met by the state.[1] Besides the fact that consumers of medicines may not have to pay for them directly, there are several other features of the market in prescribed medicines which make it a highly unusual one. There is a very unusual degree of 'information asymmetry' between the consumer (i.e. the patient) and the supplier (i.e. the drug manufacturer), hence purchasing decisions are made by an agent (i.e. the doctor). Because they are such unusual commodities with substantial risks if misused, the trade in medicines is very highly regulated all along the way from manufacture, through marketing, to supply. There is also artificial price regulation through agreements between the pharmaceutical industry, as represented in Ireland by the Irish Pharmaceutical Healthcare Association (IPHA), and the Department of Health and Children. The latest Drug Pricing and Supply

Agreement was announced in July 2006 and runs until 2010.[2] In the jargon of economics, it is a very 'imperfect market'. There may be other more sinister ways in which the market in medicines may be distorted. Using the restaurant analogy, the situation would be a less satisfactory one for the consumer and the purchaser if the person ordering the food was a close friend of the restaurateur and was in regular receipt of free meals from him. If the person paying for the food actually gets the money indirectly from the diner and also has a vested interest in the financial viability of the restaurant, things begin to look a little less straightforward. The interests of the various players in the business of prescription medicines, while overlapping, may also be conflicting. Even a patient appearing to receive his or her medicines at no immediate cost may not be best served by a system in which there are conflicts of interest between the other parties.

The interests of the pharmaceutical industry

The pharmaceutical industry is motivated, like other industries, by making a profit and winning market share from competitors. However, it is obliged to market primarily to doctors and their ability to market to their end users, patients, is severely restricted. This restriction is becoming less accepted by the industry. Advertising directly to consumers is now allowed, subject to certain conditions, in some countries (most notably the United States of America) and the multinational pharmaceutical industry now lobbies recurrently for the removal of the ban on direct-to-consumer advertising that currently applies in Europe.[3] The pharmaceutical industry is keen to maintain a good image with the general public, even though the bulk of its marketing endeavour for prescription-only medicines is directed at doctors. Thus, in addition to the marketing of specific products, companies also promote their corporate image in a variety of ways, including sponsorship of various community activities and support of patient and other health-focused groups. A new trend, notable in Ireland, is also emerging of pharmaceutical companies sponsoring public information campaigns on various diseases. Examples include the public information initiative of the Alzheimer Society of Ireland sponsored by Pfizer and the Novartis-sponsored television advertisements on fungal nail infections. As part of their general need to garner good publicity and maintain their commercial reputation, pharmaceutical companies do have an interest in their products being used safely and effectively. Thus, companies endeavour to convey a general interest in patient well-being, as well as a specific interest in the uses of their particular products, and involve themselves extensively in the education of healthcare professionals, especially doctors. They also have an interest in the proportion of both national and individual resources expended on healthcare and on the proportion that medicines represent within healthcare expenditure. Thus, as well as striving to stress the modest proportion of all expenditure represented by medicines spending, they are eager to convey the message that spending on medicines represents value for money and ought to be prioritised within national and individual spending.[4] Because medicines hold potential dangers if not used correctly and because the costs of medicines can get out of control if not constrained, there are restrictions placed on the trade in prescription medicines. These include the requirement for a doctor's prescription, supply only by a pharmacist and restrictions on advertising. The pharmaceutical industry may be ambivalent about these restrictions. While they may benefit from the increased safety accrued from these measures, they can also see them as restraints on their profitability and may sometimes lobby for reductions in some of the legislative restrictions on their business.

The interests of doctors

All doctors will profess to prioritising the interests of patients over their own. This is part of their professional role and self-image. The truth, however, is that their motives can be a good deal more complex. The desire to relieve the suffering of patients is maximised where this is associated with a degree of professional satisfaction. It may, however, be curtailed where the patient's personality, condition or circumstances tend to deny the doctor this sense of satisfaction. Most doctors are, undoubtedly, motivated by a degree of altruism. However, they would not be human were they not also motivated to some degree by the prospect of remuneration. Indeed, it has been shown that doctors' clinical behaviour can be influenced by patterns of remuneration or packages of financial incentives and disincentives.[5] Thus, they are, as one would expect, motivated by self-interest as well as patient interest. They are, of course, also interested in maintaining the high esteem in which they are generally held by patients. Doctors, as a self-regulating profession, are also subject to the influence of their fellow professionals. The Medical Council in Ireland acts to enforce the obligation of doctors to act in the best interest of patients and to constrain the extent to which they act in self interest where this conflicts with patients' interests. Doctors are, of course, cognisant of the general expectations of their peers in regard to the balance between patients' and doctors' self-interest and will be influenced by these as well as just the limited enforcement capacities and procedures of the Medical Council.[6]

Within the gap between the patients' interest and those of their doctors there is a degree of latitude. Doctors, being susceptible to the same venial pleasures as anyone else, are apt to avail of opportunities presented to them by pharmaceutical marketing. Besides the direct-marketing techniques of advertising and sales pitches of pharmaceutical representatives, they may be enticed by the thrill of the new and the fascination of the different. All these influences can affect their prescribing while not being perceived as conflicting with patients' interests. Indeed, doctors may see their engagement in education about medicines, even if provided by the industry, as being motivated by patients' interests. As workers in the healthcare industry, doctors are, naturally, interested in seeing that industry receive priority in government spending and in seeing barriers restraining personal and public spending on healthcare minimised. Given the prominent role of medicines within the panoply of healthcare technologies, doctors share with the pharmaceutical industry an interest in seeing medicines expenditure, in particular, receive priority.

The interests of patients

The interests and motivations of patients would appear, superficially, to be fairly straightforwardly related to achieving relief from their suffering. However, patients have financial interests in the medicines trade too and, obviously, will also be keen to minimise their exposure to healthcare costs. They will wish for healthcare expenditure by the state or other third-party payers to receive a high priority. Patients also have a keen interest in their access to medicines not being unduly constrained. While clearly interested in ensuring the safety of their medicines, patients are also interested in reducing the costs to them of medicines and gaining more ready access to medicines. Thus, they may not always appreciate the professional intervention of a pharmacist, which can be perceived as an additional cost and a barrier to access to medicines. Patients also have an interest in there being investment in the development and improvement of healthcare technologies, including medicines. In this regard, patients increasingly act collectively through organisations that fundraise for medical research and lobby for investment in healthcare. Recent research on health advocacy organisations in Ireland identified 167 such organisations, many of which are active in supporting medical research.[7] Patients are also mindful of their relationships with their healthcare professionals and are usually eager to maintain good relations, fearing, probably subconsciously most of the time, negative consequences for them if they do not.

The interests of the state

The state has complex relationships with each of the other players – industry, doctors and patients. As major third-party payers, they have an interest in keeping healthcare costs, including medicines costs, to a minimum. But they may be ambivalent in this, especially in a country like Ireland, where the pharmaceutical industry is such a major contributor to the general economy. The pharmaceutical industry in Ireland contributes to the employment of nearly 50,000 people and Ireland is the largest net exporter of pharmaceuticals in the world.[8] Too active a drive to reduce public expenditure on medicines would run the risk of marring relations with the industry, which could, potentially, retaliate by reducing investment in the Irish economy, even though the impact of restrictions on medicines expenditure in Ireland would in all likelihood have a very modest impact on the profitability of a transnational pharmaceutical industry. The approach to cost containment of medicines expenditure by the state tends to deploy indirect and subtle techniques. Drug budgeting, which seeks to incentivise prescribers to reduce the medicines expenditure incurred in respect of drugs they prescribe, has had only a fairly modest impact on containing medicines costs.[9] Schemes to encourage prescribers to be more cost aware and to moderate their prescribing expenditure are combined with higher-level agreements such as the Drug Pricing and Supply Agreement with the IPHA. This agreement seeks to constrain overall medicines expenditure by the state while not unduly restricting the industry's profitability, its capacity to grow new markets, or its ability to promote individual medicines. Thus, the state, while needing to be seen to act in patients' interests and to safeguard its healthcare coffers, also needs to avoid conflict with the pharmaceutical industry. The state also has a similarly problematic relationship with the medical profession. While there may be a desire to limit expenditure, it can be difficult to curtail the enthusiasm of the profession for new and invariably more expensive healthcare technologies. In common with the other players, the state has an interest in the reduction of patients' suffering but is probably more conflicted in this desire. Endeavours to relieve patient suffering invariably incur costs, which immediately give rise to the need to balance expenditure in this area with the many other calls on government resources. In a democracy like Ireland, the issues raised by these conflicts of interest become particularly difficult, as unpopular decisions may be the subject of political opprobrium. The real challenge to democrats can be to persuade their constituencies of the merits of decisions that involve restrictions in expenditure on medical technologies.

Common interests

The various players also have certain interests in common. In addition to an interest in the relief of patient suffering, each of the players has a general interest in maintaining good relations and avoiding conflict with the others. All share a common belief in the benefits of medicines in relieving patient suffering and all are generally content to see the pharmaceutical industry thrive. Thus, all players are reconciled to seeing expenditure on medicines rising year on year, although they will differ in their attitudes to this. Patients and third-party payers will wish to see this rise remain low or modest, whereas industry would prefer it remained buoyant. Doctors are probably relatively indifferent to medicines expenditure. There is also a shared perception that medicine is on a continuous upward curve of improvement driven by research and development of ever more innovative and effective medicines. The different perspectives of the various players tend to be seen more in the priority given to the different concerns about medicines than in major differences regarding the intrinsic value of medicines to healthcare. Thus, the industry, while not disinterested in issues of medicines safety and effectiveness, will tend to place the highest priority on profitability. Doctors will tend to be most concerned with the efficacy and safety of medicines. Specialists dealing with more dangerous or life-threatening conditions may place greater priority on efficacy and be prepared to deem certain risks associated with medicines worth taking. GPs dealing with less serious and often self-limiting illness may place more emphasis on safety and be prepared to forego efficacy to a certain extent. Patients tend to want the most efficacious medicine regardless, although this may be because of a lack of awareness or an understandable reluctance to acknowledge that drugs can be unsafe. The state, at least where it is paying for the medicines, will, obviously, place much more priority on the cost or relative costs of medicines.

Forms of entanglement

This complex web of interests contributes to the way the medical profession and the pharmaceutical industry interact. Pharmaceutical companies are obliged to market to doctors, who, while potentially a barrier between them and the end customer – the patient, at least have the advantage of often being relatively price insensitive.[10] Their interactions, therefore, are primarily those of a vendor and a purchaser and are shaped by common business practices widespread throughout the economy, being broadly similar to the way goods and services are promoted and marketed to customers in general. The promotional effort, though, has to be somewhat more subtle in its approach than for other commodities, not least because the patients and third-party payers (such as the state) have substantial interests in the transactions between doctors and the pharmaceutical industry. A trend has been noted by many commentators whereby the number and extent of interactions between doctors and the pharmaceutical industry have become more numerous and complex and the source of greater conflicts of interest than was the case in the past. For example, Kassirer, a former editor-in-chief of the *New England Journal of Medicine*, describes a multitude of ways in which doctors can be made to feel beholden to the pharmaceutical industry, through various forms of largesse they may have received, and the widespread conflicts of interests that many leading figures in medicine may encounter in deciding on the best treatments for their own and colleagues' patients.[11] Likewise, Marcia Angell, another former editor-in-chief of the *New England Journal of Medicine*, sounds a similar warning of how doctors are in receipt of 'hard sell, lures, bribes and kickbacks' from the drugs industry and how marketing to doctors can masquerade as education and research.[12] The interaction between doctors and the pharmaceutical industry has been described by Moynihan in terms of an 'entanglement'.[13] This entanglement takes many different shapes and occurs at various levels of the industry and the profession.

Visits of pharmaceutical company representatives
The commonest site of interaction is the encounters between pharmaceutical industry representatives ('drug reps') and individual doctors that take place at the doctor's workplace. At these encounters, as well as providing doctors with information about their products, representatives will give gifts, usually bearing the name of a drug being promoted and/or the logo of the company. Irish Pharmaceutical

Healthcare Association (IPHA) guidelines state that health professionals should not be given gifts unless they are inexpensive and relevant to the practice of medicine or pharmacy. Needless to say, companies can be very inventive with regard to what is 'relevant to the practice of medicine or pharmacy' and they can take a fairly generous view of what is 'inexpensive'.[14] Thus, although gifts such as tongue depressors, examination torches, surgical gloves, pens and post-it notes are commonplace and arguably come within the guidelines, other gifts, such as stethoscopes or blood pressure manometers, probably stretch the concept of 'inexpensive'.[15] Gifts of hand cream and penknives would also seem to stretch the concept of 'relevant to the practice of medicine'.

International evidence suggests that the vast majority of doctors encounter pharmaceutical representatives and many see them about once every two weeks.[16] Figures from Ireland suggest much more frequent contacts, in the range of two to seven per week, although there are no data on what proportion of GPs see representatives.[17] My own impression would be that it is the overwhelming majority. There is also little doubt that doctors' prescribing habits are influenced by these interactions, although many doctors deny such influence. While the larger the gift the greater the sense of obligation it may impose, there is evidence from psychology that any gift of any size invokes a need to reciprocate.[18] It has been further noted that the gift of food, which is a very common element of the interactions between pharmaceutical representatives and doctors, impels a particularly strong sense of obligation. Another important element of the visits of representatives is the offer, often accepted by doctors, of free samples of medicine being marketed. Many doctors feel that accepting these free samples is ethically more acceptable than accepting other sorts of gifts.[19] However, doctors who take such free samples have been shown to develop more expensive prescribing habits and their patients may end up paying more for their drugs in the longer term.[20]

Medical meetings

Doctors are also regular recipients of hospitality from the pharmaceutical industry at a variety of educational and other meetings. This is also subject to guidelines which, in the case of the IPHA guidelines, state that the hospitality should be 'reasonable in level and secondary to the main purpose of the occasion'.[21] They further state that the hospitality should not be extended to persons other than health professionals (e.g. spouses are excluded) and that the cost of the hospitality offered must not exceed that level which the recipients might normally adopt when paying for themselves. However, here, too, there is an incentive to the representatives in the struggle to gain market advantage and to be inventive. They may be tempted to stretch the similarly vague concepts of 'reasonable in level' and 'secondary to the main purpose of the occasion'. Certainly, the industry sometimes takes a lavish view of the expenditure doctors are prepared to incur when paying for themselves. Other forms of generosity from the industry to the profession may be more indirect. Thus, the industry, sometimes working through third parties such as professional bodies, will offer sponsorship to doctors and other professionals to help with expenses of research or travel.

Pharmaceutical companies have a very major involvement in the provision of postgraduate educational and continuing professional development in Ireland, as in many other countries. The industry most commonly sponsors meetings organised by doctors or doctors' professional associations or representative bodies. These include large national events such as annual meetings of medical colleges and large regional events such as GP study days laid on by faculties of the Irish College of General Practitioners. They also include smaller more local events such as meetings of clinical societies. While a small charge may be levied, in most cases the majority of the expenses involved in laying on the meeting, including hospitality, will be met by pharmaceutical sponsors. It has been said that without the sponsorship provided by industry, professional development of doctors would barely survive. As well as sponsoring meetings organised by doctors in relation to their own self-perceived learning needs, meetings are laid on by the industry without necessarily consulting the profession in advance. These tend to be more explicitly associated with the marketing of a particular product and are driven more explicitly by the industry's need to get a message across to prescribers. A speaker will usually be provided by the company and the hospitality is laid on entirely by the pharmaceutical company. The level of hospitality at such pharmaceutical company arranged meetings is considered to be 'corporate hospitality'. The guidelines for levels of such 'corporate hospitality' are even vaguer than those applying to meetings organised by the professions but sponsored by the industry. Moderation, though, is urged.

The role of the industry in continuing medical education is hotly debated. In the past few years there have been active discussions between representatives of medical education accreditors in the United States and Europe.[22] They have developed the first global standards for continuing medical education, which seek to create a greater distance between doctors and pharmaceutical funding in the continuing medical education sphere. They have proposed a global fund for continuing medical education to be funded by the industry collectively to reduce the impact of marketing of particular products to doctors under the guise of continuing medical education. Others argue, though, that all links should be cut entirely and continuing medical education be funded by doctors themselves or from the public purse.[23] In Ireland there is a programme of small-group continuing medical education for general practitioners that is funded from the public purse, but it competes with the much more lavishly funded educational events sponsored by the pharmaceutical companies.

Research

The pharmaceutical industry depends on a major research endeavour to develop and test new products. While initial drug development research may be conducted 'in-house' or contracted out to subsidiaries or research companies, drugs eventually have to be tried on patients. Research involving patients, though, requires access to patients and so clinical research is conducted in conjunction with the medical profession, mostly through academic institutions. This takes the form of drugs trials in which large numbers of patients with a particular condition are randomly allocated to receive treatment with either a new (experimental) treatment or an existing treatment (or sometimes a dummy treatment or placebo, where there is no existing treatment deemed truly effective). The two groups are compared at some later point in time to see if the group receiving the new treatment improved relative to a control group of patients who did not receive the experimental treatment.

The involvement of clinicians in such studies brings into being another form of entanglement which is very multi-faceted and complex. Institutions and clinicians involved in such research do require payment, as being involved incurs costs over and above those of ordinary clinical care. However, the level of this payment may be generous and, while it ought not to be, it is sometimes suspected of being more generous than required to meet the incurred costs.[24] Furthermore, regardless of the absolute level of such payments, clinical research usually represents a substantial investment on the part of any drug company concerned and so there is a considerable temptation to try and avoid the risks of potentially negative findings from such research by trying to control the research process or, in other ways, limit the independence of the researchers to disseminate all the findings of a research project. There are parallel temptations for clinical researchers to ensure that results are favourable to the sponsor. Evidence that the involvement of the pharmaceutical industry in research distorts the results has been summarised in two recent reviews. Bekelman, Li and Gross found a 'significant association between industry sponsorship and pro-industry conclusions' in biomedical research, and Lexchin et al. showed that studies sponsored by pharmaceutical companies were four times more likely to have outcomes favouring the sponsors' products than studies funded by other sources.[25] While there is no evidence that industry funding produces studies of lower methodological quality, it may be that, by setting the research agenda, determining the trial design and suppressing or delaying unfavourable findings, the industry subtly influences the impression of drug therapies under research. Naturally, there are guidelines to try and control both parties and to try and ensure that results are not incomplete or distorted and that negative findings will be published and that regulators and other policy-makers are given all appropriate insights into the product(s). Enforcing such guidelines, though, is difficult and it has been argued that, in some instances, regulators and policy-makers are, themselves, compromised.[26]

In recent years, efforts have been made to try to provide clinicians with independent assessments of research to guide their treatment of patients. Prime among the groups promoting this evidence-based medicine approach has been the Cochrane Collaboration. This is an international group of researchers who collate, assess, summarise and interpret clinical research. Although the group had an explicit policy of not accepting direct funding from a single source with a vested interest in the results of the review, it was discovered that there were two reviews of anti-migraine drugs on the group's database that had been sponsored by Pfizer.[27] The group has subsequently had to tighten its rules to maintain its reputation for integrity and independence.[28]

Besides basic research and clinical research, the pharmaceutical industry also conducts market research. This may involve doctors, too, and may entail a payment, albeit a more modest one, to doctors involved in such research.[29] It can be argued that any such payment potentially compromises the independence of the doctor when he or she comes to prescribe. It is also suspected that sometimes the research is really just another way of encouraging the doctor to try a new drug and is hence just another form of marketing.[30] One of the freedoms doctors enjoy as prescribers is that they can use any drug for any patient they choose, although drugs can only be licensed for specific indications. The use of a drug for unlicensed indications is referred to as 'off-label' use. Pharmaceutical companies are prohibited from advertising or promoting off-label use, but there have been instances where such marketing has nevertheless occurred. In a now infamous case, Parke-Davis was found to have encouraged doctors to prescribe its anti-epilepsy drug Neurontin for a variety of off-label uses by paying experts to put their names to dubious research that was said to prove the benefit of the drug for these other conditions.[31]

Other forms of entanglement

Doctors can become involved with pharmaceutical companies in other ways, too. For instance, companies will often assemble consultative panels involving doctors. This is outside normal marketing procedures and so there are no particular restrictions on levels of payment or hospitality involved in these activities. Companies may also employ doctors individually as consultants. Most doctors have sufficient autonomy within their other positions (e.g. in the publicly funded health services) to take on these consultancies. Any associated financial gain may be accrued personally, though many will share with or donate such fees to their employing institution. Doctors, like other members of the public, are entitled to hold shares in publicly listed companies, which include virtually all the pharmaceutical companies. Although such a stockholding might be thought to create obvious and probably recurrent conflicts of interest, there is no absolute restriction on doctors holding shares in pharmaceutical companies.

Doctors collectively are also multiply entangled with the pharmaceutical industry. Professional bodies of many kinds, including specialist colleges, special interest groups, professional educational institutes and so on, seek and accept sponsorship from the industry for specific and, sometimes, general activities. This can take the form of sponsorship of meetings, sponsorship of specific initiatives and projects or joint ventures which can be educational, research, or other. Many professional journals also raise part or, sometimes, all of their finances through industry sponsorship or advertising. Doctors are also involved in patient organisations and associations, especially when related to their clinical discipline. These organisations increasingly get sponsorship from the pharmaceutical industry – sometimes, indeed, through the offices of their medical members. Doctors in academia can have particularly intensive interactions with the industry, typically around research. In addition to sponsorship of specific research projects as mentioned above, there have been instances of collaboration between the industry and academic institutions at the highest level. In these cases, the level of sponsorship can run to the cost of new buildings, endowment of chairs and other forms of support of the institution's research and educational endeavours. At this level, the stakes for both parties are pretty high and this can add to pressure on doctors working within these institutes to be particularly sensitive to the needs of the industry – both to produce research favourable to the company and to avoid dissemination of research that might be unfavourable. Likewise, doctors working in academic institutions can be constrained by the relationships between their institution and the pharmaceutical industry. Kassirer quotes the example of a Boston researcher who, during negotiations with a pharmaceutical company regarding a multi-million-dollar research grant, was pressurised by officers from his own institution (that stood to gain a substantial overhead from the grant) to relent on his insistence on having access to primary data generated by the research. The researcher only managed to win over his institution when he got confirmation from journal editors who would consider publishing his research that they would only do so if he had access to all the data.[32]

Entanglement in the Irish context

There are features of the healthcare environment in Ireland that may make entanglement more likely and the attendant dangers somewhat greater than might be the case in other countries. Medicine is a more explicitly commercial enterprise in Ireland than is the case in many other European countries. In countries with a predominantly socialised healthcare system, such as in Scandinavia and the UK, there is a more general mistrust of commercialism in medicine and, perhaps, a greater wariness about being seduced by marketing. In Ireland there is a distinctive mix of public and private medicine, with a generally positive attitude to private medicine that seems to be agreed between the medical profession, the government and the public. While there may be token efforts to control costs and, hence, a tacit interest in avoiding entanglement in the public sector, there is active disinterest in what goes on in the private sector and a general acceptance that commercial practices and marketing techniques deployed in other sectors are acceptable in the private medicine arena too. One way to minimise or avoid entanglement is to introduce regulation of marketing practices. This may be by way of a voluntary code of practice or on a legislative footing. Ireland, as a society, seems to have a reluctance to legislate or regulate unless pushed to do so. Furthermore, even where regulation or legislation is in place, there has, at least historically, been a tendency to adopt a fairly *laissez-faire* attitude, except where there are potentially politically visible consequences.

There are positive political and economic advantages to being liberal towards the pharmaceutical industry in Ireland. Successive Irish governments have pursued a policy of encouraging inward investment and have been particularly successful in attracting pharmaceutical manufacturers. The pharmaceutical sector is a very important part of the Irish economy and is a particularly significant contributor to foreign earnings. Net exports of pharmaceuticals are valued at over €14.75 billion annually, making Ireland the largest pharmaceutical exporter in the world.[33] The industry also employs 24,000 people directly and a further 24,000 indirectly. Thus, the Irish government is reluctant to act in ways that might be seen to be contrary to the interests of the pharmaceutical industry. State contracts with pharmacists in Ireland have also been cited as failing to encourage generic prescribing.[34] Under the GMS, a pharmacist must supply a branded medicine when one is prescribed by the doctor (i.e. generic substitution is not allowed).[35] The pharmacist is refunded the trade price of such a medicine plus a dispensing fee. Where a doctor prescribes generically, the pharmacist can dispense any brand. In relation to other State schemes, namely the Drug Payment Scheme and the Long-Term Illness scheme, pharmacists are paid a mark-up of 50 per cent on the trade price plus a dispensing fee. This is effectively an incentive for the pharmacist to dispense the most expensive brand when the doctor prescribes generically, as the absolute value of the mark-up is greater on more expensive medicines.

These factors probably contribute to a relatively low rate of generic prescribing in Ireland.[36] Feely et al. have remarked on how generic prescribing rates in the Republic of Ireland in 1993 (as witnessed in the GMS, the only part of the Irish healthcare system for which accurate data are readily available) were 17.4 per cent compared to 38 per cent in the UK National Health Service.[37] Since then, generic prescribing rates in the UK have risen to 76 per cent (in 2002), driven by a variety of government initiatives to encourage and reward generic prescribing by GPs. By contrast, the generic prescribing rate in the GMS in 2001 was only 22 per cent.[38] It was also noted by Tilson et al. that for 18 per cent of medicines dispensed there was a generic equivalent available and, had even just the commonest of these been prescribed instead of the proprietary brand, savings in excess of €5 million could have been made.[39] The same point has recently been reinforced by a statement from the Association of Pharmaceutical Manufacturers of Ireland (who make generic drugs). Their chairman, Rory O'Riordan, is quoted as saying that savings of €15 million could be made on generic prescribing of cholesterol-lowering drugs alone.[40] This consistently high rate of proprietary name prescribing persists in spite of the indicative drug target scheme, which was meant to stimulate generic prescribing. Any suggestion of generic substitution, whereby a pharmacist would be required to dispense a generic brand unless specifically directed not to by the doctor, is opposed by the Irish Pharmaceutical Healthcare Association, which claims to be supported in this stand by the Irish Medical Organisation.[41]

Ireland is a small country, with the result that all sectors and professional groups in Ireland tend to be quite small compared to those in larger countries such as the UK, the US, France or Germany. Thus, there are greater chances of people in two quite small professional groups such as doctors and pharmaceutical company representatives having links with each other, other than purely professional ones. Furthermore, in Irish society professional and social relationships generally are not always kept so separate as they are in other societies. Thus, it is easier for representatives of pharmaceutical companies to engender a more social aspect to their relationships with doctors. A small qualitative study of doctors in north-west Ireland gives some credence to this view.[42] Doctors surveyed described their meetings with pharmaceutical representatives as providing them with valued social contact and relief from a stressful job. Older GPs meeting with well-established representatives particularly commented on this social value of contacts. In this study, respondents also reported having between two and seven contacts with representatives per week taking between ten and seventy minutes, which would appear to be an increase from the figure previously reported by O'Mahony and higher than figures reported in surveys from other countries.[43]

In Ireland the involvement of pharmaceutical companies in professional development and continuing education is also quite extensive. It has been estimated that 80–90 per cent of postgraduate education in Ireland is sponsored by the pharmaceutical industry and the nature of this sponsorship is sometimes quite generous, with the industry funding Irish doctors to go to international meetings.[44] The extent of the involvement of the pharmaceutical industry in research in Irish hospitals and third-level institutions is not well researched and no data on this could be located by the author. However, there certainly is a large amount of industry-sponsored research going on and the industry has been involved in the sponsorship of personnel and equipment in Irish hospitals and academies over the years. Recent examples include the involvement of Procter and Gamble in the Alimentary Pharmacobiotic Centre in University College Cork, sponsorship of a researcher to the Department of Clinical Pharmacology at University College Dublin by Astra Zeneca, and the sponsorship of the Newman Scholarship, also by Astra Zeneca, at University College Dublin. All the signs of entanglement observed elsewhere can be seen in the Irish healthcare system.

Responses to the dangers of entanglement

There are two basic approaches to limiting the potential dangers of entanglement. One is to try to use voluntary or mutually agreed approaches and one is to legislate. The voluntary approach tends to be pursued with the greatest enthusiasm when there is the perceived or actual threat of a legislative approach in the offing. The voluntary approach is already quite well developed in Ireland. The Irish Pharmaceutical Healthcare Association (IPHA) has in place two codes of practice.[45] One of these relates specifically to advertising and the other to marketing more generally. These codes cover issues relating to the marketing of pharmaceuticals, particularly to doctors, as direct-to-consumer advertising is, as yet, not allowed in Ireland. The codes cover such issues as the content of advertisements and other promotional materials, the behaviour of representatives, gifts, hospitality and sponsorship and relations with the general public. The code is policed by a Code of Marketing Panel, who consider complaints made to them about the marketing of drugs or the promotional behaviour of pharmaceutical companies and make recommendations. The wording of many clauses of the code is somewhat vague and a judgement is often required before it can even be established that there is a complaint.

Somewhat belatedly, it would seem the medical profession is becoming aware of the need for such codes of practice. In the sixth edition of its Ethical Guidelines to doctors, the Medical Council has, for the first time, made explicit reference to what is considered to be an appropriate type of financial support by the pharmaceutical industry for doctors, namely non-promotional educational grants.[46] It also recognises the potential for conflicts of interest arising where doctors are remunerated by or have financial interests in particular pharmaceutical companies, but it only advises that doctors must ensure that any such remuneration or financial interest should not be allowed to influence them when recommending therapy for patients. The Irish College of General Practitioners has also recently produced a code of practice on pharmaceutical company sponsorship of meetings.[47] This code also states that unrestricted educational grants are an acceptable form of financial support for meetings. It further warns against allowing the body of a meeting to be used to promote any particular company or product. The code also warns that doctors should always acknowledge that involvement of the pharmaceutical industry can give rise to a conflict of interest and recommends that any such conflict of interest be acknowledged. The code also requires a clear separation between any promotional activities and the educational content of the meeting. For instance, it specifically states that pharmaceutical representatives should not speak during the educational component of the meeting.

Conclusion

It is clear that the relationship between the medical profession and the transnational pharmaceutical industry is a complex one. The most innocent interpretation is that the industry and the profession are merely *entwined*, i.e. closely interconnected, but not in a way that they could not be easily separated without any significant consequences to either party. It would seem more likely that they are *entangled*, i.e. closely interconnected in ways that would suggest that any attempt to separate them would have consequences and would likely be resisted. A more sinister view would be that the profession has been *ensnared* by the industry such that they would individually and collectively find it very difficult to separate and that the industry is having much more influence on the profession than vice versa. While ensnarement is a possibility, there is little hard evidence to support such a malign view. That the relationship is more entangled than merely entwined is fairly clear given the extensive involvement of the industry in continuing medical education and in research in Ireland and the paucity of critical voices or professionally imposed constraints on industry-marketing activities. Furthermore, the relationship between the industry and the profession may reasonably be characterised as an essentially commercial one in which there are many incentives and few restraints towards a close or even collusive relationship. Other parties with an interest in and bearing on the relationship seem to share the ambivalence of doctors regarding the need to restrict or regulate the promotional activities of a large and powerful pharmaceutical industry. There is an over-reliance on rather vague and weak codes of practice which require a high level of trust in the industry to avoid risks to patients from over-enthusiastic use of medicines – especially newer medicines. This is a system in which cost containment does not feature very prominently and in which issues of patient safety receive less scrutiny than they deserve.

CHAPTER 8

The Dominance of Drug-Based Mental Health Care in Ireland:

A Personal Account of a General Practitioner Turned Psychotherapist

Terry Lynch

Introduction

I qualified as a medical doctor at University College Cork in 1982. I then trained to become a General Practitioner (GP) and worked as a GP in Limerick until 1997. For the first ten years or so of my medical working life, I enthusiastically embraced and accepted my medical training as being highly scientific, reliable and trustworthy, providing the public with the best available healthcare. In this chapter, I outline my personal experience as a provider of mental health services. Based on this experience, I explore the relationship between the medical profession and the pharmaceutical industry, the prescribing of antidepressants in Ireland, and the quality and effectiveness of drug regulation in Ireland. I discuss the medical press in Ireland, the education of GPs in mental health (more accurately, the lack of mental health education for GPs), and the effectiveness of antidepressants, and my own personal journey from being a convinced and enthusiastic GP to seeing mental health problems from a much broader perspective.

In the early 1990s, doubts about many aspects of my training and the everyday practice of medical care began to creep in. These doubts increased over the years, to the point that, in 1997, I decided to change the way I worked. Over the years I had become particularly interested in mental health, and had become increasingly concerned about the medical approach to mental health and mental health problems. Over the following three years, I retrained in psychotherapy and I now work exclusively in the area of mental healthcare. My book, *Beyond Prozac – Healing Mental Suffering Without Drugs*, was published in Ireland in 2001 and in Britain in 2004.[1] This book became a best-seller in Ireland in 2001. *Beyond Prozac* was welcomed by many mental health service users and many working within the field of mental services, with the exception of the majority of psychiatrists and many GPs. I have received several thousand phone calls from mental health service users and their loved ones from all over Ireland, all expressing their desire to meet with me, having read *Beyond Prozac*.

I continue to receive up to twenty letters and forty phonecalls a week from people desperately seeking help with mental health issues. Whilst approximately ten GPs have told me privately that they share my concerns regarding the medicalisation of human distress, none were prepared to express this in public for fear of reprisals from colleagues. Such is the power of the 'brotherhood' within medicine to conform to mainstream beliefs. I have written widely in Irish newspapers and magazines since the publication of the book in 2001 and I have been asked to speak at many mental health fora, but I have yet to be asked to speak at a medical meeting.

In 2003 I was appointed to the Irish government's Expert Group on Mental Health Policy. This group, appointed by the Minister of Health and Children in Ireland, was established to formulate and direct mental health policy in Ireland for the next ten to fifteen years. The group consisted of eighteen members from a diversity of backgrounds ranging from psychiatry to mental health service user representation. An important thread within the working of the Expert Group was to be mindful of the views and experiences of mental health service users and carers, as well as providers of services. To this end, the Expert Group embarked upon a major consultation process, the results of which have been taken into account and honoured within its report, *A Vision for Change*, launched in January 2006.[2]

This report and its recommendations have been welcomed across a wide range of stakeholders within mental health. Among the key recommendations of *A Vision for Change* are that: a recovery orientation should inform every aspect of service delivery; there should be significantly greater involvement of mental health service users and carers in every aspect of service development and delivery; a far greater emphasis needs to be placed on mental health promotion; a community-based mental health service needs to be developed; and the evaluation of mental health services using meaningful performance indicators should be introduced. Other recommendations include that: mental health service users and carers should have ready access to a wide variety of relevant information; systematic evaluations on all forms of interventions in mental health should be undertaken and this information should be widely disseminated; and far greater involvement of mental health service users at every stage of the research process, including the development of research agendas, commissioning, overseeing, conducting and evaluating research, as well as supporting the use of the emerging evidence base in policy and practice, should be promoted. Since the publication of this report, I have been appointed to the Independent Monitoring Group, whose remit is to oversee the implementation of this report.

The 'special' relationship between doctors and the pharmaceutical industry

The link between the pharmaceutical industry and the medical profession has not been the subject of much research in the Irish context.[3] I became very concerned about the relationship between the drug companies and doctors early in my medical career. I began to question the appropriateness of drug representatives calling to see me on a regular basis, plying their wares. It would not be unusual for three to six drug company representatives to call to see me in a given week. Typically, this would be a cordial, friendly meeting, where the company representative would present glossy, colourful information about their company's products and drop in some sample packs of drugs.

Over the years, I became suspicious of this approach, and I began to question the representatives as they came to see me. An experience with one drug company representative brought it home to me that my approach to 'drug reps' was the exception rather than the rule. This particular drug representative had been calling to me for several years. One day, I noticed that he looked quite nervous as he sat in front of me and I asked him why. He replied that I ask him a lot of questions about his products. He said that this was most unusual. Indeed, he told me that, within the geographical area he covered for his company, I was the only GP who questioned him to any degree about his products. He said that all most GPs want is a chat about anything but medicine, that most GPs see his visit as a break from the routine of seeing patients. I learned more from that drug representative's visit to me than from any other before or since.

The links between the medical profession and the pharmaceutical industry are far too close for comfort. Over the past fifty years, the pharmaceutical industry has steadily increased its influence and its presence within medicine. I believe that the pharmaceutical industry has figured out how best to influence doctors and has been working from that agenda for many decades. Many of these ways are so subtle that they go unnoticed by most doctors. The Medical Council, the Royal College of Psychiatrists and the pharmaceutical industry have issued guidelines as to proper conduct within the doctor–drug company relationship. However, the issues in question are not, in my opinion, adequately addressed within these guidelines.

For decades, many doctors have practised as though the agenda of the pharmaceutical companies and of the medical profession are identical. Cleverly and with considerable stealth over many decades, drug companies have deliberately sought to ingratiate themselves with doctors, seeking to become seen by doctors as a helping, concerned ally in a joint effort to alleviate pain, illness and distress. Not uncommonly, doctors speak of the 'special relationship' which exists between doctors and the pharmaceutical industry. An example is an article published in *Irish Medical News* in 2004 entitled 'Special Relationship between Doctors and Drug Companies'.[4] The author of this article, a well-known and rightly respected Irish GP, wrote that what works best in Ireland – in terms of doctor-drug company representative interaction – might be: 'light-hearted banter with a gentle reminder about a product. It is a *friendship* and a relationship thing knowing that doctors are pressed for time and in need of a bit of *light relief*. What it is not about is delivering charts and graphs and figures' (my emphasis).[5]

Why should there be a 'special' relationship between doctors and the drug industry? Are doctors sufficiently aware of the downside of such 'special' relationships? One rarely sees an article in the medical media outlining special relationships between doctors and, say, psychotherapists and counsellors, or doctors and dieticians. Why, for example, do doctors not arrange similar meetings with members of the counselling professions on a regular basis to truly familiarise themselves with other, non-drug, interventions?

People or groups who have special relationships sometimes lose their sense of objectivity towards each other. They may be inclined to defend each other somewhat independently of the facts, as family members or friends may do, for example. A common adage within medicine is that it is not generally wise for doctors to treat members of their own families. The closeness of the relationship blurs both objectivity and boundaries. The doctor–patient relationship – within which both doctor and patient instinctively know and understand the nature of this relationship – becomes blurred and complicated. In a typical doctor-patient relationship, both doctor and patient know where they stand and what their role is. When a doctor treats family members, the doctor is now both a doctor to and a close family relative of the patient. This can lead to health decisions being made not solely on the basis of the health requirements of the situation, but rather influenced by feelings existing between doctor and patient, and other aspects which would not normally be present within a doctor-patient relationship. The same risks apply when health carers (e.g. doctors) have 'special relationships' with the manufacturers of one form of intervention in healthcare (e.g. medication).

In May 2004, I was involved in an Irish television documentary which looked at the relationship between doctors and the pharmaceutical industry.[6] On that programme, a number of doctors expressed concern about entanglement between the medical profession and the pharmaceutical industry. With regard to doctors being taken to luxurious locations for educational purposes at the expense of pharmaceutical companies, Tom O'Dowd, Professor of General Practice at Trinity College Dublin, commented: 'Well, it is bribery, I mean, taking doctors away on those kinds of expensive trips is bribery.'[7] On the same programme, Richard Smith, former editor of the *British Medical Journal*, said that:

> Doctors are wined and dined a great deal by pharmaceutical companies. They are taken to conferences abroad, they are given gifts . . . The relationship between doctors and drug companies is probably too close for comfort, and the world would be a better place, and it certainly would be better for patients, if we [doctors] were to disentangle ourselves [from the pharmaceutical industry].[8]

Further commentaries offered by Irish medical professionals aired in this documentary are discussed below.

The prescribing of antidepressants in Ireland

I would like to outline an extended interaction in which I was involved with the Irish Medicines Board. Before, during and after this interaction, I had considerable concerns regarding the regulation of drugs in Ireland and indeed internationally. For several years, there has been considerable concern internationally regarding the safety of the SSRI (Selective Serotonin Reuptake Inhibitors) class of drugs, the newer class of antidepressants, of which Prozac and Seroxat are amongst the most commonly known. One antidepressant in particular – Seroxat – has been the source of particular concern. There has been considerable concern regarding the potential of this drug to cause withdrawal problems, which can be severe, and the possibility that Seroxat may cause some people to become violent and/or suicidal within weeks of commencing this drug. In October 2002, in light of considerable international and Irish media focus on the antidepressant drug Seroxat, I decided to take a close look at the Seroxat patient information leaflet. Two things jumped out at me as I read the leaflet. The first concerned emphatic statements regarding how Seroxat worked. On two occasions in the patient information leaflet, it was stated as a matter of fact that Seroxat worked by bringing the levels of serotonin back to normal: 'This medicine works by bringing the levels of serotonin back to normal.' And later in the patient information leaflet, it is stated: 'Seroxat is one of the antidepressants that work by returning your serotonin levels to normal.'

From my research over many years, I knew that these claims were dubious. Yet, these statements had been in the Seroxat patient information leaflet since its launch in the early 1990s until October 2002. I therefore wrote to the Irish Medicines Board. The following was part of my letter, in which I outlined why this wording should never have appeared on the patient information leaflet:

> Patients put on Seroxat *never* have their serotonin levels measured prior to treatment to assess whether their serotonin levels are normal or abnormal to begin with. Patients *never* have their serotonin levels checked while on treatment to see whether their so-called 'abnormal' serotonin levels have returned to normal. It has not been scientifically established what the normal range of serotonin levels actually is; and obviously if we don't know what constitutes 'normal' serotonin levels, our scientific knowledge of 'abnormal' serotonin levels is inevitably seriously deficient.
>
> When treatment with Seroxat (and the other SSRIs) is stopped, no attempt is made by the doctor to assess serotonin levels. If Seroxat was working all along by 'returning your serotonin levels to normal' as the leaflet so emphatically states, what happens to one's serotonin level when Seroxat is stopped? Does it now somehow miraculously remain 'normal' in the absence of treatment? Or does it become 'abnormal' again? The bottom line here is that we doctors haven't a clue what happens to our patients' serotonin levels when the drug is stopped because we have no way

of measuring our patient's serotonin levels, and we do not know what constitutes 'normal' or 'abnormal' levels. The bottom line is that we doctors have no idea whether the patients we treat with Seroxat (and other SSRIs) have a normal, low or raised serotonin level at any stage of the entire process of diagnosis and treatment. And we have absolutely no idea how our patients' serotonin levels are responding to the treatment on an ongoing basis. In 20 years as a medical doctor, I have never, ever heard of a patient anywhere having their serotonin levels checked.[9]

In their reply to my letter, the Irish Medicines Board did not contest my comments:

> The Irish Medicines Board has been reviewing this matter with its experts for some time and is in agreement that the statement that SSRIs 'work by bringing the levels of serotonin back to normal' is not consistent with the scientific literature. The company has been asked to review the patient information leaflet accordingly.[10]

The second issue which struck me as I read the Seroxat patient information leaflet in October 2002 was another emphatic statement: 'Remember, you cannot become addicted to Seroxat.' From my own investigations, I immediately knew that this sentence was seriously misleading and should never have appeared in the patient information leaflet. For years, I had been well aware of the considerable medical and pharmaceutical company resistance to the distinct possibility that Seroxat and other SSRI drugs might be addictive. However, it was the certainty of this statement that struck me forcefully, particularly since I was aware – thanks to the excellent work of Charles Medawar on the Social Audit website[11] – that neither Seroxat nor other SSRI drugs had ever been systematically tested for their addictive potential. I raised this issue with the Irish Medicines Board. Several months after my initial letter, the manufacturers of Seroxat changed the wording with regard to both issues I had raised. The reference to it being impossible to become addicted to Seroxat was removed from the patient information leaflet. The wording regarding how Seroxat worked was also changed. I am not suggesting that the company changed the wording on foot of my letters, given the considerable international focus on and concern about Seroxat. In my opinion, I believe that the manufacturers of Seroxat removed the wording about addiction to protect themselves from further lawsuits – class actions have already begun in several countries, taken by people who believe they have become addicted to Seroxat. These inaccuracies had appeared on the Seroxat patient information leaflet since the drug first arrived on the market in the early 1990s. Millions of people worldwide (and thousands in Ireland) would have read this inaccurate wording and believed it.

As outlined by Charles Medawar,[12] over the past 200 years there has been a series of débâcles regarding medication prescribed for mental health problems, all of which have followed the same pattern:

- the production of a new group of drugs for mental health problems
- widespread enthusiasm for the drug within medical and pharmaceutical circles and among the public
- widespread prescribing of the drug
- gradual, growing awareness of problems associated with the drug, including addiction, dependency and withdrawal problems
- denial and dismissal of these problems for decades by the medical profession and pharmaceutical industry, in spite of widespread user experience of such problems and
- eventual and belated admission of addiction and dependence associated with the drug, by which time millions of people worldwide have needlessly become addicted to the drug in question. Typically, by this time, there is a new wonder drug on the market which becomes the focus of pharmaceutical, medical and public hope and attention.

This pattern is reflected in the histories of drugs such as alcohol, opium, barbiturates and amphetamines. The most recent public addition to this list has been the benzodiazepine tranquillisers (e.g. Valium). These drugs first came on the market in the 1950s, and for decades were seen much as SSRIs have been seen for the past ten years – as a major breakthrough in the treatment of emotional and mental distress. It took the medical profession and the pharmaceutical industry almost thirty years to acknowledge what millions of users of benzodiazepine tranquillisers worldwide had known for years, had put to their doctors, who dismissed the issue: that these drugs are in fact highly addictive.[13] I believe that we are currently well into an eerily similar process with SSRI antidepressants. These drugs first came on the market in the late 1980s. Concerns about addiction and withdrawal problems emerged within a few years of the launch of this class of drugs, and it has recently emerged that there was evidence of withdrawal problems within the original studies prior to their launch. Over the years, many thousands of people worldwide had expressed to their doctors their experience of great difficulty and unpleasant experiences coming off the drugs. For many years, doctors dismissed these findings. In recent years, the prevailing medical wisdom is that SSRI drugs cause 'discontinuation' symptoms, but they do not cause 'withdrawal' problems, and they most definitely are not addictive. In reality, this is an exercise in semantics.

In my opinion, the approach of both the pharmaceutical industry and the medical profession to potential addiction problems of SSRI drugs is deeply disturbing, irresponsible, and requires accounting for. One would think that, following the benzodiazepine débâcle, the medical profession and the pharmaceutical industry would become far more vigilant and aware of possible addiction problems with future wonder-drugs. The opposite has been the case. The definition of addiction was changed, to make it much more difficult for a drug to be called 'addictive'. In 1980, the then current edition of the *Diagnostic and Statistical Manual*[14] defined drug dependence as either tolerance (needing more of the drug to get the same effect) or withdrawal symptoms. However, in the updated version of the *Diagnostic and Statistical Manual*,[15] the American Psychiatric Association changed the definition of drug dependence, making it more difficult to define drugs as addictive. Both tolerance and withdrawal are now required to satisfy the definition of addictiveness. Ironically, according to this definition, benzodiazepine drugs would not necessarily be described as addictive, since many people taking these substances remain on the same doses for years, without feeling the need to increase the dose over time.

Drug companies did not systematically test the SSRIs for addictive potential. Nor did the medical profession, or the drug regulatory authorities, insist that SSRIs be assessed for their addictive potential, surely a major error of judgement given the litany of addictiveness problems with a series of drugs used to 'treat' emotional distress and mental health problems over the past 200 years.[16]

The bulk of medical problems are dealt with by GPs. For example, in the area of mental health, approximately 10 per cent of mental health problems which present to GPs are referred for specialist intervention, the remainder being dealt with by the GP. It would therefore seem appropriate that GPs ensure that they have a steady stream of independent information about the drugs they prescribe, upon which to base their decisions about treatment and interventions. According to a 2004 survey,[17] it would seem that GPs in Ireland rely on the drugs industry as their primary source of information in this regard. When asked the question 'Where do you get most of your information on new drugs?', 48 per cent of GPs responded that they obtained this information from the drug representatives who call to them on a regular basis. A further 47 per cent identified medical journals and publications as their principle source of information on new drugs. Many such publications are funded to a major extent by the pharmaceutical industry. Five per cent referred to other sources of information. The Cochrane Collaboration[18] is internationally recognised as a major, trustworthy, independent source of information on drugs and the effectiveness of interventions. Of the 100 GPs surveyed, not a single respondent mentioned the Cochrane Collaboration as a source of information on new drugs. This was not a major survey, in that it involved only 100 GPs. Nevertheless, it does provide some indication of trends regarding the sources of information and education available to GPs in Ireland.

The medical press in Ireland

Three of the most prominent medical publications in Ireland are the *Irish Medical Times*, the *Irish Medical News*, and *Medicine Weekly*. Funded largely through advertising fees from the pharmaceutical industry, these medical newspapers are circulated free of charge to all doctors in Ireland weekly or bi-weekly. As a general rule, these publications convey a positive image of the medical profession, of the pharmaceutical industry and of the 'special' relationship which exists between both parties. In general, there is a feel-good sense (from a medical and drug company perspective) to the articles within these publications. Photo-shoots of doctors and pharmaceutical company representatives at meetings or social gatherings are a regular feature. Rarely do issues which are challenging either to the medical profession or the pharmaceutical industry appear within these pages. For example, I was aware of the paucity of information in these three publications regarding the various changes in the wording to the Seroxat leaflet, including the removal of the sentence discussed above, 'Remember, you cannot become addicted to Seroxat', a change made by the company in 2003.

In the documentary on the relationship between doctors and the pharmaceutical industry mentioned above,[19] this issue was alluded to: 'In the month after GlaxoSmithKline removed the wording 'Remember, you cannot become addicted to Seroxat' from its patient information leaflet, none of the Irish medical newspapers/magazines reported the issue directly'.[20] Also on that programme, Tom O'Dowd, Professor of General Practice in Trinity College Dublin, commented :

> If you have pharmaceutically driven updating and continuing medical education, it's not something they are going to mention quickly. And I, for example, heard about the difficulties of coming off SSRIs on the radio. I didn't hear about it in the medical literature. It didn't come across to me in the normal [medical] circles.[21]

I have long been uncomfortable about the level of advertising within these three Irish medical publications. I decided to estimate just how much space within these publications was devoted to the advertisement of drugs, picking one edition of each at random. In the 13 September 2004 issue of the *Irish Medical News*, approximately 35.25 out of a total of fifty-six pages (approximately 63 per cent of the entire publication) were taken up with pharmaceutical company advertisements for drugs. Given that a further 2.5 pages consisted of photo-shoots of various meetings, less that one-third of the entire space of the publication remained for news and articles. In the 21 July 2004 edition of *Medicine Weekly*, approximately 23.75 pages out of a total of forty-eight pages (approximately 49 per cent of the publication) were devoted to pharmaceutical company advertisements for their products. Two pages of this edition were given to Doctors' Awards 2004, the sponsors of which were prominently displayed, fifteen out of sixteen of whom were pharmaceutical companies. Photographs of various meetings occupied a further page, leaving approximately 44 per cent of the entire publication available for news and articles. Similarly, in the 18 June 2004 edition of the *Irish Medical Times*, drug company advertisements took up approximately twenty-eight out of the total of forty-eight pages (equivalent to roughly 58 per cent of the entire space within the publication). The only non-drug company advertisement in this edition of any significant size was one relating to physiotherapy, which occupied roughly one-fifth of one page. As is the trend with all such publications, photographs of meetings occupied one and a half pages, and advertisements for non-drug alternatives received little or no coverage.

A recurring trend regarding the photographs of meetings is to include a mix of doctors and drug company representatives, again fostering the image of co-operation and shared vision between the two groups. Another recurring trend in the medical press is to include a large advertisement for a drug adjacent to an article on a particular topic. For example, a full-page, colourful, attractive advertisement for an antidepressant drug will frequently appear next to an article on depression. An article on schizophrenia will typically be adjacent to a full-page attractive advertisement for a major tranquilliser drug used by doctors as an intervention for people diagnosed as suffering from schizophrenia. I have never seen an advertisement for a non-drug treatment appear alongside an article about mental health in this fashion.

Mental health education of GPs

Given the rather ad-hoc nature of GP education in mental health, I was not surprised at the following rather alarming finding from an Irish 2004 publication:

> A review of mental health service delivery at primary care level in South West Dublin has called for specific mental health skills training for GPs. Nearly 70% of the GPs surveyed indicated that they had no specific training in mental health, despite the majority of GPs stating that at least a tenth of their case-load had mental health issues.
>
> 68% of GPs indicated that they had no specific training in mental health, while 32 % had training consisting of between 3 and 9 months on the job and/or during their hospital rotation. To address the problem, more than 70% of GPs indicated that they were interested in future studies in the area of mental health.[22]

Surely, it is alarming that roughly 70 per cent of GPs have had no specific training in mental health. Of those who have had mental health training, this generally consists of between three and nine months working within a psychiatry department in a hospital. Training during this time tends to be psychiatry-based, focusing primarily on the medical model or biological approach to mental health problems. GPs enter their working life with little or no exposure to other perspectives on mental health and mental health problems. Yet, GPs are considered to be adequately prepared to deal with the majority of mental health problems without referral to specialist services. I have similar concerns regarding the training of psychiatrists, whose training tends to be predominantly focused on biology, and less so on the psychological and social aspects of mental health and mental health problems.

For the past ten years, prescriptions for antidepressant drugs have been rising steadily, year on year. In 2002, an estimated 300,000 people in the Republic of Ireland were prescribed antidepressants.[23] The vast majority of these prescriptions were written by GPs. How can the public be sure that the prescribing of such medication is indeed the right course of action to deal with their distress, given that the majority of GPs may not even be sufficiently trained in mental health to make a competent decision, either about what the problem truly is, or the appropriate intervention?

One might presume that there is solid scientific evidence for such widespread medical enthusiasm for prescribing antidepressant drugs. This is not the case. Since the introduction of the SSRI antidepressants in the late 1980s, virtually all of the evidence points to a worsening of the problem which is defined as depression, both in Ireland and internationally. As Dermot Walsh, former Inspector of Mental Hospitals, outlined in the *Prime Time* programme:

- Despite the increase in the use of antidepressants in Ireland over the past ten years, a higher number of people are being admitted to psychiatric hospitals. According to the [Irish] Health Research Board, one-third of all psychiatric admissions are now because of depression. This trend of increased hospital admissions due to depression in the period 1989–2004 is consistent with the situation in other developed countries internationally.

- The length of stay of each hospital admission has not declined during this period, as one would expect if antidepressants were as effective as they are often claimed to be.

- The incidence of suicide, which is closely related to depression, has not declined over this time period. Graphs of increased antidepressant prescription and of increase in suicide run almost in parallel.[24]

Given the considerable medical enthusiasm which exists for prescribing antidepressant drugs, I find it quite disconcerting that one rarely hears a doctor outline (either in public or to patients) what I would call the real facts about the effectiveness of these drugs. The reality is that antidepressant drugs reduce symptoms – which does not necessarily result in recovery, or in the person getting their life back on track satisfactorily – in about 50–65 per cent of cases, that placebo reduces symptoms in 35–50 per cent of cases, and that counselling and psychotherapy, in many studies, have been shown to be as effective as antidepressant medication.[25] The jury is still out as to whether the combination of medication and counselling is superior to either intervention used on its own.

From general practice to psychotherapy

As is the case in many Western countries, treatment of mental health problems in Ireland revolves around the prescribing of medication. In the 1990s, as I became increasingly concerned about this, I realised that morally I could not continue to work in this manner. I went back to university and undertook a three-year MA degree in psychotherapy at the University of Limerick, which I completed in 2002. I now feel I have a far more rounded education in mental health than the vast majority of my GP colleagues, and perhaps some of my psychiatrist colleagues.

Since *Beyond Prozac* became widely known across Ireland in 2001, I have heard several thousand stories of people's experiences, which virtually all share a common thread. The person became overwhelmed at some point in their lives. They went to their GP, who made a psychiatric diagnosis, and/or referred the person to a psychiatrist, who made a psychiatric diagnosis. Medication was initiated and continued, often for years, and in the vast majority of cases medication was the sole form of intervention offered. The difficulties which created the problem in the first place received little or no attention. The person feels consigned to a 'no man's land', a twilight existence, and loses hope for the future.

Typically, when people attend me for the first time, they have already seen a psychiatrist and/or a GP, sometimes several of each. Many will be on a variety of different medications. Ironically, over time (provided it is appropriate to do so in the circumstances of the individual), reducing the medication prescribed by other doctors is often an important part of the person's recovery process. This needs to be done with care, patience and medical supervision. I am not anti-medication. Medication has its place within mental healthcare.

I have worked with enough people to realise that the medical approach to mental health problems is seriously deficient. In my work, I set out to establish a safe, therapeutic relationship with the person. In the process, we become a team working together, with the express purpose of aiding the person to get their life back on track. Traditionally, the medical approach views mental health problems as discrete diagnoses, and tends to place little importance on the life of the person. In my opinion, this is a misguided approach to mental health. The life of the person and the mental and emotional distress they experience are intricately interwoven.

A common thread running through the mental health problems experienced by people is loss of selfhood. For various reasons, people can lose their sense of self – self-empowerment, self-confidence, self-esteem, self-assuredness and self-expression. I have found that working with a person towards recovering a lived sense of selfhood is usually a prerequisite to recovery. Yet, selfhood as a key issue is repeatedly overlooked within the medical approach to mental health problems.

Conclusion

Filled with a passionate desire to establish psychiatry as a scientific, respectable branch of medicine, many pioneering psychiatrists over the past 100 years have made a major error of judgement. They first arrived at their conclusions, and subsequently set up their research to establish that their conclusions were correct. Deciding that mental health problems were caused by a physical brain defect (rather than, for example, major emotional distress), they designed their research to establish that this was the case. Thus, the cart (the outcome) was put before the horse (the hypothesis), an approach which is inherently unscientific.

Doctors do not readily engage with people who question the beliefs and practices of the profession. My book *Beyond Prozac* has become widely known in Ireland. As noted earlier, I have been invited to speak at a wide range of meetings since my book was published, but I have yet to be asked to speak at a medical meeting anywhere in Ireland. In the weeks following the conference in Cork from which the seeds of this book emerged, 'Health, Democracy and the Globalised Pharmaceutical Industry: Exploring the Politics of Drug Regulation Internationally and in Ireland', (University College Cork, 16–17 September 2004), two of the above-mentioned Irish medical publications referred to the conference. Neither report mentioned that I had been speaking at the conference. In contrast, two Irish national newspapers, both of which gave substantial coverage to the conference, made several references to my talk and its content. The mainstream press, it appears, is more likely to give coverage to critical commentaries on mental healthcare than the medical press.

I am encouraged to see that an important high-level and official British publication has expressed concern about the influence of the pharmaceutical industry. In April 2005, the House of Commons Health Committee published a report entitled *The Influence of the Pharmaceutical Industry*.[26] As a relatively lone voice within Irish medicine publicly expressing concern regarding the influence of the pharmaceutical industry, it was a strange experience for me to read this report. Coming from such an august source, it felt almost eerie to read so many of my concerns expressed within this document. There is little reason to believe that such an inquiry would not be appropriate in Ireland.

In conclusion, I have many concerns about the lack of true democracy which exists within Irish healthcare. The deep entanglement between the pharmaceutical industry and the medical profession is a major cause for concern. Action must be taken to ensure that, in the interest of the public, excessive links between the medical profession and the pharmaceutical industry do not compromise the quality of healthcare. A comprehensive investigation into the influence of the pharmaceutical industry, similar to that carried out by the House of Commons, would be a good start.

PART THREE

Controversy and Change: Medicines Regulation in Canada, Britain and Australia

CHAPTER 9

New Directions in
Canadian Drug Regulation:

Whose Interests are Being Served?

Joel Lexchin

Introduction

The Canadian healthcare system is characterised by the division of responsibility between the federal and provincial governments. While the federal government provides a substantial amount of the funding for the system, it does not regulate the practice of medicine, with control over hospitals and the services provided by healthcare practitioners resting with provincial governments. The federal government attempts to maintain some national uniformity in the system by attaching a series of conditions to the money it provides to the provinces: public administration of the system, no economic barriers to the receipt of care, people insured in one province must be able to receive services in all other provinces, all medically necessary services must be covered, all residents of Canada must be covered. Should provinces not enforce these conditions, then the federal government can withhold part or all of its cash contribution.

At the level of medications there is also a split between the two levels of government. The federal government is not involved in paying for medications, except for members of the military, people in federal prisons and Native Canadians. Each of the provinces has established its own distinct public payment system for drugs. Prescribing and dispensing medications are considered part of the practice of medicine that puts them under provincial control. On the other hand, the federal government has sole jurisdiction over the drug regulatory system that is the focus of this chapter.

There are two competing visions of what the prime function of a drug regulatory authority should be. One, put forward by the pharmaceutical industry, holds that the main function is to facilitate industry's efforts to develop new products and to approve them as quickly as possible. In this view, medications are commodities and the regulatory authority exists to provide a service to the industry. The second view, espoused by consumer groups and public health activists, sees the primary purpose as appropriately evaluating products to ensure a high standard of effectiveness and safety. Here medications are seen as an essential element of the healthcare system and the regulatory authority exists to provide a service to the public.

These visions are not completely polar opposites. Industry would agree that marketed medications should also be safe and effective, but it also is very clear that marketing authorisation should not be held up by what it sees as undue delays in evaluating the trial data that it submits. To this end, in many countries drug companies fund part or all of the regulatory authority through user fees and in return expect timely approvals for their products. Companies also regard their data as proprietary and expect regulatory authorities to keep it confidential so as not to jeopardise their commercial activities. Consumer groups and health activists, on the other hand, concede that the drug companies are necessary to develop new products, but they are mainly focused on the quality of the products that emerge from the approval process and are more interested in a thorough review than a rapid one. They are also generally in favour of transparency in the regulatory review process. Disease-focused groups sometimes differ from consumer groups on the question of the speed of drug approvals. While they are still concerned with safety, they often want what they see as new therapeutically important medications approved as quickly as possible.

The Therapeutic Products Directorate – changing priorities?

In Canada, government regulation of drug safety, quality and efficacy is almost solely the responsibility of the Therapeutic Products Directorate (TPD), an arm of Health Canada.[1] But the state does not possess the wherewithal to undertake the elaborate clinical and pre-clinical trials required to meet the objective of providing safe and effective medications. Nor is the state willing or able to mobilise the resources that would be necessary to undertake these tasks. Therefore, a tacit political decision is made to relinquish some authority to the drug manufacturers, especially with respect to information that forms the basis on which regulatory decisions are made. In this model, called 'clientele pluralism',[2] the state relinquishes some of its authority to private-sector actors, who, in turn, pursue objectives with which officials are in broad agreement.

Despite the lack of functional authority in some areas implied in the clientele pluralism model, the TPD would still nominally seem to side with consumer groups when it comes to decision-making around drug efficacy and safety. The front page of its bi-monthly bulletin contains the following mission statement: 'We contribute to the health of Canadians and to the effectiveness of the health-care system by assessing the safety, efficacy and quality of pharmaceuticals . . . in a timely manner.'[3]

In the past, financing for the TPD and its predecessors came solely from government appropriations, but, over the past decade, financing for the TPD has shifted and is now being split about equally between government and user fees from pharmaceutical companies.[4] This shift in the financing of the regulatory body has raised concerns, based on principal–agent and capture theories, about whether the TPD's primary commitment is still to public health. Principal–agent theory proposes that there is a relationship between a principal who has a task that needs to be performed and an agent who is contracted to do the task in exchange for compensation. Prior to the introduction of user fees, the principal was the public and the agent was the relevant regulatory authority. However, since 1994 a new principal has been added: the pharmaceutical industry that is now providing a substantial fraction of the money needed to run the drug regulatory system. Regulatory capture theory asserts that, over time, regulators tend to become advocates for the industry they are supposed to regulate as a result of conflict avoidance and influence from the industry. The theory predicts that, over time, regulatory authorities will become less receptive to the needs of the public and will more closely align their mission with that of the pharmaceutical industry.[5]

One example of how principal–agent theory may be operating is the change in the regulation of advertising of over-the-counter products to consumers. Up until March 1997, all promotion through radio or television had to be pre-cleared[6] by Health Canada staff and print advertisements were reviewed by Health Canada if there were complaints about them. Those functions have now been turned over to a private-sector agency, Advertising Standards Canada, a body whose fourteen-member board of directors includes representatives of some of the largest advertising agencies in the country, with only a single person from the Consumers Association of Canada to represent the public interest and no representatives from the health community. At the same time as this transformation was taking place, Dann Michols, the Director General of the Therapeutics Product Programme (TPP), the predecessor to the TPD, circulated an internal bulletin in which he discussed the question of who the TPP's client is. In the context of cost recovery Mr Michols advised staff that 'the client is the direct recipient of your services. In many cases this is the person or company who pays for the service.' The one-page document focused on service to industry relegating the public to the secondary status of 'stakeholder' or 'beneficiary'.[7]

The apparent reorientation of the TPD in favour of business interests is further reflected in its Business Transformation Strategy (BTS) that is being implemented. The BTS was introduced in early 2003 and 'builds on the commitments made by the Government of Canada to "speed up the regulatory process for drug approvals", to move forward with a smart regulations strategy to accelerate reforms in key areas to promote health and sustainability, to contribute to innovation and economic growth, and to reduce the administrative burden on business'.[8]

One of the key phrases in the BTS is 'smart regulation'. Smart regulation means that Canada should 'regulate in a way that enhances the climate for investment and trust in the markets'.[9] While health is not ignored, the emphasis is clearly on creating a business-friendly environment. The federal External Advisory Committee on Smart Regulation explicitly states that risk management has an essential role in building public trust and business confidence in the Canadian market and regulatory system.[10] Once again, the business agenda takes a prominent position.

When applied to drug regulation, risk management would mean weighing potential negative effects against potential advantages. Potential negative effects would be adverse health effects that could occur under reasonably foreseeable conditions.[11] The shift from the precautionary principle to risk management is subtle but unmistakable. The precautionary principle says that if products cannot be shown to be safe then they should not be marketed or, if they are allowed onto the market, it should be under restricted conditions. Risk management, on the other hand, says that things should be assumed to be safe unless there is information to the contrary and, therefore, in general, products should be allowed unfettered access to the market and once there largely left unattended. Risk management usually involves a risk–cost–benefit approach, which, according to the Royal Society of Canada,[12] has a 'built-in bias in favor of technological benefits, which are immediate, highly predictable and quantifiable (otherwise, the technology would have no market), and against the risk factors, which are discounted because they tend to be long term, less certain and less easily quantified'. The Royal Society goes on to point out that the precautionary principle is proactive, in the sense that it assumes that:

> It is better to design and deploy the technologies in ways that prevent or avoid the potential harms, or guarantees the management of these risks within limits of acceptability, than to move ahead with them on the assumption that unanticipated harms can be ameliorated with future revisions or technological 'fixes'.[13]

Wiktorowicz[14] believes that previous changes in regulatory policy, such as the move from doing a detailed review and analysis of clinical trial data to an examination of summary information with selective requests for follow-up data re-analysis in identified areas, has already pushed Canada's regulatory system from one where new drugs were considered potentially harmful until proven safe to one where they are considered safe until proven harmful. Explicitly incorporating risk management as defined by smart regulation would make this slide even more pronounced.

Past statements and practices can offer a guide to an agency's current orientation, but a much more nuanced understanding is gained by examining present actions. In the remaining portion of this chapter I propose to look at four programme areas that are the subject of ongoing implementation inside the TPD: timeliness of drug approvals, drug safety, transparency in the regulatory process and direct-to-consumer advertising of prescription medications. I will begin with a description of each programme and then present representative positions on each of these areas from the viewpoint of industry and the public interest. The objective is to see whether principal–agent theory is operating by analysing whether the TPD's orientation aligns more closely with public or private interests.

Timeliness of drug approvals

The TPD is devoting significant organisational resources towards the goal of speeding up the drug approval process. In the budget speech outlining government spending for the 2003 session of the federal parliament, $190 million[15] was allocated over a five-year period mostly to improving 'the timeliness of Health Canada's regulatory processes with respect to human drugs'.[16] Forty million out of the $190 million was allocated for fiscal 2003/4. Out of that amount, 78 per cent ($31.2 million) went towards 'improved regulatory performance', mainly an effort to eliminate the backlog in drug approvals and to ensure timeliness in getting drugs onto the market.[17]

At a December 2003 meeting of the TPD Advisory Committee on Management, I questioned what the priorities were in directing the money and was offered four rationales: 1) if there was no improvement in the area of timeliness and the backlog then it would be difficult to move ahead in other areas; 2) this is an area where the TPD has the capacity to take action; 3) the emphasis on this particular issue in the Speech from the Throne;[18] 4) timeliness and the backlog are the areas where the TPD has received the most criticism.

Who is criticising the TPD and why is timeliness so important that it reaches the throne speech? Patient groups are naturally concerned if effective treatments are being delayed and Canada does lag behind other countries in the speed at which it approves drugs given priority status.[19] However, fewer than 9 per cent of the new active substances marketed in Canada qualify as either breakthrough products or significant therapeutic improvements.[20] The loudest and most influential voice calling for faster drug approvals comes from the brand-name industry. In a recently released document, Canada's Research-Based Pharmaceutical Companies (Rx&D), the industry organisation representing the brand-name companies[21] in Canada, emphasises the excessive length of time that it takes to get a drug approved.[22]

From the point of view of return on investment, industry's preoccupation with timeliness makes perfect sense, but whether that applies when a public health point of view is adopted is questionable. If most new drugs offer only little or no therapeutic gain over existing treatment options, who benefits from getting these newer drugs onto the market faster? Furthermore, it is these newer products that are driving rising drug costs. The average price of a prescription for a new patented medication went from $54.68 in 1997 to $77.06 in 2001. At the same time, prices for existing medications remained virtually stable, going from $32.18 to $33.68.[23]

Timeliness in the approval process may take on even greater importance in the near future. In spring 2004, the private members' Bill C-212 was passed in the Canadian parliament to deal with the user fees that various arms of government collect from industry for delivering services. Strong private-sector interest in this legislation was expressed through the Business Coalition on Cost Recovery which included the brand-name pharmaceutical companies. The coalition was particularly supportive of aspects of the bill that are meant to ensure that user fees are consistent with the level and value of the services provided.[24] In this regard, Bill C-212 provides for Canadian services to be compared with similar ones offered by Canada's major trading partners. If services are not adequate, government departments stand to forfeit part of the user fees. Setting and measuring timelines for drug approvals are relatively straightforward; but how do you set time standards for how long it should take to act on adverse drug reaction[25] reports? In order to avoid financial penalties, Health Canada may direct even more resources into ensuring that drug approval times are met at the expense of its other responsibilities.

Drug safety

In contrast to the $31.2 million given over to faster approvals, only $2.5 million of the $40 million was allocated for the Marketed Health Products Directorate (MHPD), which is charged with monitoring the safety and performance of drugs already approved. This discrepancy in the allocation of money came at a time when the MHPD was only receiving one-fifth of the annual monetary appropriations compared to the TPD[26] and had to stop routinely trying to assign causality when evaluating adverse drug reaction reports. Information from each adverse drug reaction report that is received is entered into a number of fields in the Canada Adverse Drug Reaction Information System (CADRIS) database. Now, because of increased workload and funding constraints, the number of essential fields in the CADRIS database has been reduced, such that the 'causality' field is no longer being systematically used.[27]

Another indication of possible resource problems in the MHPD is the shift in the origin of adverse drug reaction reports away from its five regional reporting centres. In 1998, 31.4 per cent and 47.2 per cent came from the centres and manufacturers, respectively;[28] by 2005, the percentages were 33.3 per cent and 62.3 per cent.[29] The likely explanation for this change is that the regional centres were unable to process the volume of reports that people were trying to make and therefore reporting shifted to the manufacturers with their greater capacity for receiving reports.

Moreover, the current system of notifying doctors about serious safety concerns appears to be ineffective. As early as July 1996 Health Canada advised doctors about five cases of cardiac arrhythmias[30] associated with the combination of cisapride (a drug marketed for gastrointestinal disorders) and products that inhibit certain liver enzymes.[31] A second report in early 2000 discussed seventy serious adverse drug reaction reports including thirty-five involving heart rate and rhythm disorders.[32] Despite these alerts and the serious nature of the reactions, during the latter half of the 1990s cisapride consistently remained among the top forty most prescribed drugs in Canada.[33] (Cisapride was subsequently withdrawn from the Canadian market for safety reasons in August 2000.)

The move to speed up drug approvals may be further compromising safety standards. Abraham and Davis[34] compared drug withdrawals in the United Kingdom and the United States in the period 1971 to 1992 and reported a ratio of 2.67:1 (24 drugs:9 drugs). Their explanation for the lower number of withdrawals in the United States was that the longer period spent examining the data in the US allowed regulators there to detect serious safety problems before products were marketed.[35]

Further evidence that shorter approval times might adversely affect safety standards comes from a survey of US regulatory officials. User fees paid to the Food and Drug Administration (FDA) by the brand-name pharmaceutical industry were tied to quicker approvals by the FDA, with times dropping for new molecular entities from twenty-seven months in 1993, when user fees were instituted, to nineteen months in 2001.[36] The Washington-based Public Citizen's Health Research Group (HRG) surveyed FDA reviewers in 1998 for their reaction to the changes in the agency. Nineteen out of fifty-three medical officers identified a total of twenty-seven new drugs in the past three years that they thought should not have been approved but were; seventeen said that standards were 'lower' or 'much lower' than they had been three years previously.[37] A subsequent survey by the Office of Inspector General confirmed some of these findings. Although 64 per cent of FDA respondents had confidence in the FDA's decisions regarding the safety of a drug, at the same time 40 per cent who had been at the FDA at least five years indicated that the review process had worsened during their tenure in terms of allowing for in-depth, science-based reviews.[38]

Pharmaceutical companies place a premium on rapid drug approvals in order to start recouping their investment in their products. Their interest in post-marketing surveillance is decidedly secondary. When companies in the US agreed to supplement the FDA budget with user fees, they stipulated that the fees could only be used to hire new reviewers; none of the money went to post-marketing surveillance. Most of the Phase Four (post-marketing) studies[39] that industry committed itself to do have gone uncompleted, according to a report from HRG. From 1990 through 1994 a total of eighty-eight new molecular entities (NMEs) were approved which had at least one post-marketing commitment. Only 13 per cent (eleven of the 88) were classified by the FDA as complete as of December 1999. For the 107 NMEs with Phase Four commitments approved between January 1995 and the end of 1999, not one drug had been classified by the agency as having completed commitments as of 23 December 1999.[40] The HRG conclusions were reinforced by an FDA report. Looking at post-marketing commitments made between 1991 and 2000 the FDA found that only 882 of 2,400 (37 per cent) commitments for pharmaceuticals and forty-four of 301 (15 per cent) for biologics[41] had been completed.[42]

In Canada, one indication of the interest in drug safety comes from an analysis of the website for Rx&D. A search of the site in late 2003 found only a single page dealing with drug safety as opposed to 207 pages concerned with drug approvals. The item in question was a news release playing down the significance of a story that had been aired on a television show.

In contrast to the pharmaceutical industry, independent bodies have argued for more emphasis on safety issues. The *Canadian Medical Association Journal* was so disturbed by Health Canada's delay in issuing a warning to doctors about fatal side effects associated with the use of cisapride that it decided to monitor warnings issued by the FDA and publish them in the event that Health Canada did not issue similar cautionary statements in a timely manner.[43] The *Canadian Medical Association Journal* also editorially called for the creation of a new agency, independent of Health Canada, that would proactively investigate suspected safety problems rather than waiting for voluntary reports from doctors, pharmacists and others to arrive.[44] Consumer groups such as Women and Health Protection[45] have recommended that Health Canada develop a comprehensive strategy for post-market safety of women's experiences with prescription drugs. Such a strategy should be developed in consultation with the women's health community and include the principle of the right to be warned and informed.[46] After conducting hearings across Canada, the all-party Health Committee of Parliament issued a report calling on Health Canada to 'increase resources for post-market surveillance so that the infrastructure has the capacity to receive, analyse and respond to consumer and health professional reports and complaints about adverse drug reactions'.[47]

Transparency in the regulatory process

Drug regulation in Canada is shrouded in secrecy. Even the names of drugs in the approval process are not disclosed and all of the information that industry submits, including clinical trial data on safety and efficacy, is deemed confidential and can only be released with the permission of the company, even with an Access to Information request. The importance of the fact that confidentiality, which is of prime importance to the pharmaceutical industry, is privileged over openness, an elemental value in any democratic society, is something that cannot be emphasised too strongly.

There are clearly good reasons why manufacturing information should be protected by the TPD. This is proprietary knowledge and if it became public it could adversely affect the financial status of a company by providing competitors with an unfair advantage. Personal data that enters the files of regulatory agencies like the TPD can include the identity of individual patients or health professionals as well as information on the illness from which the patient is suffering. Information that might lead to the identification of individual patients or health professionals should also not be disclosed to any party.[48]

These arguments do not apply when it comes to health and safety data. There is no good evidence to show that the interests of companies would be harmed by the disclosure of this type of information; specifically, confidentiality is not necessary to foster research and innovation.[49] Research builds upon the work of others; hindering the transfer of knowledge may actually lead companies to repeat mistakes, causing research to take longer and be more costly. On the other hand, non-disclosure has serious disadvantages for the TPD, health professionals and the public. If information submitted to regulatory agencies is never disclosed, then this data will never enter the normal peer review channels and is therefore not subject to scrutiny by independent scientists. Without this type of feedback, TPD reviewers may be more prone to misjudge the accuracy or usefulness of the data submitted; the scientific atmosphere in the agency may be stifled and the professional growth of its staff severely inhibited. Deprived of any independent access to information, health professionals have to accept the TPD's judgement about the safety and effectiveness of products. In the case of well-established drugs this is probably not much of a concern, but it may be different with new drugs where experience is limited.[50]

The level of secrecy in the TPD has been criticised a number of times, and in response in early 2004 the TPD announced a new initiative, the Summary Basis of Decision (SBD). When a new drug or medical device is approved, the SBD would outline the scientific and benefit/risk-based reasons for the TPD's decision to grant market authorisation for a product. The key part of the SBD of importance to prescribers and consumers is the clinical information on drug effectiveness and safety. Is enough information provided to allow for safe and rational use of new medications or the extended indications for previously approved drugs? Between 2001 and 2003 there have been a number of cases where an examination of the data submitted to drug regulators has allowed the identification of information that was either unavailable or misrepresented within the published literature.

These same discoveries would not have been possible using the new SBDs because they lack crucial information:[51] the study protocol is unavailable; there is no information about baseline characteristics of trial participants, the number of participants who withdrew and reasons for withdrawal; there is no data about primary and secondary[52] efficacy outcomes or fatal and non-fatal serious adverse events by the treatment arm.[53]

A model for the minimum level of reporting already exists in FDA approval packages. Once a drug has been approved in the United States, the FDA posts on its website a detailed summary of the information that the company has submitted, including the clinical trial data, along with commentaries from FDA reviewers. Instead of adapting this model to the Canadian situation, Health Canada proposed a 'reading room where people could review all the data submitted by the manufacturer but not transcribe or copy it, or otherwise make that data available to interested members of the public.'[54]

The pharmaceutical industry has consistently argued that safety and efficacy data are proprietary information that must be kept confidential to protect the commercial interests of the companies. This line of reasoning is reflected in a 2004 article authored by a vice-president of Merck, one of the largest pharmaceutical companies in the world. Writing in the *Canadian Medical Association Journal* he stated that 'Merck (like other companies) is obliged to protect proprietary information and intellectual property, including aspects of the design of clinical trials of investigational agents and the very existence of certain studies'.[55]

In contrast to the industry position, a 2000 report by the ad hoc Committee on the Drug Review Process[56] of Health Canada's own Science Advisory Board stated: 'in our view and that of many stakeholders, the current drug review process is unnecessarily opaque. Health Canada persists in maintaining a level of confidentiality that is inconsistent with public expectation and contributes to a public cynicism about the integrity of the process.'[57] To remedy this situation the Committee recommended 'that [Health Canada] should set new standards of access to information at all stages of the drug review process, enhancing transparency and public confidence'.[58] Likewise, the report of the Parliamentary Health Committee supported the development of mechanisms to enable greater public disclosure of information about clinical trials.[59]

Direct-to-consumer advertising (DTCA) of prescription drugs

The Canadian government has historically been reluctant to use the legislative powers granted to it under the Food and Drugs Act[60] to regulate pharmaceutical promotion.[61] Partly, this hesitancy is a reflection of the clientele pluralist model of regulation, but, as Lexchin and Kawachi[62] note, there are two major theoretical drawbacks to government regulation – one financial, the other practical. Increasingly, fiscal pressures in almost all countries have prevented government agencies from effectively policing pharmaceutical promotion. Government regulatory agencies rarely have the resources to make it economically rational for individual firms *not* to cheat. The other major drawback to government regulation is a lack of necessary expertise compared to industry. Voluntary self-regulation therefore seems an attractive option because, lacking government–industry contention, it is a more flexible and cost-effective option. Government regulators also reason that, in a highly competitive industry, the desire of individual companies to prevent competitors from gaining an edge can be harnessed to serve the public interest through a regime of voluntary self-regulation run by a trade association. However, although misleading advertising may to some degree inhibit competition, it is also far more often good for business.

Regulations issued under the Food and Drugs Act only allow companies to advertise prescription drugs to the extent that the name, quantity and price of the product can be displayed.[63] Policy statements in 1996 and 2000 reinterpreted this regulation to mean that companies were allowed to run 'disease awareness' advertisements as long as the name of a product was not mentioned or firms could name a medication as long as its use was not discussed. The only type of advertising that remained prohibited was one where both a product was named and its use was given.[64]

Continuing with its policy of indirect regulation, Health Canada has been reluctant to enforce even this loose reinterpretation of its own rules. A commentary in the *Canadian Medical Association Journal* notes that: 'Response to complaints tends to be slow, probably reflecting Health Canada's under capacity to regulate DTCA, and, arguably, ineffectual.'[65] The authors go on to describe how a television advertisement promoting bupropion (Zyban) for smoking cessation was allowed to run for months even though Health Canada deemed that it violated the regulations. No penalty of any type was imposed on GlaxoSmithKline, the company responsible for the advertisement.[66]

Advertisements for Diane-35, an oral contraceptive marketed by Berlex and approved in Canada only for use as a second-line agent[67] for resistant acne, were plastered on bus shelters in Montreal and other cities across Canada with the message 'the acne solution for women only'. Although the ad did not directly name the drug, the woman featured in the ad was given the name 'Diane'. Women and Health Protection sent a letter to Health Canada complaining about this and other ads in March 2001, following Berlex's launch of a new national billboard, television and cinema ad campaign for Diane-35. An Access to Information request revealed that eighteen months after this letter was sent there had not been any communication between Health Canada and the company. Meanwhile, the Diane-35 ad campaign continued. Print ads continued to run in *Healthy Woman*, a Canadian magazine produced to be read by patients in family physicians' and gynaecologists' waiting rooms.[68]

The experience with DTCA in the US shows that rules governing this practice are frequently and repeatedly broken;[69] magazine ads rarely have any information such as the nature of illness-related precursors, illness prevalence or common misconceptions about the condition or its treatments. Furthermore, alternative treatments were discussed in less than 30 per cent of advertisements and less than 10 per cent of advertisements stated the treatment's success rate.[70]

In a paper published in February 2002, Mintzes and colleagues[71] used a cross-sectional survey[72] to examine the relationship between patients' requests for medications and physicians' prescribing decisions. In order to assess physicians' confidence in their prescribing decisions, they asked doctors 'If you were treating another similar patient with the same condition, would you prescribe this drug?' An answer of 'very likely' indicated confidence in choice and 'possibly' or 'unlikely' indicated some degree of ambivalence. Physicians were ambivalent about the choice of treatment in about half the cases when patients had requested advertised drugs compared with 12 per cent for drugs not requested by patients. The authors concluded that, if physicians prescribe requested drugs despite personal reservations, sales may increase but appropriateness of prescribing may suffer.

DTCA has also been associated with significant increases in drug spending. The 50 most heavily advertised drugs were responsible for $US9.94 billion of the $US20.8 billion increase in US retail prescription drug spending from 1999 to 2000, or nearly half of the total.[73] Not only is DTCA encouraging the use of more expensive medications, but it also promotes the use of potentially unsafe drugs. Of the 548 new drugs introduced into the United States between 1975 and 1999, 2.9 per cent were withdrawn for safety reasons and 8.2 per cent acquired one or more black box warnings. The latter is the strongest type of warning required by the FDA, used to alert physicians to serious and/or life-threatening drug risks. Over half of withdrawals for safety reasons occurred within the first two years post-market launch, and over half of black box warnings within seven years.[74] Although only a small minority of drugs is withdrawn for safety reasons, considerable numbers of people may be exposed, particularly if drug use is heavily promoted soon after launch, before risks are fully known. Nearly 20 million Americans took one or more of the five drugs withdrawn from the market between September 1997 and September 1998.[75]

At the same time that this evidence about the consequences of DTCA has been accumulating, Health Canada has been engaged in a project to re-examine and revise Canadian health safety legislation. As part of its review, the agency has issued a document outlining policy options for new legislation. The document lays out four options for direct-to-consumer advertising of prescription drugs; two of the four, including the one that is given the most prominence in terms of space, are favourable to DTCA,[76] while none of the four actually advocates enforcing the current legislation as it was written (i.e. advertising only name, price and quantity). It is of particular note that Health Canada's reinterpretation of the legislation was a unilateral action taken without any debate in parliament, public consultation or discussion paper being issued. The fact that in a wide-ranging review of pharmaceutical legislation Health Canada did not feel it necessary to even mention that it had effectively changed the meaning of the regulations governing DTCA speaks volumes about the priority that the organisation places on openness and public dialogue.

The main groups in favour of DTCA in Canada are the ones that stand to gain the most from it. Rx&D, representing the brand-name companies, has a position paper claiming that 'advertising can raise awareness of effective new therapies and improve the overall health of the nation by helping Canadians recognise early symptoms and informing them about potential treatment options' and that 'advertising medication would ultimately, and most importantly, give the Canadian consumer a choice. Canadians would be empowered to take charge of their health like never before.'[77] Media organisations that would be the recipients of new advertising revenue have called on the federal government to lift the ban on DTCA so that Canadians 'can participate in decisions that affect their health'.[78] The coordinator for Advocare, a body that bills itself as a network of consumer-based health organisations and receives funding from the pharmaceutical industry, wrote in the *Globe and Mail*, a national newspaper, that 'direct-to-consumer advertising can contribute significantly to health education and promotion'.[79]

Groups that either refuse money from the pharmaceutical industry or that maintain an independent policy despite receiving industry funding have condemned DTCA as antithetical to the public interest.[80] The *Canadian Medical Association Journal* has come out editorially against DTCA, calling instead for the money to be spent 'in providing unbiased "consumer" information about drugs and alternative non-drug therapies and prevention'.[81] In doing so it echoed the positions of the Canadian Medical Association, the Canadian Pharmacists' Association and the Consumers' Association of Canada, all of which are strongly opposed to the practice.[82]

Drug regulation in an international context

If the bias by regulators in favour of industry was just confined to drug regulation in Canada, that would be cause enough for concern, but a brief examination of the situation in other countries reveals that regulatory agencies there are mirroring what is happening in Canada. In Australia prior to the late 1980s, the position of the Therapeutic Goods Administration (TGA)[83] was to protect consumer welfare without primary concern for the profits of multinational drug manufacturers. However, this position started to be undermined with the establishment of a subsidy system operated by the Department of Industry aimed at encouraging investment in manufacturing, research and development, and exports. Cost recovery was introduced with the goal that 50 per cent of the funding of the TGA should come from industry by 1996/7 and full cost recovery began in 1998. Further alignment of the TGA with industry came with the introduction of cost recovery in the mid-1990s and a report from the Industry Commission. According to Lofgren and de Boer: 'Its terms of reference signaled the reduction of processing times, that business should be relieved of unduly complicated regulatory requirements, and that more extensive use should be made of evaluation reports and decisions from overseas agencies.'[84]

Drug safety is treated the same in the US and the United Kingdom (UK) as it is in Canada. In 1999, the FDA had 1,408 employees to review new drug applications, and seventy-two handling the post-marketing surveillance of nearly 50,000 medications.[85] The UK Medicines and Healthcare products Regulatory Agency puts its main efforts into analysing pre-marketing data and gives too little attention to post-marketing surveillance to evaluate the effects of medicines in the normal clinical setting.[86]

The European Medicines Agency (EMEA) produces European Public Assessment Reports (EPARs) after a drug has been approved. These are supposed to reflect the assessment file submitted by the manufacturer, its analysis by the EMEA's scientific advisory body and the reasons underlying that body's opinion.[87] An analysis of nine EPARs issued between September 1996 and August 1997 found a striking lack of standard presentation of information in these documents. The reporting of clinical trials was not always clear and none of the nine EPARs mentioned references to published trials.[88] A subsequent analysis that covered all EPARs published in 1999 and 2000 revealed that the EPARs were not harmonised, reliable, or correctly updated.[89]

Changes made by the FDA regarding broadcast DTCA in 1997 saw the amount spent in this area of promotion rise from $US1.07 billion in 1997 to $US3.24 billion in 2003.[90] However, as of June 2002, the FDA had only five staff dedicated to reviewing DTCA material which included 248 television ads and an unknown, but certainly large, number of print ads.[91] New Zealand is the only other 'developed' country that allows DTCA of prescription drugs. Industry practices are regulated by a Code of Therapeutic Advertising that is administered by the Advertising Standards Complaints Board (ASCB), a body appointed by the Advertising Standards Authority (ASA), an advertising industry body. Coney[92] gave an example of what happened when her organisation, Women's Health Action Trust (WHAT), complained about a DTC advertisement. Although this complaint was ultimately upheld, it took from June 1999, when it was initially lodged, until December 1999 for WHAT to be told that the complaint was successful. During this period WHAT was required to respond to several requests by the ASCB for more information, sign a waiver that it gave up any right 'to take or continue any proceedings against the advertiser, publisher or broadcaster concerned', and adhere to a requirement not to make the result public before the ASA did. In addition, Coney points out that the ASCB's decisions are not binding or enforceable.

Conclusion

Drug regulation is not an exact science. There are many areas of uncertainty that call for judgements to be made about effectiveness and safety when deciding whether to approve a new drug or remove an old one from the market. As in any policy area there are only limited available resources, be they monetary allocations or personnel, while the array of tasks in drug regulation is almost endless. How these limited resources are distributed can be seen as a reflection of the priorities of the regulatory agency. Regulatory agencies are privileged with a wide range of data about the products that they supervise – releasing that information might have negative economic consequences for regulated industries, but a positive one for public health. Having laws and regulations in place is necessary in a regulatory environment, but not sufficient if the authority chooses not to enforce them. When there are choices to be made, they reflect a set of underlying values – values that can be analysed. In the Canadian context, when the values of the TPD are examined with respect to timeliness of drug approvals, safety, transparency and direct-to-consumer advertising, in each case those values are more closely aligned with the interests of private industry than they are with those of public health.

Private values are antithetical to democracy; they speak to the need to make a profit, not to protect public health. While the two can at times be synonymous, that happens mostly by coincidence rather than by design. Within the private sector, competition and the profit motive may be the best way to get newer and better computers or washing detergent. However, medications are not ordinary consumer products and government is intimately and necessarily involved with almost all aspects of medications because of their importance in healthcare. When government adopts the values of private industry in drug regulation, it is in essence telling its people that the needs and values of the private sector take precedence over their health. Democracy is not just the right to vote in an election, it means the ongoing and active participation of the citizenry in determining the policies of the government with an expectation that government will acknowledge the views being put forward and incorporate them into its actions. Within the Canadian drug regulatory system, democratic values such as openness, safety and objective information are being championed by organisations reflective of a wide range of the Canadian public. This chapter has shown that the Canadian government has largely decided to ignore those democratic values, opting instead for a drug regulatory system that reflects the interests of private industry.

CHAPTER 10

Turbulence in UK Medicines Regulation:
A Stink about SSRI[1] Antidepressants that Isn't Going Away[2]

Andrew Herxheimer

Introduction

In the UK, comprehensive medicines regulation began officially in 1971 when the 1967 Medicines Act came into force. Initially it was operated by the Medicines Division of the Department of Health, but in 1989 the work was hived off to a new separate Executive Agency of the Department, the Medicines Control Agency (MCA). Instead of being funded from the departmental budget, the MCA operated a Trading Fund and became largely self-funding from the fees that companies have to pay for product licences and other services. The agency was so successful in streamlining its work that in the 1990s it was able to reduce the level of fees substantially. In 2003, the MCA was merged with the previously separate body regulating medical devices to form the Medicines and Healthcare products Regulatory Agency (MHRA).

The very labour-intensive work of examining applications from companies seeking approval for new products is done in the Licensing Division, and accounts for the bulk of the MHRA's work and is its main source of income. All the Member States of the EU share this work. Under the mutual recognition procedure, one national agency takes the lead for evaluating a particular product. Companies anxious to have their licence applications processed quickly and efficiently to minimise the erosion of patent life 'shop around' among the major European regulatory agencies for the one with the best performance. The MHRA thus effectively competes with the others.

The MHRA is responsible also for the safety of medicines after they have been marketed. This is the task of the Post-licensing Division; it accounts for 20 per cent to 30 per cent of the total MHRA budget and largely supports the 'Yellow Card' adverse drug reaction (ADR) reporting scheme. The greater emphasis in regulation on scrutiny of new drug applications, rather than post-marketing surveillance, suggests that industry does not regard the monitoring and analysis of safety issues as an especially important use of its fees.

For most of its life the MHRA and its predecessors have had a rather low public profile. This is partly due to the technical and legal complexities of its work, which interests relatively few outsiders, but a major reason has also been a culture of secrecy. This civil service tradition was much strengthened by the notorious clause 118 of the Medicines Act, which, until 2005, made the disclosure of *any* information obtained by, or furnished to, a person in pursuance of this Act a punishable offence. This clause applied both to officials and to the members of advisory committees. As a result, even interested people in the outside world knew too little to be able to ask useful questions that could legally be answered. Clause 118 of the Medicines Act was repealed with the introduction of the Freedom of Information Act, at the start of 2005, but this new act also restricts much disclosure of commercially sensitive information and is not expected to make any great difference. Secrecy remains a major obstacle to effective accountability and participation, pretty much throughout the EU.

Medawar and Hardon[3] have helpfully outlined how drug regulation developed in the UK, and also describe examples of industry influence on regulation.[4] They have focused on difficulties with SSRI antidepressants, particularly fluoxetine (Prozac, made by Lilly) and paroxetine (Seroxat, made by GSK [GlaxoSmithKline]), because these brought to light serious inadequacies in the British drug regulation system, and also prompted a reshaping of the system.

The SSRI problems began to emerge in the early 1990s, and Healy[5] has also described their history and evolution. The introduction of SSRIs in the UK led to a threefold increase in antidepressant prescriptions between 1990 and 2000, and soon after their introduction two major problems began to surface. First, fluoxetine (brand name Prozac) was suspected of causing suicidal and violent behaviour which was unrelated to the suicidal thoughts that are a recognised feature of severe depressive illness. Then evidence accumulated that treatment with paroxetine (brand name Seroxat in UK, Paxil in USA) could lead to dependence on the drug: some people found it impossible to stop taking the drug because of severe withdrawal symptoms. The incidence of suicidal behaviour is much lower than that of withdrawal problems. It is now clear that both problems occur to some extent with all the SSRIs and similar drugs; the details differ for individual drugs.

The regulators: emerging from the shadows into the limelight

The MCA and its main official advisory committee until 2005, the Committee on Safety of Medicines (CSM), investigated these problems repeatedly. It first formally reviewed suicidality in 1990/1, and withdrawal reactions in 1993, 1996 and 1998. Each time they found nothing that seemed to require much action. This is not surprising, since they relied mainly on the Yellow Card reports[6] in their database, and on responses from the manufacturers of the drugs concerned; they refused to consider reports from patients. Price et al.[7] summarised the regulators' 1996 review of withdrawal reactions: they did not try to distinguish symptoms of withdrawal from those due to relapse of depression, and wrongly assumed that withdrawal symptoms were rare, mainly because of the low frequency of reporting per thousand prescriptions. This MCA/CSM study also wrongly characterised withdrawal symptoms as 'relatively mild'.

The first BBC *Panorama* programme on these issues, *Secrets of Seroxat*, broadcast on 19 October 2002, precipitated a flood of complaints and led to questions in parliament. The *Panorama* team was astonished to receive 1,374 emails in response to the broadcast. Charles Medawar and I analysed these.[8] While we were doing this, the MCA/CSM set up a further 'Intensive Review' of both problems, but this was abandoned in April 2003 after it emerged that one key member of the review team had undeclared interests in companies that made an SSRI, and that two other team members (both CSM members) held shares in GSK, the manufacturer of Seroxat.[9] In May 2003 the MHRA replaced it with another inquiry, an independent review by an Expert Working Group (EWG) of the CSM, none of whose members had links with any of the pharmaceutical companies. The EWG included two consumer representatives, which was unprecedented (only one of them was able to play a significant part). Their work on the EWG was warmly acknowledged, but one of these two members left soon after it began. The other, Richard Brook, the chief executive of Mind,[10] resigned in protest halfway through. (He was protesting against the EWG's refusal to publish an interim warning about clear problems it had already identified.) A third lay member was appointed eight months later, by which time, however, the report was almost complete.

While the EWG was doing its work, Charles Medawar and I had been able to analyse the Yellow Card (YC) reports concerning paroxetine that the CSM/MCA had received between 1990 and 2002, and to compare them with the emails received by *Panorama*. We found a remarkable correspondence between the phenomena reported by doctors and users of paroxetine. The descriptions from patients were, however, more detailed and direct; those from doctors were brief and technical, using medical terms.[11] The YC reports contained important information that the MCA's analysis had not picked up about the nature of prominent withdrawal effects, their relationship to dosage and dose changes, and their timing during and after use of paroxetine. We suggested that the YC scheme was 'in important respects chaotic and misconceived'. The agency apparently felt too aggrieved to contact us or the editor of the journal, and instead on its website brushed off our 'concerns about the miscoding of reactions reported through the Yellow Card Scheme and about proper follow up of reports. The criticisms of the coding and follow up of reports are unfounded. MHRA has robust procedures in place to ensure that reports of adverse reactions are accurately coded and where necessary, further information is obtained from the reporter.' However, after some months this statement disappeared from the website and a grudging apology was finally received. Originally the EWG was expected to report back in three months, but it transpired that it needed much longer, and its final report appeared in early December 2004.[12]

Meanwhile, GSK had applied for a licence to market Seroxat for use in children, and soon after the appointment of the EWG they submitted supporting evidence to the MHRA. The MHRA suspected a problem, asked for further data, and in June 2003 suddenly and unexpectedly issued a warning against the use of the drug in children. Three months later a similar warning was issued about a closely related drug, venlafaxine (brand name Efexor)[13], and in December 2003 the warning was extended to all SSRIs except Prozac. The reason was not only a significantly increased risk of drug-induced suicidal behaviour, but lack of evidence of effectiveness in children.

For many months this diverted the EWG from its original task of examining withdrawal problems and possible suicidality in adults. Its final report found a significant lack of important data, a clear and substantial risk of sometimes severe withdrawal reactions, and no clear evidence of a greater risk of SSRI-induced suicidal behaviour compared with tricyclic antidepressants (which had preceded the SSRIs). The EWG softened the earlier warnings about using SSRIs in children, and also concluded that the 'benefit:risk profile' of SSRIs was positive in adults – in spite of acknowledging (publicly for the first time) that 'The effectiveness of SSRIs in mild depression has not been clearly demonstrated in RCTs' (randomized clinical trials). Without clinical trials in mild depression it is not possible to assess the balance between benefit and harm for these drugs in this indication. Prescriptions for 'mild depression' account for two-thirds of all SSRI prescriptions for depression.[14]

In June 2004 the House of Commons Health Committee set up an inquiry into the influence of the pharmaceutical industry on health policies, health outcomes and future health priorities and needs. Two major reasons for this were concern about the increasing medicalisation of life – the notion that 'there is a pill for every ill' – and the inevitable harms resulting from the overuse of medicines. The timing of the investigation coincided with the MHRA's investigation into the safety of the SSRIs, and the committee referred to this case to illustrate some of its concerns.

Effective warnings had been lacking regarding the frequency of withdrawal symptoms experienced with Seroxat. Both the manufacturers and the regulators claimed they had always acted promptly and appropriately in this respect. However, working papers seen by the EWG state that the original licence application (submitted in the early 1990s) recorded Seroxat withdrawal reactions in 30 per cent of patients. The regulators denied this. It also emerged in the inquiry that the MHRA/CSM had failed from the outset to warn of the lack of evidence of SSRI effectiveness in mild depression, suggesting that, as noted above, most users might expect minimal benefit while exposed to significant risks.

The EWG identified a lack of basic data, and several other shortcomings:

- The data on Prozac suicide-related events provided by Lilly excluded many controlled trials performed outside the US. The EWG noted that Lilly had proposed to retrieve these data, but this could not have been done in time for its report, which would have 'to be updated when data are available'.
- The Dutch company Organon 'excluded many seemingly relevant studies' from the data on suicidality with Zispin (mirtazapine). The EWG had requested Organon to provide these data and awaited a response.

- Three companies (Lilly, Solvay and Wyeth) could produce no clinical trials specifically designed to establish the prevalence and severity of withdrawal reactions related to their drugs.
- The MHRA very much relied on company analyses and summaries of data rather than raw data. (The EWG did not state how far its findings were based on re-examination of data held by regulators for years. This appears to have been the case to a significant extent.)

The EWG working papers suggested that companies may not comply with requests for relevant information, and that the MHRA often cannot require them to. For example, GSK, the Marketing Authorisation Holder, argued first that it had fully investigated Seroxat withdrawal problems, then later resisted the regulator's proposal to warn that Seroxat appeared particularly troublesome, on the grounds that no clinical trials had been done to establish this. All the available evidence pointed to a singular risk with Seroxat, but the warnings eventually proposed by the MHRA/CSM did not mention it.[15]

The MHRA is still investigating the withholding of information by the makers of Seroxat as a possible criminal offence. At the time of writing, the investigation has been in progress for 3.5 years, with no end in sight. Medawar[16] speculated that it might never happen:

> The reality is that any prosecution of the Company would put the Agency itself – and Chairman Breckenridge in particular too squarely in the frame. What was it he told *Panorama* for the second of their four splendid programmes? (11 May 2003) – *"What you can say with great firmness is that these drugs do not increase the risk of suicidal thought and they do not increase the risk of suicide."* If that's the Agency's best assessment after more than a decade of drug investigation, personally spearheaded by the blunt tool, Breckenridge, why should the law expect GSK to do any better?' The priority and urgency of this investigation is of course secret.

The EWG report has not been widely reviewed. However, an analysis by Charles Medawar, posted on the Social Audit[17] website in 2005, led to the following main conclusions:

> It seems clear from the launch and the volume of spin that the report of the Expert Working Group (EWG) on the Safety of SSRI Antidepressants was never intended for peer review, nor is it fit for it:
> - its scope is impossibly limited
> - it is remarkably incomplete

- the authorship is uncertain
- key source data are unavailable
- bias is unacknowledged
- perspectives are skewed
- and it is tortuous to read

The legacy of the EWG report will probably have little to do with the safety of SSRI antidepressant users. Moreover, the EWG's failure to analyse raw data, and its reliance on companies for this, proved fatal. Later, the US FDA required GSK to commission a completely independent reanalysis of the data; this demonstrated a significant risk of drug-induced suicidal behaviour for adults too.[18]

Its findings and recommendations – other than those relating to the need for research – still lag well behind common sense. The real significance of this report is to do with the rich evidence it gives of the inadequacy of present systems of drug control.

It will take time to unpick and mine all the data in this report, and who knows how long it will take for all the implications to sink in. One day, it will surely be obvious that the present system of drug regulation fails, both as a health endeavour and as a democratic enterprise. In the meantime, this report explains both why the dissolution of the system is nowhere nigh and long overdue.[19]

Meanwhile, the official information for prescribers and patients from the regulators and the companies on how to use SSRIs appropriately and safely continues to be unclear and inadequate. This is in spite of the fact that the MHRA is (widely and reasonably) regarded as one of the best regulatory systems in the world – which also implies that in some countries the situation would be even worse.

Wider implications of the SSRI experience[20]

The antidepressant controversy still continues, but it has already profoundly affected the shape of medicines regulation as well as the reputation of the industry. The lasting impact of the story relates to greater recognition of:

- the limitations of clinical trials in predicting the benefits and harms of medicines in routine medical practice
- extensive 'ghostwriting' of research papers by company personnel, published in the name of purportedly independent senior academics and clinicians
- the prevalence and significance of bias resulting from non-publication of negative trial results

- the essential importance of feedback from users about drug effects, and the importance of the Internet in facilitating this;
- the significance of intensive drug promotion and PR management in shaping perceptions of drug benefit and risk[21]
- the pervasiveness of conflicts of interest of all kinds, and their significance as factors that affect the quality of drug prescribing; and
- the need for greater transparency of data and clarity in regulatory warnings and other communications.

Recent and future changes in medicines regulation

Policy changes related to the reporting of adverse reactions were initiated while the EWG was doing its work. The first was an independent review of the Yellow Card scheme, the first since it started in 1964.[22] In its terms of reference it was in effect charged with answering one question: 'Who should *not* have access to the data?' The inquiry by Jeremy Metters, a former deputy Chief Medical Officer at the Department of Health, seemed to have been triggered by alarm at the request from Charles Medawar and myself for access to the anonymised Yellow Card data for all the SSRIs. We had a detailed discussion with Dr Metters and his colleagues; the official minutes are on the Social Audit website. The report recommended requiring approval of any request by separate scientific and ethical committees. It was completed in 2003 and the recommendation was implemented in April 2006.[23]

The second policy change was the decision to accept reports direct from users of medicines. A new website, www.yellowcards.gov.uk, was set up for the purpose, a CSM Working Group considered how to organise Patient Reporting of Adverse Drug Reactions, and pilot schemes have been started. In April 2006, the NHS Research and Development Methodology Programme and the MHRA jointly invited proposals for an evaluation of the patient reporting component of the Yellow Card system, to run for two years from September 2007.

Other steps were not directly related to the reporting of adverse effects. One was the creation of a CSM Working Group on Patient Information, to 'consider how the quality of the information provided with medicines could be improved'. It began work in November 2003 and reported in 2005.[24] It makes many good recommendations; an appendix summarises an interesting focus group discussion of a new Seroxat patient information leaflet. Another new move, on 31 January 2005, was the appointment to the MHRA of a communications director, a post that had not existed before and that was glaringly needed.

The most recent and most important event was the announcement of plans to restructure the MHRA.[25] This immediately followed publication on 5 April 2005 of the House of Commons Health Committee's report on the influence of the pharmaceutical industry,[26] which found the agency complacent and lacking the competence to act as a licensing authority. Among many recommendations, this all-party committee proposed an independent review of the agency, and also the transfer of 'sponsorship' of the pharmaceutical industry from the Department of Health to the Department of Trade and Industry. On 7 April 2005, the government introduced a proposal to abolish the agency's two key advisory bodies – the Medicines Commission and the Committee on the Safety of Medicines – both established in 1971. The following week national advertisements invited senior professionals and representatives of patients and consumers to fill posts in the new system. The MHRA also promised the Health Select Committee to make public the basis for each decision to award a licence. This may affect the advisory system.

The Medicines Commission (which never really served its purpose) and the Committee on the Safety of Medicines have been replaced by the Commission on Human Medicines (CHM). This new committee deals only with drugs for use in humans and has four functions. It advises ministers on licensing policy in general and on the licensing of individual drugs in particular; has overall responsibility for drug safety issues; advises on the appointment of members of the other professional bodies serving the MHRA; and hears initial appeals from drug companies against rejection of a licence application. The CHM has nineteen members, including a chair, who is a clinician or from a profession allied to medicine, and two lay members. The remaining members are senior professionals in fields such as general medicine, paediatrics, clinical pharmacology, analytical chemistry, biological science and herbal medicine. All members and their close families are barred from having any personal interests such as shares in the pharmaceutical industry or earnings from it.

The new commission is advised by three standing committees and around fifteen expert advisory groups, each of which includes at least two lay members. The standing committees deal with biologicals and vaccines, pharmacovigilance, and pharmacy and standards. The expert advisory groups are constituted for each application, will probably have a dozen or so members, including four or five specialists, and will call on advisers from other expert advisory groups or from outside as required. Some members, such as statisticians, lay representatives and industry experts, are drawn from pools held by the MHRA. These expert advisory groups scrutinise the licence application and ultimately recommend to the CHM whether it should be accepted. Chairs of the standing committees and expert advisory groups are also not permitted to have personal interests in the pharmaceutical industry. Others who have interests must declare them and may sometimes be debarred from taking part in a discussion.

The government responded to the Health Committee's report in September 2005.[27] It supported some recommendations, said it was already doing much to deal with problems highlighted by the committee, but opposed the two key recommendations – the call for an independent review of the MHRA and the recommendation that government sponsorship of the industry should move from the Department of Health to the Department of Industry, to avoid some conflicts of interest. The House of Commons debated the government's response on 8 December 2005.[28] The Health Committee changed substantially after the general election of May 2005 and is unlikely to return to the subject. Its new chairman has, since 1997, been Chair of the All Party Group on the Pharmaceutical Industry.

Meanwhile responsibilities for medicines regulation are steadily moving to the EU, and the EMEA, European Commission and European Parliament are having to grapple with many of the same issues and the same actors. Inadequate transparency and conflicts of private and public interests will remain major problems.

In May 2006, the SSRI story took another lurch forward: under pressure from the US FDA, GSK admitted that the suicide rate in clinical trials of Seroxat in major depressive disorder was six times higher on the drug than in the comparison groups taking placebo.[29] This happened because the FDA had insisted on an independent analysis of the original trial data. Previously, regulatory agencies, including the MHRA in its many lengthy investigations, had all started from the companies' own summaries and data analyses without checking the methods of analysis or the primary data. It transpired that the regulators had accepted the company's analysis, which had been based on an inappropriate statistical method and had not made use of the 'serious adverse event narratives' or the comments noted on the case report forms from the trials. GSK has kept the initiative by producing its briefing document: it skilfully presents the data and conclusion in ways that try to minimise damage to the product, notably by suggesting – as previously trailed – that the problem of drug-induced suicidality affects mainly young adults (as well as children). This is not so. On past form, some regulators are quite likely to accept the company's data and conclusion, which stresses as always that the drug is a valuable treatment. No regulatory body has yet acted on the lack of evidence of SSRI effectiveness in treating 'mild' depression, yet such cases account for two-thirds of all prescriptions.

These new revelations mean that all the work done by the EWG and by the EMEA on SSRI antidepressants has to be redone properly, that clear and definitive decisions may not be made for several more years and that the precautionary principle continues to be largely ignored.

The need for a public enquiry into drug regulation remains paramount so long as regulatory bodies are permitted to act in secret and as judge and jury in their own case. It follows that calling for an enquiry is futile so long as health professionals and politicians are satisfied with that.

Conclusion

The major problems with SSRI antidepressants, which took many years to be accepted as real by the medicines regulators in the UK and other countries, are not yet fully recognised and remain inadequately investigated. In the UK they led to the discovery of serious deficiencies in the regulatory system, both in its legal basis and in the way in which the regulations are applied. This came as a shock, because the MHRA is regarded as one of the world's leading drug regulators, and the UK pioneered the Yellow Card system of voluntary reporting of suspected adverse drug reactions. Efforts are now being made to improve this system as well as other regulatory procedures.

These events will inevitably affect medicines regulation in other countries, not only in the EU, but internationally. Regulators will have to ensure that pharmaceutical companies which develop and market new products can no longer put their own interests before those of patients and the public. Both regulators and industry must become publicly accountable. All this is bound to take time, but delays cannot be accepted.

I conclude with a quote from the transcript of the third BBC *Panorama* programme 'Taken on Trust', broadcast on 3 October 2004:

> DR MIKE SHOOTER, President, Royal College of Psychiatrists: Oh no it has huge implications, I think once again we're seeing the SSRI's being the

focus for something much wider in psychiatry and we're seeing psychiatry being the focus for something much much wider in medicine as a whole. I think, you know, a few years down the line we're going to be talking about this with many more sorts of medication than psychotropic medication.[30]

PRESENTER: So you think this has ramifications right through medicine as a whole?

SHOOTER: Right through medicine. Right through medicine.

Acknowledgment. I warmly thank Charles Medawar for his valuable comments on drafts of this paper.

CHAPTER II

Is Australia's National Medicines Policy Failing?
The Case of COX-2 Inhibitors[1]

Agnes Vitry, Joel Lexchin and Peter R. Mansfield

'The importance of precautionary measures should not be played down on the grounds that the risk is unproved.' (The BSE Inquiry, 2000)[2]

Introduction

Following the worldwide withdrawal of Vioxx (rofecoxib), commentators in the USA, Europe and Asia raised questions about the ability of drug regulatory agencies to fulfil their public health responsibilities.[2] At the time of the withdrawal, rofecoxib sales represented more than 40 per cent of the total Australian government expenditure on non-steroidal anti-inflammatory drugs (NSAIDs).[4] NSAIDs are aspirin-like drugs that reduce pain and inflammation in conditions such as arthritis. These drugs also have many adverse effects, including bleeding from the stomach. Most NSAIDs work by inhibiting the cyclo-oxygenase-1 and 2 enzymes (COX-1 and COX-2). Rofecoxib was a new NSAID that selectively inhibited COX-2 much more than COX-1 and this was thought to be why it could cause less bleeding from the stomach, but also why it could cause more heart attacks. Two other new NSAIDs, celecoxib and meloxicam, are less COX-2 selective than rofecoxib, but more selective than most of the older non-selective NSAIDs. Before rofecoxib was withdrawn, spending on rofecoxib, celecoxib and meloxicam represented more than 90 per cent of the total Australian government NSAID expenditure. However, Australian studies showed that the prescribing of these COX-2 selective inhibitors was not in accord with quality use of medicine principles.[5] According to some experts, rofecoxib may have caused several thousand extra cardiovascular events in Australia.[6]

Australia is often praised as one of the rare countries in the 'developed' world to have introduced and implemented a National Medicines Policy, with one of the main objectives being to ensure quality use of medicines. What actions were taken by the different stakeholders to protect Australia from the COX-2 inhibitor disaster? What improvements should be made to protect Australians from such disasters in the future?

The Australian National Medicines Policy

The stated aim of the Australian National Medicines Policy (NMP) is to 'meet medication and related service needs, so that both optimal health outcomes and economic objectives are achieved'. There are four main objectives:[7]

- medicines meeting appropriate standards of quality, safety and efficacy
- timely access to the medicines that Australians need, at a cost individuals and the community can afford'
- quality use of medicines; and
- maintaining a responsible and viable medicines industry.

The main agency responsible for the quality, safety and efficacy objective is the Therapeutic Goods Administration (TGA). TGA approves drugs for marketing in Australia and sets the approved uses and product information. The TGA is a government agency but is now funded entirely by user fees from drug companies. The access objective is the responsibility of the Pharmaceutical Benefits Scheme (PBS). After a drug has been approved for marketing the drug company can apply to the PBS for a subsidy covering the entire Australian population. Drugs are subsidised if they are priced to provide an acceptable cost–benefit ratio. Many agencies contribute to the quality use of medicines objective, but the bulk of government funding goes to the National Prescribing Service (NPS). The NPS provides health professionals with education and quality assurance activities that allow them to reflect on their own practice and explore and apply best practice therapeutic guidelines. The Department of Industry provides subsidies to make pharmaceutical manufacturing in and export from Australia more financially viable. The government has delegated responsibility for regulation of prescription drug advertising to the pharmaceutical industry association, Medicines Australia.

Failures of drug regulatory authorities

The Australian Therapeutic Goods Administration (TGA) approved the marketing of celecoxib (Celebrex) in June 1999 and rofecoxib (Vioxx) in October 1999 using standards similar to those of other regulatory agencies in the industrialised world and which suffer from the same shortcomings: new drugs can be approved on the sole basis that they are more effective than placebo. There is no requirement for manufacturers to provide data showing that new drugs have better efficacy or safety than existing treatments.[8] A single study showed a small benefit in terms of gastrointestinal safety for rofecoxib compared with some other NSAIDs,[9] but none for celecoxib.[10] There were no studies comparing COX-2 selective inhibitors with commonly used treatments for osteoarthritis such as paracetamol. Nor were there any studies in patients at high risk of gastrointestinal adverse effects comparing COX-2 selective inhibitors with a combination of a less selective NSAID and a cytoprotective drug to protect the stomach lining. The Australian registration data were not publicly available, but the FDA registration data showed no clinical advantage of COX-2 inhibitors over other NSAIDs.[11]

The VIGOR trial, published in 2000, compared rofecoxib with a non-selective NSAID, naproxen. This trial showed a gastrointestinal safety advantage for rofecoxib,[12] but this advantage was negated by a significantly greater risk of cardiovascular events.[13] In 2001, a review of all published English-language randomised controlled trials on COX-2 inhibitors concluded: 'It is mandatory to conduct a trial specifically assessing cardiovascular risk and benefit of these agents.'[14] In October 2001, eleven months after publication of the VIGOR trial, the Australian Product Information for Vioxx was amended but with a statement that minimised the VIGOR findings: 'the risk of serious cardiovascular thromboembolic adverse events was significantly lower in patients receiving naproxen'. Two years later an Adverse Drug Reactions Advisory Committeee (ADRAC) bulletin reviewed the cardiovascular risk of COX-2 inhibitors and concluded: 'At present the evidence for an association between rofecoxib and a risk of cardiovascular events is inconclusive and indirect.'[15]

Given the clear early evidence of serious safety concerns with rofecoxib compared to naproxen, it is important to ask why the TGA did so little and so late. There are several possible explanations. First, since 1 July 1998 the TGA has been required to fully recover its operating costs for all activities, including its public health responsibilities. Assessments made by drug regulatory authorities are not purely technical and can be influenced in different ways.[16] There are strong arguments that too often the balance is weighed in favour of the interests of manufacturers rather than those of patients.[17] A significant minority of European regulators believe that dependence on fees from industry distorts regulatory assessments against the public interest.[18] A US survey found that almost 20 per cent of Food and Drug Administration reviewers felt they were pressured to approve or recommend approval of a new drug despite reservations about the safety, efficacy or quality of the drug.[19] Second, the extent of the regulatory power of the TGA may be limited. John McEwen, the then principal medical adviser for the TGA, was quoted as saying that 'it's in dispute that we [the TGA] would have the power to force those [safety] studies once a drug is on the market'.[20] Third, under-reporting of adverse drug events and the lack of adequate post-marketing surveillance studies undermine the regulatory system. While data on the distribution of funds between drug approval and post-marketing surveillance sections of the TGA is lacking, in Canada, a country with roughly similar resources, post-marketing surveillance receives about one-fifth the personnel and funding as the arm of Health Canada that approves new drugs.[21] Other methods of monitoring drug safety, including linkage of large databases, have not yet been adequately funded and implemented. Fourth, the lack of transparency of the TGA's decision-making process and the confidentiality of the clinical dossiers submitted by drug companies prevent professional organisations and health information providers from carrying out their own drug evaluations. The rationale for the TGA decisions cannot be assessed, since no one else, aside from the pharmaceutical companies, has access to the data. End users have no opportunity to provide input into the process (e.g. requesting improvement in product information documents).

Failure of the Pharmaceutical Benefits Scheme to contain unjustified drug expenditures

All COX-2 selective inhibitors were eventually listed on the Pharmaceutical Benefits Scheme (PBS) as of restricted benefit for osteoarthritis and/or rheumatoid arthritis. In theory this means that the drug would only be subsidised if the patient had osteoarthritis and/or rheumatoid arthritis and not for other medical conditions such as non-specific pain or sports injuries. At the time of the listing of Celebrex in 2000, the then Health Minister, Dr Michael Wooldridge, publicly claimed 'a major breakthrough in arthritis therapy'.[22] The Pharmaceutical Benefits Advisory Committee (PBAC) – an independent expert committee which advises the Health Minister on which drugs should be available as pharmaceutical benefits – recommended that the price of Celebrex should be $1.00 a day and should be halved when an agreed number of tablets had been sold.[23] However, the Health Minister accepted a recommendation from the pricing authority that the price be 20 per cent higher than the PBAC had suggested, with no price adjustment at higher sales.[24]

In 2003, an Australian study showed that large numbers of patients used COX-2 selective inhibitors for reasons that did not comply with PBS restrictions, including non-specific pain and sprains and sports injuries.[25] Between 36.7 per cent and 63.3 per cent of these patients had not been prescribed any pain medication in the previous year. Again, no effective action was taken. By contrast, in some jurisdictions, including US states and Canadian provinces, the implementation of prior-authorisation programmes – requiring physicians to submit patient information for review before reimbursement approval – slowed the uptake of COX-2 selective inhibitors.[26] The provincial government of British Columbia chose not to subsidise rofecoxib at all. Prior-authorisation programmes for COX-2s may have generated extra costs such as those associated with the bureaucracy required, but the general consensus seems to be that overall they both reduce costs and improve clinical care.[27]

One may question whether it is the PBS' role to encourage the quality use of medicines. If the answer is yes, then decisions for PBS listing and restrictions should not only be based on cost and efficacy considerations, but should take into account public health outcomes. The PBS did little to discourage COX-2 inhibitor use. Rather than requiring doctors to phone for authority, the PBS merely requested doctors to observe a restriction to prescribe only for 'symptomatic treatment of osteoarthritis' and with celecoxib also allowed for 'symptomatic treatment of rheumatoid arthritis'. These restrictions were very similar to the listing of other NSAIDs ('chronic arthropathies [including osteoarthritis] with an inflammatory component'). Neither the restrictions nor the note that the use of COX-2 selective inhibitors 'is not subsidised through the PBS' for 'acute pain, soft tissue injury, arthrosis without an inflammatory component' was likely to have much impact on prescribing.[28]

Intense and misleading drug promotion

Marketing campaigns for COX-2 selective inhibitors have been among the most intense ever seen. Reportedly, Merck spent on direct-to-consumer advertising of Vioxx (rofecoxib) in the USA in 2000 more than PepsiCo spent on promoting Pepsi ($160.8 million and $125 million respectively).[29] In Canada, Merck spent over $CAN6 million in 2000 promoting rofecoxib, including 50,000 visits by sales representatives to doctors and over one million samples left behind.[30] In Australia, COX-2 selective inhibitors were heavily promoted in ways that implied superior safety and efficacy over other NSAIDs, despite the fact that studies of the COX-2 selective inhibitors had not shown any *overall* safety or efficacy advantages. The advertising focused on promoting these drugs as having a gastrointestinal (GI) bleeding safety advantage. Vioxx was presented as 'A new world of GI safety in pain relief'.[31] The first advertisement for Celebrex (celecoxib) claimed that it was 'Potentially the most exciting therapeutic advance in the treatment of inflammation and pain since the advent of NSAIDs . . . Powerful relief, safely delivered.'[32] A later advertisement for Celebrex showed a blood transfusion pack with the headline 'This is the price thousands of patients are paying for arthritis relief'.[33] It is true that every year in Australia thousands of patients need blood transfusions because of GI bleeding caused by NSAIDs. However, there is no evidence that patients would be safer overall if they took celecoxib instead of a non-selective NSAID.

Branded direct-to-consumer advertising of prescription products is banned in Australia, but television advertisements urged arthritis sufferers to ask their general practitioners about the new drugs. Marketing campaigns for COX-2 selective inhibitors enrolled the most influential Australian rheumatologists on to advisory boards.[34] In 2002, the *Medical Journal of Australia* published a position statement on 'Considerations for the Safe Prescribing and Use of COX-2-specific Inhibitors', authored by the Australian COX-2 Specific Inhibitor Prescribing Group, stating that 'whether any [COX-2 specific inhibitor] poses a risk to cardiovascular safety remains subject to debate'.[35] Fifteen members (65 per cent) of the twenty-three members of this group, including eight (100 per cent) of the rheumatologists involved, declared current financial links with the companies marketing celecoxib and rofecoxib: Pfizer and Merck.[36]

Promotional materials for rofecoxib in several countries were found to be false or misleading. In Australia in 2001, the manufacturers of celecoxib and rofecoxib were both fined $10,000 for breaching the code of conduct for the ethical marketing of prescription pharmaceutical products.[37] Fines of this amount are unlikely to act as deterrents to prevent companies from breaching the code. After the publication of the VIGOR study, drug companies forcefully denied any cardiovascular safety concerns. In

September 2001, the US Food and Drug Administration issued a Warning Letter to Merck requesting it to cease immediately all promotional activities which misrepresented the safety profile of rofecoxib by minimising the cardiovascular safety concerns, making unsubstantiated superiority claims against other NSAIDs, and promoting Vioxx for unapproved uses and at an unapproved dosing regimen.[38]

After the withdrawal of Vioxx, Pfizer sent a letter to Australian doctors claiming that 'the cardiovascular safety profile of Celebrex has been extensively studied' and 'the data do not indicate significant cardiovascular safety concerns with Celebrex'. After a long-delayed appeal process, the Medicines Australia Code of Conduct Committee fined Pfizer $30,000 in May 2005, but failed to ask Pfizer for a corrective letter, so if doctors were misled by those claims they would remain misled.[39] An analysis of the code of conduct showed that the control of drug promotion in Australia is mainly based on a voluntary complaint reporting system administered by a twelve person committee, of whom five members come from the industry.[40] The code of conduct has no clear provisions for active monitoring of drug promotion and sets no limits on the amount of money companies can spend to influence prescribers.

Weakness of independent drug information

At the time COX-2 selective inhibitors were launched in Australia, most of the information available to health professionals was provided by drug companies. There were only a few publications provided by independent information providers, mainly the National Prescribing Service (NPS) and the *Australian Medicines Handbook (AMH)*.[41] Since 2002, all annual *AMH* editions have included summaries of the VIGOR and CLASS studies and warned about the increased cardiovascular risk. In October 2001, the National Prescribing Service (NPS) newsletter published a full edition on the COX-2 selective inhibitors, with an extensive summary of the scientific evidence at that time. It stated that 'Evidence is accumulating that selective inhibition of the COX-2 enzyme may be associated with prothrombotic effects.'[42] However, by contrast with this critical statement, later messages sent out by the NPS failed to warn prescribers appropriately of the increasing safety concerns for rofecoxib. The NPS regularly writes to Australian general practitioners giving them feedback about how their prescribing compares with their peers. The December 2001 NPS prescribing feedback letter about NSAIDs did not mention the cardiovascular risks of the COX-2 selective inhibitors.[43] The 2003 NPS

Prescribing Practice Review stated that 'it remains unresolved whether COX-2 selective NSAIDs are prothrombotic compared to other NSAIDs'.[44] Immediately after the withdrawal of rofecoxib, the NPS released a fact sheet that recommended: 'Use lower risk NSAIDs (e.g. celecoxib, diclofenac and ibuprofen) in preference to higher risk agents.'[45] This recommendation was made even though the fact sheet correctly noted that there were no long-term placebo-controlled studies of celecoxib.

Some independent drug information providers overseas published much stronger messages. As early as July 2000, the French journal *Prescrire* concluded that rofecoxib was 'a disappointing NSAID analgesic' and mentioned cardiac risks.[46] In January 2002, the *Canadian Therapeutics Letter* concluded that, on the basis of FDA data from the CLASS and VIGOR studies, COX-2 selective inhibitors were 'associated with an increased incidence of serious adverse events as compared to non-selective NSAIDs'.[47] *Butlleti Groc*, a Spanish independent drug bulletin, was sued by Merck because of their article entitled 'The So-called Advantages of Celecoxib and Rofecoxib: Scientific Fraud'.[48]

The reach and the strength of information provided by independent organisations in Australia are limited. Fewer than 10 per cent of Australian general practitioners are *AMH* users. Fewer than 8 per cent of GPs participated in the NPS case study on COX-2 selective inhibitors.[49] It is unlikely that independent messages could overturn the influence of the intense propaganda from drug companies. Furthermore, many articles in other medical journals tended to emphasise the benefits of COX-2 selective inhibitors and minimise risks.

Provision of independent drug information is a key feature of the National Medicines Policy and is a necessary element in the promotion of the quality use of medicines. However, on its own it is insufficient in the face of the millions of dollars spent on advertising by drug companies. Future policies regarding quality use of medicines need to take account of this extreme imbalance.

Directions for the future

The development of the National Medicines Policy is an ongoing interactive process where all stakeholders, governmental bodies, drug companies, prescribers and consumers share common responsibilities. There are currently signs of positive development with the initiatives of the Pharmaceutical Health and Rational Use of Medicines (PHARM) committee – PHARM is an expert advisory committee which oversees the

Quality Use of Medicines (QUM) component of Australia's National Medicine Policy – to support the inclusion of quality use of medicines aspects in the Medicines Australia Code of Conduct and in the PBAC decision-making process. However, the increasing entanglement between health professionals and drug companies is a cause for concern.[50]

Health professionals should not be passive victims of misinformation campaigns or deficient regulatory systems. They need to proactively request strong evidence of therapeutic benefit before prescribing new drugs and choose independent sources of information over industry-funded medical education. The education of healthcare professionals in the proper use of evidence should start in the professional schools and continue in postgraduate training. Programmes such as the one developed at McMaster University in Canada that restricted contact between medical residents (registrars) and the industry continued to exert its effect once these residents finished their training and were out in practice. They were more sceptical of sales representatives and had fewer contacts with them than their colleagues who had not participated in the programme.[51]

Patients need to be better informed of the risks of new drugs and should demand more accountability and transparency from public agencies. Instead of allowing companies to run 'help-seeking' advertisements, the government should engage these same advertising experts to help design material that will truly provide information to patients.

Core elements of the National Medicines Policy require major reappraisal if we want to avoid similar disasters in the future. Requiring mandatory registration of all clinical trials in a publicly available registry would help ensure that it will be easier to spot when partial results are published, as was the case with celecoxib and the CLASS study.[52] The TGA needs to commit to releasing all clinical data on safety and efficacy once it has made a decision on whether or not to approve a new drug. Post-marketing surveillance should be recognised as being equally as important as pre-marketing approval and given the necessary resources to do the proper job. The TGA should have the power to require mandatory post-marketing studies where there are safety concerns or where pre-marketing trials did not include active comparators. Another idea worth considering is a five-year licence renewal for drugs where their initial benefit to harm ratio could be re-evaluated. Such a system is employed by the European Medicines Agency.[53] Finally, there should be a government-funded, publicly accountable agency responsible for regulation of promotion rather than relying on industry self-regulation.

Australian citizens deserve better from all of those who are entrusted with safeguarding the medicines system.

Glossary

Adverse drug reactions

An adverse drug reaction (ADR) is an unintended, negative consequence associated with the use of drugs.

Biologics

Biologics are derived from living sources and include blood products, vaccines and products that come from the use of biotechnology.

Celtic Tiger

The economic boom in the Irish economy since the 1990s has led some commentators to characterise Ireland as the Celtic Tiger.

Clinical trials

Clinical trials are the main form of research used in the investigation of the benefits and harms of medicines. In clinical trials patients are typically randomly allocated to a treatment group, but do not know to which group they belong; each group receives the drug being tested, a comparator medication or a placebo. There are four phases in clinical trials. In Phase One drugs are tested in healthy volunteers to determine the metabolic and pharmacological actions of the drug in humans, the side effects associated with increasing doses and, if possible, to gain early evidence on effectiveness. Phase Two testing takes place in several hundred people and consists of controlled clinical studies conducted to obtain some preliminary data on the effectiveness of the drug for a particular indication or indications in patients with the disease or condition. Phase Three testing usually involves several hundred to several thousand patients and is intended to gather the additional information about effectiveness and safety that is needed to evaluate the overall benefit–risk relationship of the drug. Post-marketing studies are referred to as Phase Four tests.

Compulsory licensing

Compulsory licensing laws allow governments to issue a licence to a domestic manufacturer to manufacture a drug without the consent of the patent holder.

Corporatism

Corporatist policy-making is based on the belief that state-coordinated dialogue between diverse 'stakeholders' can resolve conflicts of interests and produce win-win consensualist policy-making.

Dáil Éireann

The Irish parliament (the Oireachtas) consists of two houses, Dáil Éireann and Seanad Éireann. A member of the Dáil is a Teachta Dala (TD) and the prime minister is the Taoiseach.

G8

G8 refers to the Group of Eight, an international forum of the governments of the 'leading industrial nations', which holds annual summits to discuss policies of mutual concern and the global economy. Current members are Britain, France, Germany, Italy, Japan, Russia and the USA.

Generic drugs

A generic drug is a drug which has the same qualitative and quantitative composition in active substances and the same pharmaceutical form as a patented drug, and whose bioequivalence with the patented drug has been demonstrated by appropriate bioavailability studies. Generic drugs tend to be substantially cheaper than patented ones. In some countries, generic substitution is allowed whereby a pharmacist can (and is usually encouraged to) dispense the cheapest brand available even when the doctor has used a brand name – although such systems do allow the doctor to insist, usually by some additional endorsement on the prescription, on a particular brand being prescribed.

Globalisation

There is no agreed definition of globalisation. For precision, some use the prefixes of 'capitalist' or 'neo-liberal' to refer to the contemporary era of capitalism, and to distinguish it from what they regard as other democratic forms of globalisation, termed globalisation 'from below'. Capitalist globalisation is characterised by market-driven policy-making and the increased mobility of international investment due to new information and communications technologies. A key feature of this new phase of capitalism is increased competition between nation states and regions for transnational corporation investment.

Intellectual property rights

Intellectual property rights are the rights given to persons over creations of the mind such as inventions, works of art and literature and designs. Intellectual property rights, such as patents, trade marks and copyright, grant the creators of an object an exclusive right over the use of their creation for a certain period of time, usually twenty years. In order for a patent to be granted, the invention must fulfil the criteria of being novel, innovative and useful. For some, intellectual property rights are synonymous with monopoly privileges.

Neo-liberalism

Neo-liberalism is the political ideology that became dominant internationally in the 1980s and that underpins mutually reinforcing public policies such as redirecting public spending away from social welfare, reducing tax rates, free trade and privatisation of public companies, services and utilities.

Parallel importation

Parallel importation allows governments to sanction the importation of pharmaceutical products when the price being charged by the patent holder in that jurisdiction is higher than the price being charged elsewhere.

Patented drug

When medicines are first launched on the market and are still under patent, there is only one brand available, so that, even if the medicine is prescribed by its generic (or non-proprietary) name, the branded product will have to be dispensed. However, when the drug comes off patent, a number of brands of the same medicine may become available.

Pharmacovigilance

Pharmacovigilance is the practice and science of drug safety monitoring that involves the collection and evaluation of case reports of suspected adverse drug reactions (ADRs). Its purpose is to detect previously unknown or poorly understood adverse effects of medicines.

195

Precautionary principle

According to the precautionary principle, if a new technology, including drugs, cannot be shown to be safe then it should not be marketed or, if it is allowed onto the market, it should be under restricted conditions. In contrast, in risk management drugs are assumed to be safe unless there is information to the contrary. Therefore, in general, products should be allowed unfettered access to the market and, once there, largely left unattended.

Notes on Contributors

John Abraham is professor of sociology, co-director of the Centre for Research in Health and Medicine (CRHaM) and head of the Health, Medicine and Science Research Group at the University of Sussex.

Michael Barry is a senior lecturer/consultant clinical pharmacologist at the University of Dublin, Trinity College. He is the clinical director of the National Centre for Pharmacoeconomics in Dublin. His research areas of interest include economic evaluation and health technology assessment.

Colin Bradley is professor of general practice at University College Cork. He has a long-standing research interest in the prescribing of general practitioners. He is a member of a large European research group investigating users' perspectives on psychotropic medicines.

Gerard Downes is a Government of Ireland postgraduate scholar at the University of Limerick, where he is researching a PhD on the WTO's TRIPs Agreement and its implications for global governance.

Kathy Glavanis-Grantham is a lecturer in sociology in University College Cork. Her publications have focused on issues of rural development and gender in the Middle East.

Andrew Herxheimer is emeritus fellow at the Cochrane Centre in Oxford. He worked for some years as a medical doctor before turning to clinical pharmacology and teaching at medical schools. He is the founder of the *Drug and Therapeutics Bulletin*, which he edited for many years. He currently works on DIPEx (Database of Individual Patients' Experiences, www.dipex.org).

Joel Lexchin has been an emergency physician at the University Health Network in Toronto for the past eighteen years. He is currently an associate professor in the School of Health Policy and Management at York University. He has been a consultant on pharmaceutical issues for the province of Ontario, various arms of the Canadian federal government, the World Health Organization, the government of New Zealand and the Australian National Prescribing Service.

Terry Lynch is a Limerick-based general practitioner and psychotherapist. He was a member of the Irish Department of Health and Children's Expert Group on Mental Health Policy.

Peter R. Mansfield is a South Australian general practitioner and founder of Healthy Skepticism Inc., an international organisation aiming to improve health by reducing harm from misleading drug promotion (www.healthyskepticism.org). He is also a research fellow, Discipline of General Practice, University of Adelaide.

Stephen McCloskey is director of the Centre for Global Education (formerly the One World Centre) in Belfast and a long-term activist in the field of international development.

Orla O'Donovan is a lecturer in the Department of Applied Social Studies, University College Cork, where her research and teaching are centrally concerned with the politics of healthcare.

Denis O'Hearn is professor of sociology at Queens University Belfast and for many years was chair of the West Belfast Economic Forum.

Máirín Ryan is a pharmacist at the National Centre for Pharmacoeconomics and lecturer in pharmacoeconomics in the Department of Pharmacology and Therapeutics, Trinity College Dublin. Her research interests include cost data generation in the Irish setting and economic incentives in pharmaceutical policy in Ireland.

Lesley Tilson is a pharmacist at the National Centre for Pharmacoeconomics in Dublin. She is a lecturer in pharmacoeconomics in Trinity College Dublin and her research interests include economic evaluation of pharmaceuticals in the Irish setting, pharmaceutical pricing and reimbursement strategies, policies to promote generic markets, international pharmaceutical pricing, analysis of drug utilisation and expenditure trends.

Agnes Vitry is a senior lecturer at the School of Pharmacy and Medical Sciences, University of South Australia, a researcher at the Quality Use of Medicines and Pharmacy Research Centre, a consultant editor with the *Australian Medicines Handbook*, the main Australian medicines formulary, and an active member of Healthy Skepticism Inc., an international organisation aiming to improve health by reducing harm from misleading drug promotion (www.healthyskepticism.org).

Notes and References

Notes to Introduction

1. Nuria O'Mahony's campaigning efforts resulted in the establishment in 2006 by the Irish government of the Oireachtas Sub-Committee on the Adverse Side Effects of Pharmaceuticals. See Houses of the Oireachtas Joint Committee on Health and Children, Eighth Report, *The Adverse Effects of Pharmaceuticals*, April 2007.
2. B. Mintzes, *Educational Initiatives for Medical and Pharmacy Students about Drug Promotion: An International Cross-Sectional Survey* (World Health Organisation and Health Action International, 2005).
3. J. Law, *Big Pharma: Exposing the Global Healthcare Agenda* (New York: Carroll & Graf, 2006).
4. See, for example, A. Hardon, 'Contesting Contraceptive Innovation: Reinventing the Script', *Social Science and Medicine,* vol. 62, no. 3, 2006, pp. 614–627; C. Medawar and A. Hardon, *Medicines Out of Control? Antidepressants and the Conspiracy of Goodwill* ([Amsterdam]: Aksant, 2004); E. 't Hoen, 'TRIPs, Pharmaceutical Patents, and Access to Essential Medicines: A Long Way from Seattle to Doha', *Chicago Journal of International Law,* vol. 3, no. 1, 2002, pp. 27–46.
5. M. Klawiter, 'Risk, Prevention and the Breast Cancer Continuum: The NCI, the FDA, Health Activism and the Pharmaceutical Industry', *History and Technology,* vol. 18, 2002, pp. 309–353.
6. P. Farmer, *Pathologies of Power: Health, Human Rights and the New War on the Poor* (Berkeley: University of California Press, 2003).
7. Pharmacovigilance is the practice and science of drug safety monitoring that involves the collection and evaluation of case reports of suspected adverse drug reactions (ADRs). Its purpose is to detect previously unknown or poorly understood adverse effects of medicines.
8. I. Illich, *Limits to Medicine. Medical Nemesis: The Expropriation of Health* (London: Marion Boyars, 1976, 1995).
9. Health Action International is a non-profit organisation and global network of individuals and organisations that works to increase access to and rational use of essential medicines.
10. Healthy Skepticism is an international non-profit organisation that strives to improve health by reducing harm due to misleading drug promotion.
11. C. Van Egeraat, 'The Pharmaceutical Industry in Ireland: Agglomeration, Localisation or Simply Spatial Concentration?', NIRSA Working Paper No. 28 (Maynooth: National Institute for Regional and Spatial Analysis, 2006).

12. Irish Pharmaceutical Healthcare Association, *Industry Report Pharma Ireland: Developing and Delivering Medicines* (Dublin: Irish Pharmaceutical Healthcare Association, 2005).
13. G. Deegan, 'Investigation Urged into Health Patterns after Firm is Fined', *The Irish Times,* 16 February 2006.
14. Government of Ireland, *Towards Better Regulation* (Dublin: Department of the Taoiseach, 2002), p. 2.
15. For example, see the work of John Abraham and his colleagues, such as J. Abraham, *Science, Politics and the Pharmaceutical Industry: Controversy and Bias in Drug Regulation* (London: Routledge, 1995); J. Abraham and G. Lewis (eds.), *Regulating Medicines in Europe: Competition, Experts and Public Health* (London: Routledge, 2000), and J. Abraham and H. Lawton (eds.), *Regulation of the Pharmaceutical Industry* (London: Palgrave, 2003).
16. Irish Pharmaceutical Healthcare Association, *Industry Report,* 2005.
17. D. Staunton, 'Bono Calls for "Conscientious Commerce"', *The Irish Times,* 27 January 2006.
18. Democracy Commission, *Briefing Paper on Themes for the National Consultative Conference 2005 New Directions for Irish Democracy* (Dublin: Democracy Commission, 2005).
19. See P. Brown and S. Zavestoski, 'Social Movements in Health: An Introduction', in P. Brown and S. Zavestoski (eds.), *Social Movements in Health* (Oxford: Blackwell, 2005).
20. V. Navarro, 'Policy without Politics: The Limits of Social Engineering', *American Journal of Public Health,* vol. 93, no. 1, 2003, pp. 64–67.

Notes to Chapter 1

1. W. Robinson, *Transnational Conflicts: Central America, Social Change, and Globalization* (London: Verso, 2003), p. 13.
2. L. Sklair, *The Transnational Capitalist Class* (Oxford: Blackwell, 2001).
3. Robinson, 2003, p. 20.
4. Ibid., pp. 61–62.
5. G. Arrighi, *The Long Twentieth Century* (London: Verso, 1994).
6. *Maquiladoras* are foreign-owned factories that operate in the free-trade zones of Mexico, mainly along the border with the United States.
7. A good collection of studies of commodity chains is found in G. Gereffi and M. Korzeniewicz (eds.), *Commodity Chains and Global Capitalism* (Boulder, CO: Westport, 1994).
8. J. Williamson, 'What Should the World Bank Think About the Washington Consensus?' *World Bank Research Observer,* vol. 15, no. 2, 2000, pp. 251–264.
9. A critical element of property rights that strongly affects the drugs industry is intellectual property rights, wherein corporations make claims to products and designs, protecting them by patents and other means, usually with the aim of increasing their profits for a period of time.

10. The Jubilee Debt Campaign (JDC) is a coalition of local and national organisations calling for an end to unpayable debt. Useful statistics and a history of the debt issue can be found on the Jubilee Debt Campaign's website http://www.jubileedebtcampaign.org.uk.

11. Jubilee Debt Campaign estimates that Cameroon, Ethiopia, Gambia, Guinea, Madagascar, Malawi, Mauritania, Senegal, Uganda and Zambia all spent more on debt servicing in 2002 than on health or education. The JDC also cites examples of where debt cancellation is working, such as Benin, where 54 per cent of the revenue saved through debt relief has been spent on health, including rural primary health care and HIV programmes. See http://www.jubileedebtcampaign.org.uk.

12. UNAIDS, *Report on the Global AIDS Epidemic*, available from the World Health Organisation's (WHO) Statistical Information System, 2004, http://www.who.int/research.

13. UNAIDS is 'The Joint United Nations Programme on HIV/AIDS' and the 'main advocate for accelerated, comprehensive and co-ordinated global action on the epidemic'; UNAIDS, '$22 billion needed in 2008 to reverse the spread of AIDS', press release issued on 21 June 2005, http://www.unaids.org.

14. Jubilee Debt Campaign website: http://www.jubileedebtcampaign.org.uk.

15. In 2005, the G8 agreed a package of so-called debt relief, mainly for African countries, in which relief was contingent on 'tackling corruption', 'boosting private sector development' and 'eliminating impediments to private investment'. In other words, debt relief was yet another form of conditionality, by which the wealthy Western countries were attempting to force the Washington Consensus on poorer countries. Significantly, among these countries was Bolivia, which has been at the forefront of the fight against the Washington Consensus and, especially, against privatisation of natural resources such as gas and water. For a critique of the G8 package, see G. Monbiot, 'A Truckload of Nonsense: The G8 Plan to Save Africa Comes with Conditions that Make It Little More than an Extortion Racket', *The Guardian*, 14 June 2005.

16. For a review of measures of world inequality, which shows convincingly that the world has steadily become more unequal since the Second World War, see R. Wade, 'Is Globalization Reducing Poverty and Inequality?', *World Development*, vol. 32, no. 4, 2004, pp. 567–589.

17. UN, *Human Development Report 2001* (Oxford and New York: United Nations Development Programme, 2001).

18. CSO, *National Income and Expenditure 1997* (Dublin: Central Statistics Office, 1998).

19. Foreign Policy, 'Measuring Globalization: Who's Up, Who's Down?' *Foreign Policy*, January–February 2003, pp. 60–72.

20. D. O'Hearn, 'Economic Growth and Social Cohesion in Ireland', in M. Dauderstadt (ed.), *Economic Growth and Social Cohesion in Europe* (Bonn: Friedrich Ebert Foundation, 2001).

21. E. Mulqueen, 'The Price You Are Forced to Pay', *The Irish Times,* 27 January 2004; Office of the United States Trade Representative, 'Bilateral Trade Agreements', http://www.ustr.gov/Trade_Agreements/Bilateral/Section_Index.html; IPHA, 'Ireland is World's Biggest Pharmaceutical Exporter', *Medicines Matter,* newsletter of Irish Pharmaceutical Healthcare Association, February 2005. Low expenditures on drugs might be a good thing if they reflected better health in the population or alternative (preventative) public health strategies. In the case of Ireland, they do not.

22. On the social results of Irish growth since 1994, see O'Hearn, 2001, 'Economic Growth'.

23. GATS, a multilateral trade agreement, should not be confused with GATT, the international financial organisation that preceded and was replaced by the World Trade Organisation (WTO), about which see below.

24. World Development Movement, *Briefing on Regulating TNCs: Making Investment Work for People, an International Framework for Regulating Corporations* (London: World Development Movement, 1999).

25. The Catholic Agency for Overseas Development (CAFOD) has produced a series of useful briefing papers on the WTO and its negotiations. They are available from the CAFOD website: www.cafod.org.uk.

26. CAFOD, *The Rough Guide to the WTO: A CAFOD Briefing* (London: CAFOD 2001). Low prices for home-grown maize is not the only problem caused by free trade. In 2001, scientists were amazed to find that one of the oldest varieties of Mexican maize had been contaminated by GM corn from the US, despite the fact that no genetically modified corn had been grown within 60 miles of the contaminated crops; J. Vidal, 'Mexico's GM Corn Shocks Scientists', *The Guardian,* 30 November 2002.

27. World Development Movement, *Trade Justice at Cancun? Why the WTO's Remit Should Not Be Expanded to Cover the 'New Issues'* (London: World Development Movement, 2003).

28. World Development Movement, *Briefing Paper on GATS* (London: World Development Movement, 2002).

29. The Uruguay Round was a seven-and-a-half-year round of talks (1986–1994) under the General Agreement on Tariffs and Trade (GATT). By the end of the round, 123 countries were members of GATT and signed up to its provisions, including the establishment of the World Trade Organisation (to replace GATT) and multilateral agreements such as TRIPs and GATS.

30. CAFOD, *Rough Guide to the WTO.*

31. Generic drugs are chemically identical to brand-name drugs, yet they are typically sold at substantially lower prices than the branded equivalents.

32. The argument that drug costs must be high to offset high costs of development has been effectively disputed. See O. O'Donovan and K. Glavanis-Grantham, 'Researching the Political and Cultural Influence of the Transnational Pharmaceutical Industry in Ireland', *Administration,* vol. 52, no. 3, 2004, p. 27.

33. G. Velásquez, 'Bilateral Trade Agreements and Access to Essential Drugs' in J. A. Z. Bermudez and M. A. Oliveira (eds.), *Intellectual Property in the Context of the WTO TRIPS Agreement: Challenges for Public Health* (Rio de Janeiro: Escola Nacional de Saúde Pública/WHO, 2004).

34. Article 27 of the 1917 Mexican constitution legalised village communes (*ejidos*). As part of the NAFTA agreement, the Mexican government under President Salinas de Gortari rescinded Article 27, thereby revoking collective ownership of land.

35. For further information on these issues, see the website of ETC Group (formerly RAFI), an international research and campaigning group that is dedicated to the conservation and sustainable advancement of cultural and ecological diversity and human rights, http://www.etcgroup.org/main.asp. See, especially, ETC Group, 'Oligopoly, Inc.: Concentration in Corporate Power 2003', *Communique*, no. 82, November/December 2003, http://www.etcgroup.org/documents/Comm82OligopNovDec03.pdf.

36. J. Bhagwati and A. Panagariya, 'Bilateral Trade Treaties Are a Sham', *Financial Times*, 13 July 2003.

37. Office of the United States Trade Representative, 'Bilateral Trade Agreements', http://www.ustr.gov/Trade_Agreements/Bilateral/Section_Index.html.

38. Bhagwati and Panagariya, 'Bilateral Trade Treaties'.

Notes to Chapter 2

1. R. Weissman, 'A Long Strange TRIPs: The Pharmaceutical Industry Drive to Harmonize Property Rules, and the Remaining WTO Legal Alternatives Available to Third World Countries', *University of Pennsylvania Journal of International Economic Law*, vol. 17, no. 4, 1996, pp. 1069–1125.

2. The General Agreement on Tariffs and Trade (GATT) was established in 1947 and embodies a set of rules for the conduct of international trade policy on a multilateral basis. The primary objective of GATT was to reduce barriers to trade between countries. All countries that were party to the GATT were called 'Contracting Parties'. The GATT was replaced by the World Trade Organization (WTO), which came into being on 1 January 1995.

3. States that are party to WTO agreements are called 'members'.

4. A. Lanoszka, 'Global Politics of Intellectual Property Rights, WTO Agreement, and Pharmaceutical Drug Policies in Developing Countries', *International Political Science Review*, vol. 24, no. 2, 2003, pp. 181–198.

5. J. Meek, 'Beginners Guide to Gene Patents', *The Guardian*, 15 November, 2003, p. 11.

6. Lanoszka, 'Global Politics'.

7. J. O. Lanjouw and I. Cockburn , 'New Pills for Poor People?: Empirical Evidence After GATT', *World Development*, vol. 29, no. 2, 2001, pp. 265–289.

8. K. Maskus, *Intellectual Property Rights in the Global Economy* (Washington DC: Institute for International Economics, 2000), p. 1.

9. G. Mossinghoff and T. Bombelles, 'The Importance of Intellectual Property to American Research-Intensive Pharmaceutical Industry', *Columbia Journal of World Business,* vol. 31, no. 1, 1996, pp. 38–48.

10. C. Raghavan, *Recolonization: GATT, the Uruguay Round and the Third World* (London and Penang: Third World Network and Zed Books, 1990).

11. B. Hoekman and M. Kostecki, *The Political Economy of the World Trading System* (Oxford University Press, 1995).

12. P. Drahos and J. Braithwaite, *Global Business Regulation* (Cambridge University Press, 2000).

13. Pfizer, 'Intellectual Property by Edmund J. Pratt, Chairman Emeritus, Pfizer Inc.', 2004, http://www.pfizer.com/are/about_public/mn_about_intellectualpropfrm.html. Accessed 1 July 2004.

14. H. Chang, *Kicking Away the Ladder: Development Strategy in Historical Perspective* (London: Anthem Press, 2002).

15. Panos Institute, *Patents, Pills and Public Health: Can TRIPs Deliver?*, Panos Report No. 46, 2002.

16. The International Anti-Counterfeiting Coalition (IACC) was established in 1978 as a cross-section of business groupings within the USA intent on countering intellectual property transgressions worldwide. The group has since sought to promote laws, regulations and directives that are designed to eliminate intellectual property rights violations.

17. Mossinghoff and Bombelles, 'The Importance of Intellectual Property'.

18. The US International Trade Commission (ITC) is an independent US federal agency that provides trade expertise to both the legislative and executive branches of the US government. The primary objective of the ITC is to determine the impact of imports on US industries, and to direct retaliatory actions against countries that engage in unfair trade practices such as intellectual property rights infringements.

19. S. Sell, *Private Power, Public Law: The Globalization of Intellectual Property Rights* (Cambridge University Press, 2003), p. 47.

20. USITC, 'Foreign Protection of Intellectual Property Rights and the Effect on US Trade and Industry', INV No. 332-TA-245, 1988.

21. Weissman, 'A Long Strange TRIPs', p. 1087.

22. Mossinghoff and Bombelles, 'The Importance of Intellectual Property'.

23. J. Di Masi *et al.*, 'Costs of Innovation in the Pharmaceutical Industry', *Journal of Health Economics,* vol. 10, no. 1, 1991, pp. 107–142. In a survey of twelve US-owned pharmaceutical firms the authors estimated the pre-tax average cost of new drug development at $US231 million (1987 dollars). However, the US federal Office of Technology Assessment calculated that only half of the $US231 million is tied up in funds for development; the other half is 'opportunity cost', i.e. the most valuable foregone alternative or, in this case, the return the company would have

received if it invested the money rather than spent it on R&D in developing the drug.

24. Until 1994 PhRMA was known as the Pharmaceutical Manufacturers Association (PMA).
25. Maskus, 'Intellectual Property Rights'.
26. A. Relman and M. Angell, 'America's Other Drug Problem: How the Drug Industry Distorts Medicine and Politics', *New Republic*, vol. 227, no. 25, pp. 27–41.
27. Ibid., p. 30.
28. PhRMA, 'Enforcing the TRIPs Agreement is Critically Important to US Industries', 2000. Source: http://www.phrma.org/international/resources/04.11.2000.54.cfm. Accessed 22 August 2004.
29. Drahos and Braithwaite, *Global Business Regulation*.
30. Lanoszka, 'Global Politics', p. 191.
31. Drahos and Braithwaite, *Global Business Regulation*.
32. J. Bhagwati, *In Defence of Globalisation* (Oxford University Press, 2004).
33. Weissman, 'A Long Strange TRIPs'.
34. K. Zeng, *Trade Threats, Trade Wars: Bargaining, Retaliation, and American Coercive Diplomacy* (Ann Arbor: University of Michigan Press, 2004).
35. Weissman, 'A Long Strange TRIPs', p. 1083.
36. C. M. Correa, *Intellectual Property Rights, the WTO and Developing Countries: The TRIPs Agreement and Policy Options* (Penang: Third World Network, 2000).
37. S. Sell and A. Prakash, 'Using Ideas Strategically: The Contest Between Business and NGO Networks in Intellectual Property Rights', *International Studies Quarterly*, vol. 48, no. 1, 2004, pp. 143–175.
38. C. Johnson, *Blowback: The Costs and Consequences of American Empire* (New York: Holt Metropolitan Books, 2000).
39. P. Drahos, 'Global Property Rights in Information: The Story of TRIPs at the GATT', *Prometheus*, vol. 13, no. 1, 1995, p. 421.
40. Weissman, 'A Long Strange TRIPs'.
41. Drahos and Braithwaite, *Global Business Regulation*, p. 44.
42. Sell and Prakash, 'Using Ideas Strategically', p. 145.
43. Pfizer, 'Intellectual Property'.
44. Oxfam, *Rigged Rules and Double Standards: Trade, Globalisation and the Fight Against Poverty* (Oxford: Oxfam, 2002).
45. Pfizer, 'Intellectual Property'.
46. Drahos, 'Global Property Rights'.
47. S. P. Shukla, *From GATT to WTO and Beyond* (Helsinki: UNU World Institute for Development Economics Research, 2000).
48. Sell, *Private Power, Public Law*, p. 94.
49. Drahos and Braithwaite, *Global Business Regulation*.
50. Sell, *Private Power, Public Law*, p. 147.
51. Ibid.

52. W. Pretorius, 'TRIPs and Developing Countries: How Level is the Playing Field?', in P. Drahos and R. Mayne (eds.), *Global Intellectual Property Rights: Knowledge, Access and Development* (Basingstoke: Palgrave Macmillan, 2002), pp. 183–200.

53. Correa, *Intellectual Property Rights.*

54. Pretorius, 'TRIPs and Developing Countries', p. 189.

55. Bhagwati, *In Defence of Globalisation*, p. 184.

56. J. Watal, 'Intellectual Property and Biotechnology: Trade Interests of Developing Countries', *International Journal of Biotechnology*, vol. 2, no. 1/2/3, 2000, pp. 44–55.

57. A. Subramaniam, 'Putting Some Numbers on the TRIPs Pharmaceutical Debate', *International Journal of Technology Management*, vol. 10, no. 2/3, 1995, pp. 252–268.

58. Shukla, *From GATT to WTO and Beyond.*

59. The Doha Declaration on the TRIPs Agreement and Public Health emanated from the WTO Ministerial Conference held in Doha, Qatar, from 9th to 14th November, 2001. The Doha Declaration was an attempt to negate some of the worst effects of TRIPs and affirmed that the agreement 'can and should be interpreted and implemented in a manner supportive of WTO Members' rights to protect public health and, in particular, to promote access to medicines for all' (Doha Declaration, 2001).

60. Correa, *Intellectual Property Rights.*

61. K. Balasubramaniam, 'Access to Medicines: Patents, Prices and Public Policy–Consumer Perspectives', in P. Drahos and R. Mayne (eds.), *Global Intellectual Property Rights: Knowledge, Access and Development* (Basingstoke: Palgrave Macmillan, 2002), pp. 101-102.

62. Ibid.

63. R. Mayne, 'The Global NGO Campaign on Patents and Access to Medicines: An Oxfam Perspective', in Drahos and Mayne (eds.), pp. 244–258.

64. Oxfam, *Rigged Rules.*

65. Mayne, 'The Global NGO Campaign'.

66. World Intellectual Property Organization (WIPO), *Implications of the TRIPs Agreement on Treaties Administered by WIPO* (Geneva: WIPO Publications, 1997), p. 33.

67. Mayne, 'The Global NGO Campaign'.

68. Ibid.

69. J. Ikenberry and C. Kupchan, 'Socialization and Hegemonic Power', *International Organization*, vol. 44, no. 3, 1990, pp. 283–315.

70. Brehon Law, which provided a framework of administrative practice and social custom in early medieval Ireland, originated in prehistoric times and found its closest parallel in traditional Hindu law. Brehon law derives its name from the Irish word *Breitheamh*, meaning judge.

71. Pharmachemical Ireland, 'Sector Profile', 2004, http://www. pharmachemicalireland.ie/sectors/ipcmf/webipcmf.nsf/whome?openform. Accessed 10 September 2004.

72. The Irish Patents Act of 1992 (Section 78) states that a minister may use an invention for any purpose which appears to such Minister to be necessary or expedient for the following purposes: '*(a)* for the maintenance of supplies and services essential to the life of the community; *(b)* for securing a sufficiency of supplies and services essential to the well-being of the community; *(c)* for promoting the productivity of commerce and industry, including agriculture; *(d)* generally for ensuring that the whole resources of the community are available for use, and are used, in a manner best calculated to serve the interests of the community; *(e)* for assisting the relief of suffering and the restoration and distribution of essential supplies and services in any country or territory other than the State that is in grave distress; or *(f)* for ensuring the public safety and the preservation of the State'. J. Love, 'Access to Medicine and Compliance with the WTO TRIPs Accord: Models for State Practice in Developing Countries', in Drahos and Mayne (eds.), pp. 74–89.

73. Weissman, 'A Long Strange TRIPs'.

74. European Commission, 'Communication by the European Communities and their Member States to the TRIPs Council on the Review of Article 27.3(B) of the TRIPs Agreement, and the Relationship Between the TRIPs Agreement and the Convention on Biological Diversity (CBD) and the Protection of Traditional Knowledge and Folklore' (Brussels: Directorate-General for Trade, 2002).

75. Qualified Majority Voting (QMV) is the most common voting procedure used by the EU Council of Ministers, under which each member state has a fixed number of votes according to the size of its population. Germany (population 82 million) has 29 votes in the Council, while Ireland (population 4 million) has seven votes. To pass a vote by QMV, three conditions must pertain: firstly, 232 out of the total of 321 votes in the Council have to be obtained; secondly, a majority of member states must approve the bill; and thirdly, those countries supporting the bill must represent at least 62 per cent of the total EU population. QMV is used to pass most Council decisions, while others, particularly those pertaining to highly sensitive areas such as taxation, foreign policy, social policy and defence, require unanimity among all Council members.

76. R. Shapiro, and K. Hassett, 'The Economic Value of Intellectual Property', report prepared for USA for Innovation, Source: http://www.usafor innovation.org/news/ip_master.pdf. Accessed 6 November 2005.

Notes to Chapter 3

1. This chapter is concerned with prescription drugs.

2.   R. K. Merton, 'The Normative Structure of Science', in N. Storer (ed.), *The Sociology of Science: Theoretical and Empirical Investigations* (University of Chicago Press, 1942).

3.   K. Popper, *Objective Knowledge: An Evolutionary Approach* (Oxford: Clarendon Press, 1972).

4.   E. C. Huskisson, 'Classification of Anti-Rheumatic Drugs', in E. C. Huskisson (ed.), *Anti-Rheumatic Drugs* (East Sussex and New York: Praeger, 1983), pp. 1–4.

5.   G. B. Bluhm et al., 'Radiologic Assessment of Benoxaprofen Therapy in Rheumatoid Arthritis', *European Journal of Rheumatology and Inflammation*, vol. 5, no. 2, 1982, pp. 186–97; US Court, Deposition of Gilbert Bluhm, *Clarence Borom vs Eli Lilly*, District Court for the Middle District of Georgia, Columbus Division, 27 October 1983.

6.   E. C. Huskisson et al., 'Benoxaprofen: A Clinical Trial with an Unusual Design', *Rheumatology and Rehabilitation*, vol. 17, 1978, pp. 254–58; E. C. Huskisson and J. Scott, 'Treatment of Rheumatoid Arthritis with a Single Daily Dose of Benoxaprofen', *Rheumatology and Rehabilitation*, vol. 18, 1979, pp. 110–113.

7.   FDA Department of Health and Human Services, *Guidelines for the Clinical Evaluation of Anti-Inflammatory and Anti-Rheumatic Drugs* (Washington DC: US GPO, 1977); H. J. W. Bodewitz, et al., 'Regulatory Science and the Social Management of Trust in Medicine', in M. Bijker et al. (eds.), *The Social Construction of Technological Systems* (Cambridge, MA: MIT Press, 1987).

8.   E. C. Huskisson, 'Trials of Anti-Rheumatic Drugs', in C. Good and C. Clarke (eds.), *The Principles and Practice of Clinical Trials* (Edinburgh: Churchill Livingstone, 1976), pp. 192, 196.

9.   US Court, Deposition of Gilbert Bluhm, *Clarence Borom vs Eli Lilly*, District Court for the Middle District of Georgia, Columbus Division, 27 October 1983, p. 21.

10.   Bluhm et al., 'Radiological Assessment of Benoxaprofen Therapy', p. 190.

11.   Ibid., p. 186.

12.   W. M. O'Brien, 'Radiological Evaluation of Erosions: A Quantitative Method for Assessing Long-Term Remittive Therapy in Rheumatoid Arthritis', *British Journal of Clinical Pharmacology*, vol. 22, 1986, pp. 173S–182S; US Court, Deposition of William O'Brien, *Clarence Borom vs Eli Lilly*, District Court for the Middle District of Georgia, Columbus Division, 28 September 1983.

13.   BBC, 'The Opren Scandal', *Panorama*, January 1983.

14.   E. C. Huskisson, 'Editorial', *European Journal of Rheumatology and Inflammation*, vol. 5, no. 2, 1982, pp. 49–50.

15.   W. Dawson et al., 'The Pharmacology of Benoxaprofen with Particular Reference to Effects on Lipoxygenase Product Formation', *European Journal of Rheumatology and Inflammation*, vol. 5, no. 2, 1982, p. 61.

16.   US Court, Deposition of Gilbert Bluhm, 1983, pp. 48–49.

17. US Congress, Hearings of the Intergovernmental Relations and Human Resources Subcommittee of the House of Representatives, *The Regulation of New Drugs by the FDA: The Drug Review Process*, Washington DC: US GPO, 3–4 August 1982, pp. 485–486.

18. PDAC, Transcript of Psychopharmacological Drugs Advisory Committee Meeting, FDA Headquarters, 18 May 1992, p. 95.

19. Ibid., pp. 70–85.

20. Ibid., p. 95.

21. Ibid., pp. 266–68.

22. Ibid., p. 271.

23. Ibid., pp. 309, 312.

24. Ibid., pp. 283–284.

25. Ibid., p. 315.

26. Ibid., p. 268.

27. Secular trends in reporting rates refers to the fact that overall rates of ADR reporting have varied over the years. Consequently, in comparing the numbers of ADR reports on drugs that have been introduced on to the market in different periods or eras, one should take account of such secular trends in order to sharpen the validity of the comparison.

28. PDAC, Transcript of Psychopharmacological Drugs Advisory Committee Meeting, pp. 105–111, 119–120; Y. Tsong, Statistical Comparison of ADE Reporting Rates between Triazolam and Temazepam, internal FDA memo to Chief of Epidemiology Branch, Office of Epidemiology, 1992.

29. D. J. Graham, Halcion Comparison with Temazepam, internal FDA memo, 8 May 1992.

30. T. Laughren and H. Lee, 'Review of Adverse Event Data in Upjohn Sponsored Clinical Studies of Halcion', FDA submission to PDAC, 1 May 1992, Table 6.25a.

31. PDAC, Transcript of Psychopharmacological Drugs Advisory Committee Meeting, p. 147.

32. Laughren and Lee, 1992, 'Review of Adverse Event Data'.

33. PDAC, Transcript of Psychopharmacological Drugs Advisory Committee Meeting, pp. 148, 322.

34. Ibid., p. 157.

35. Laughren and Lee, 'Review of Adverse Event Data', tables 6.26 and 6.26a.

36. PDAC Transcript, p. 363.

37. Ibid., p. 315.

38. Ibid., p. 362.

39. J. Abraham, 'Pharmaceuticals, the State and the Global Harmonisation Process', *Australian Health Review*, vol. 28, no. 2, 2004, pp. 150–160.

40. D. Poggiolini, 'Research, Development and Regulation: A Background to Harmonization', in P. F. D'Arcy and D. W. G. Harron (eds.), *Proceedings of the First International Conference on Harmonisation* (Belfast: IFPMA, 1992), pp. 13–14.

41. A. McIntyre, *Key Issues in the Pharmaceutical Industry* (Chichester: John Wiley & Sons, 1999), p. 96.

42. M. Bangemann, 'Welcome and Introduction: Welcome Address by Mr Martin Bangemann, Vice-President of the Commission of the European Communities', in D'Arcy and Harron (eds.), Proceedings, p. 4.

43. Y. Araga, 'Keynote Address', in P. F. D'Arcy and D. W. G. Harron (eds.), *Proceedings of the Third International Conference on Harmonisation* (Belfast: IFPMA, 1996), p. 19.

44. IFPMA, 'A Brief History of ICH', in *ICH: Past and Future*, 1998, at http://www.ifpma.org/ich1.html.

45. ICH, *Guideline on the Need for Carcinogenicity Studies of Pharmaceuticals*, 29 November 1995.

46. ICH, *Guideline on the Extent of Population Exposure to Assess Clinical Safety for Drugs Intended for Long-Term Treatment of Non-Life-Threatening Conditions*, 27 October 1994.

47. P. Sjoberg, 'Data to Support the Extension of Clinical Trials', in D'Arcy and Harron (eds.), Proceedings 1996, p. 345.

48. ICH, 27 October 1994.

49. ICH, 29 November 1995.

50. M. Schwarz and M. Thompson, *Divided We Stand: Redefining Politics, Technology and Social Choice* (Hemel Hempstead, Herts: Harvester Wheatsheaf, 1990).

51. J. Abraham and G. Lewis, *Regulating Medicines in Europe: Competition, Expertise and Public Health* (London: Routledge, 2000).

Notes to Chapter 4

1. B. Miller, 'IMB fails the public over SSRIs', *Depressiondialogues.ie Newsletter*, 27 July 2005 (http://www.depressiondialogues.ie/IMB/).

2. M. Angell, *The Truth About Drug Companies: How They Deceive Us and What to Do About It* (New York: Random House, 2004), p. 239.

3. J. Abraham, 'The Pharmaceutical Industry as a Political Player', *The Lancet*, vol. 360, no. 9, 2002, p. 1498.

4. J. Abraham and G. Lewis, 'Citizenship, Medical Expertise and the Capitalist Regulatory State in Europe', *Sociology*, vol. 36, no. 1, 2002, pp. 67–88.

5. P. Kirby and M. Murphy, 'Ireland as a "Competition State"', in M. Adshead, P. Kirby and M. Millar (eds.), *Contesting the Irish State* (Manchester University Press, 2007) (forthcoming).

6. For a discussion on scientised policy-making, see P. Brown and S. Zavestoski, 'Social Movements in Health: An Introduction', in P. Brown and S. Zavestoski (eds.), *Social Movements in Health* (Oxford: Blackwell, 2005).

7. B. O'Halloran, 'Spending is Key for Drug Firms to Develop Right Chemistry', *The Irish Times*, 23 April 2004.

8. J. Abraham, *Science, Politics and the Pharmaceutical Industry: Controversy and Bias in Drug Regulation* (London: Routledge,1995); M. Levine and J. Forrence, 'Regulatory Capture, Public Interest and the Public Agenda: Toward a Synthesis', *Journal of Law, Economics and Organisation,* vol. 6, 1990, pp. 167–198.

9. For example, E. Brezis and A. Weiss, 'Conscientious Regulation and Post-regulatory Employment Restrictions', *European Journal of Political Economy,* vol. 13, 1997, pp. 517–536.

10. Abraham, *Science, Politics and the Pharmaceutical Industry.*

11. Abraham, 'The Pharmaceutical Industry as a Political Player', p. 1498.

12. Abraham and Lewis, 'Citizenship, Medical Expertise and the Capitalist Regulatory State'.

13. Kirby and Murphy, 'Ireland as a "Competition State"'.

14. P. Kirby, 'The Changing Role of the Irish State', in T. O'Connor and M. Murphy (eds.), *Social Care in Ireland* (Cork Institute of Technology, 2006) p.118.

15. Ibid.

16. Ibid.

17. Dáil debate, 28 May 1968.

18. M. Wren, *Unhealthy State: Anatomy of a Sick Society* (Dublin: New Island, 2004).

19. Dáil debate, 13 December 1972.

20. Dáil debate, 20 June 1968.

21. D. Keogh, 'Ireland and "Emergency" Culture, between Civil War and Normalcy, 1922–1961', *Ireland: A Journal of History and Society (Irish Democracy and the Right to Freedom of Information),* vol. 1, no. 1, 1995, pp. 4–43.

22. Ibid., p. 5.

23. Irish Pharmaceutical Healthcare Association, *Submission to the Enterprise Strategy Group* (Dublin: Irish Pharmaceutical Healthcare Association, 2002), p. 2.

24. Government of Ireland, *Regulating Better: A Government White Paper Setting Out Six Principles of Better Regulation* (Dublin: Stationery Office, 2004), p. 1.

25. Health Action International Europe, *Patients' Reporting of Adverse Reactions.* (Amsterdam: Health Action International Europe, 2005).

26. National Drugs Advisory Board, *Annual Report 1980* (Dublin: National Drugs Advisory Board, 1981).

27. Seanad debate, 25 October 1995.

28. P. Weedle and M. Cahill, *Medicines and Pharmacy Law in Ireland* (Dublin: Kenlis Publishers, 1991) p. 19.

29. Dáil debate, 5 July 1995.

30. M. Henry, 'Vaccination and Clinical Trials', *Irish Medical News,* 16 November 2000.

31. Report on the Lindsay Tribunal, 26 November 2001.

32. C. Van Egeraat, 'The Pharmaceutical Industry in Ireland: Agglomeration, Localisation or Simply Spatial Concentration?', NIRSA Working Paper No. 28 (Maynooth: National Institute for Regional and Spatial Analysis, 2006).
33. Seanad debate, 25 October 1995.
34. Irish Medicines Board, *Annual Report and Accounts 1997* (Dublin: Irish Medicines Board, 1998).
35. Irish Medicines Board, *Newsletter*, April 2001.
36. Irish Medicines Board, *Annual Report 2004* (Dublin: Irish Medicines Board, 2005).
37. Abraham and Lewis, 'Citizenship, Medical Expertise and the Capitalist Regulatory State'.
38. Angell, *The Truth About Drug Companies*.
39. World Health Organisation, *14th Model List of Essential Medicines* (Geneva: WHO, 2005).
40. Thanks to Colin Bradley, Professor of General Practice, University College Cork, for these estimates of the rates of reporting of ADRs by Irish doctors.
41. E. Donnellan, 'Oireachtas Body to Study Adverse Effects of Drugs', *The Irish Times*, 14 April 2006.
42. Seanad Éireann, 25 October 1995
43. Irish Medicines Board, *Newsletter*, October 2000.
44. Interview with Erica Murray, Irish Association of Health Stores, 20 October 2004.
45. Fine Gael and the Labour Party, *Fine Gael/Labour Programme for Government*, 1982.
46. Dáil debate, 20 November 1985.
47. See O. O'Donovan, and K. Glavanis-Grantham, 'Researching the Political and Cultural Influence of the Transnational Pharmaceutical Industry in Ireland', *Administration*, vol. 52, no. 3, 2004, pp. 21–42.
48. L. Tilson, K. Bennett and M. Barry, 'The Potential Impact of Implementing a System of Generic Substitution on the Community Drug Schemes in Ireland', *European Journal of Health Economics*, vol. 50, 2005, pp. 267–273.
49. Dáil debate, 12 March 1985.
50. Dáil debate, 12 March 1985.
51. Irish Pharmaceutical Healthcare Association, 2002, p. 2.
52. L. Tilson et al., 'The High Cost of Medicines in Ireland', *European Journal of Health Economics*, vol. 49, 2004, pp. 341–344. See also the chapter by Barry, Tilson and Ryan in this volume.
53. M. Wall, 'Price of 800 Common Medicines to Fall 20%', *The Irish Times*, 1 March 2007. RTÉ Investigative Unit, 'Bad Medicine' (http://www.rte.ie/radio1/investigate/1130032.html) and *Pat Kenny Show*, 7 March 2007.

54. R.J. Quinn and C. O'Neill, 'Attitudes of General Practitioners to their Interactions with Pharmaceutical Companies: A Qualitative Study', *Irish Medical Journal,* vol. 95, no. 7, 2002, pp. 199-200.

55. Irish Pharmaceutical Healthcare Association, 2002, p. 4.

56. Interview, 11 January 2005.

57. L. Toop et al., *Direct to Consumer Advertising of Prescription Drugs in New Zealand: For Health or for Profit?* (New Zealand Departments of General Practice, Christchurch, Dunedin, Wellington and Auckland Schools of Medicine, 2003).

58. R. Moynihan and D. Henry, 'The Fight against Disease Mongering: Generating Knowledge for Action', *PLoS Medicine,* vol. 3, no. 4, 2006, pp. 1–4.

59. O. O'Donovan, 'Corporate Colonization of Health Activism? Irish Health Advocacy Organizations' Modes of Engagement with Pharmaceutical Corporations', *International Journal of Health Services* vol. 37, no. 4, 2007, pp. 711-733.

60. M. Houston, 'State Gets its First Independent Website', *The Irish Times,* 27 April 2004.

Notes to Chapter 5

1. This is determined by the overall number of plants and number of employees in the pharmaceutical sector located in Cork harbour and its environs. However, it is important to acknowledge that most of the Cork-based plants are part of the drug substance sub-sector (i.e. those plants that produce active pharmaceutical ingredients (APIs) as opposed to drug products). See C. van Egeraat, 'The Pharmaceutical Industry in Ireland: Agglomeration, Localisation or Simply Spatial Concentration', NIRSA Working Paper Series, no. 28, National Institute for Regional and Spatial Analysis, NUI Maynooth, February 2006.

2. This dearth has been somewhat ameliorated by the research of van Egeraat, op. cit.

3. This secrecy was confirmed during the undertaking of a Royal Irish Academy research project by Orla O'Donovan and myself in 2004–2006 on the relationship between patient groups and the pharmaceutical industry in Ireland. See the final report at www.ria.ie/committees/pdfs/tsrp/ODonovan.pdf. See also the report by Consumers International, *Branding the Cure: A Consumer Perspective on Corporate Social Responsibility, Drug Promotion and the Pharmaceutical Industry in Europe* (London: Consumers International, 2006), where lack of transparency in reporting corporate social responsibility information is noted (p. 6).

4. O. O'Donovan and K. Glavanis-Grantham, 'Researching the Political and Cultural Influence of the Transnational Pharmaceutical Industry in Ireland', *Administration,* vol. 52, no. 3, 2004, pp. 21–42.

5. Health Action International (HAI) is an independent, global network working to increase access to essential medicines and improve their rational use. See http://www.haiweb.org.

6. B. Roche, 'Why it's Boom Time in Pharmachem', *The Irish Times,* 14 August 2004.

7. IDA, *Vital Statistics* (Dublin: IDA, 2004), p. 8; D. O'Hearn, *The Atlantic Economy: Britain, the US and Ireland* (Manchester University Press, 2001), pp. 172, 194.

8. IDA, *Vital Statistics*.

9. Ibid.

10. Y. Scannell, *Environmental and Planning Law in Ireland* (Dublin: Round Hall, 1995), p. 73.

11. Enterprise Strategy Report Group, *Ahead of the Curve: Ireland's Place in the Global Economy* (Dublin: Forfás, 2004).

12. Ibid., pp. xvii–xviii.

13. Ibid., p. xx.

14. IDA, *Vital Statistics*.

15. O'Hearn, p. 173.

16. Ibid., p. 174.

17. Ibid., p. 175.

18. Ibid.

19. Ibid.

20. Ibid.

21. Ibid., p. 176.

22. Forfás is Ireland's national policy and advisory board for enterprise, trade, science, technology and innovation. It operates under the auspices of the Department of Enterprise, Trade and Employment.

23. O'Hearn, 2001, p. 184.

24. B. O'Halloran, 'R&D is Vital to Sustaining Biotech Success', *The Irish Times*, 4 July 2003.

25. O'Hearn, 2001, op. cit., p. 179.

26. IDA, *Vital Statistics*.

27. Ibid., p. 13.

28. Ibid.

29. O'Hearn, 2001, p. 187.

30. C. Dooley, 'Report Says 2003 Set a Record for Industrial Peace', *The Irish Times*, 3 September 2004.

31. IDA, *Pharmaceuticals Ireland* (Dublin: IDA, 2004).

32. G. Mullally, 'Challenging the Illusion of Powerlessness: Social Movements, the Transnational Pharmaceutical Industry and the State in the Republic of Ireland', unpublished MA thesis in the Sociology of Development, University College Cork, Department of Sociology, 1992.

33. IDA, *Pharmaceuticals Ireland*.

34. On 8 February 2007 Pfizer announced its intention to sell off part of its plant at Loughbeg in 2008 and likewise at Little Island in 2009. This will

mean a reduction in Pfizer's presence in Cork. A. Beesley, '"Cost is a Factor but it's certainly not the overriding one". No One is Safe from Unforgiving Forces of Business,' *The Irish Times*, 9 February 2007.

35. M. Dundon, 'Pharmaceutical Giant Plans 1,000 Jobs in 650m Cork Investment', *Irish Examiner*, 28 July 2004.

36. Interview with tradesperson who has worked for over twenty years in the pharmaceutical/chemical sector in Cork harbour, 10 September 2004.

37. A. Beesley, '"Cost is a Factor but it's certainly not the overriding one". No One is Safe from Unforgiving Forces of Business,' *The Irish Times*, 9 February 2007.

38. M. Parsons, 'Sanofi-Aventis to Close Waterford Plant', *The Irish Times*, 15 March 2007.

39. Irish Business and Employers Confederation (IBEC) works to shape policies and influence decision-making in a way that develops and protects members' interests and contributes to the development and maintenance of an economy that promotes enterprise and productive employment. See www.ibec.ie.

40. B. O'Halloran, 'Looking Like the New IT', *The Irish Times*, 4 July 2003.

41. M. Dundon, '1,000 Jobs Bonanza as Drugs Giant Expands', *Irish Examiner*, 28 July 2004.

42. Interview with tradesperson who has worked for over twenty years in the pharmaceutical/chemical sector in Cork harbour, 10 September 2004.

43. O'Hearn, *Atlantic Economy*. This is also confirmed by the research of Van Egeraat, 2006.

44. Cork County Development Board, *Integrated Strategy for the Economic, Social and Cultural Development of County Cork 2002–2011* (Cork, 2001), Section 5.4.

45. South West Regional Authority, *Regional Planning Guidelines* (Cork, 2004).

46. CSO Ireland, *Statistics: Seasonally Adjusted Standardised Unemployment Rates* (Cork, 2006). See www.cso.ie/statistics/sasunemprates.htm, Accessed 8 August 2006.

47. Interview with tradesperson who has worked for over twenty years in the pharmaceutical/chemical sector in Cork harbour, 10 September 2004.

48. B. Roche, 'Why it's Boom Time', *The Irish Times*, 14 August 2004.

49. Ibid.

50. *Cork Independent*, 25 May 2006.

51. IDA, *Vital Statistics*, p. 13.

52. Ibid., p. 12.

53. Proctor & Gamble's decision in March 2007 to transfer production of its skincare products from Nenagh to Lodz, Poland, making 280 workers redundant, while not within the pharmaceutical sector, may be suggestive of possible future developments within the sector. B. Roche, 'Munster Suffers Loss of Hundreds of Jobs', *The Irish Times*, 8 March 2007.

54. Interview with tradesperson who has worked for over twenty years in the pharmaceutical/chemical sector in Cork harbour, 10 September 2004.

55. 'Drug Output', *The Irish Times,* 27 July 2004.

56. Ibid.

57. IDA, *Pharmaceuticals Ireland.*

58. S. Jacobzone, 'Pharmaceutical Policies in OECD Countries: Reconciling Social and Industrial Goals' (Paris: OECD, 2000).

59. IDA, *Pharmaceuticals Ireland.*

60. Ibid.

61. Roche, 'Why it's Boom Time', *The Irish Times,* 14 August 2004.

62. IDA, *Pharmaceuticals Ireland.*

63. L. Reid, 'Waste Issue Delays New Planning Bill', *The Irish Times,* 8 September 2004.

64. 'Dáil Passes Planning and Development Bill', *Indymedia Ireland,* 5 July 2006.

65. An Bord Pleanála was established in 1977 under the Local Government (Planning and Development) Act, 1976, and is responsible for the determination of appeals and certain other matters under the Planning and Development Acts, 2000 to 2004, and with appeals under the Building Control Act, 1990, the Local Government (Water Pollution) Acts, 1977 and 1990, and the Air Pollution Act, 1987.

66. 'Dáil Passes Planning and Development Bill', *Indymedia Ireland,* 5 July 2006. For a critical assessment of the impact of this planning law, see T. Flynn, 'The Planning and Development (Strategic Infrastructure) Bill, 2006: A Critical Analysis of Its Implications for Environmental Law', Fourth Law and the Environment Conference, Department of Law, University College Cork, 27 April 2006. Available on www.ucc.ie/en/lawsite/eventsandnews/previousevents/environapr2006/Do cumentFile,16194,en.doc.

67. Mullally, 'Challenging the Illusion of Powerlessness'.

68. R. Allen, *No Global: The People of Ireland versus the Multinationals* (London: Pluto, 2004).

69. Reid, 'Waste Issue'.

70. See www.chaseireland.org for information on this organisation and the ongoing campaign against Indaver.

71. A. Lucy, 'Cork Seen as Key to Future of South West', *The Irish Times,* 1 March 2004.

72. A. Beesley, 'Green Party Calls for Appointment of New EPA Director to be Terminated', *The Irish Times,* 28 August 2004.

73. M. Brennock, 'New Code Restricts Job Moves for Civil Servants', *The Irish Times,* 10 September 2004.

74. M. Mayoshi, ' "Globalisation", Culture, and the University', in F. Jameson and M. Mayoshi (eds.), *The Cultures of Globalization* (Durham NC: Duke University, 1998), p. 267.

75. S. Krimsky, *Science in the Private Interest: Has the Lure of Profits Corrupted Biomedical Research?* (Lanham: Rowman and Littlefield, 2003).

76. For an in-depth account of the Olivieri case, see J. Thompson, P. Baird and J. Downie, *The Olivieri Report* (Toronto: James Lorimer, 2001).

77. Krimsky, 2003, p. 215.

78. Ibid.

79. Science Foundation Ireland, *Points of Excellence* (Dublin, [2004]), p. 5.

80. Ibid.

81. Department of Enterprise, Trade and Employment, *Building Ireland's Knowledge Economy: The Irish Action Plan for Promoting Investment in Research and Development to 2010* (Dublin: Government Publications, 2004), p. 3.

82. Ibid.

83. Department of Enterprise, Trade and Employment, *Building Ireland's Knowledge Economy*.

84. Enterprise Strategy Report Group, *Ahead of the Curve: Ireland's Place in the Global Economy* (Dublin: Forfás, 2004).

85. Ibid., p. xiv.

86. IDA, *Vital Statistics*, p. 3.

87. Ibid.

88. Ibid.

89. Enterprise Strategy Report Group, p. xviii.

90. Ibid.

91. Mayoshi, ' "Globalisation", Culture, and the University'.

92. Krimsky, *Science in the Private Interest*.

93. The Alimentary Pharmabiotic Centre has established a joint research partnership with GlaxoSmithKline. See press release, Science Foundation Ireland, 12 February 2007, on www.sfi.ie, accessed 16 March 2007.

94. Science Foundation Ireland, p. 8.

95. Ibid.

96. University College Cork, Office of the President, *Growing Excellence* (Cork, 2003).

97. Interview with Jean van Sinderen-Law, Director of Development, University College Cork, 31 August 2004.

98. University College Cork, *Careers Service Annual Report 2003* (Cork, 2004).

99. See http://cufdevelopment.ucc.ie/current_prog.php and http://cuf development.ucc.ie/documents/SchoolofPharmacy_001.pdf, accessed on 6 August 2006.

100. The Embark Initiative is operated by the Irish Research Council for Science, Engineering and Technology (IRCSET) and the development with Pfizer marks the start of IRCSET's 2006 Industry Partnership Programme: 'intended to *broaden* the experience of Embark scholars . . . through exposure to *commercially orientated research practices* and technological advancements within industry' (my emphasis). See www.ircset.ie/eps/pdfs/pfizer.pdf.

101. See the Pfizer Ireland website http://www.pfizer.ie.

102. Roche, 'Why it's Boom Time'.

103. See chapters nine, ten and eleven in this volume. See also Public Citizen's work on the influence of the TPI in the US at www.publiccitizen.org, as well as the excellent analysis by R. Moynihan and A. Cassels, *Selling Sickness: How the World's Biggest Pharmaceutical Companies Are Turning Us All into Patients* (Vancouver/Toronto: Greystone Books, 2005).

104. Medicines for All pamphlet [n.d.].

105. B. Woods, *Dying for Drugs*, Channel Four, 2003.

106. Medicines for All pamphlet [n.d.], op. cit.; communication with Lilian Collier, founding member of Medicines for All, 13 September 2004.

107. Medicines for All pamphlet [n.d.], op. cit.

108. Woods, 2003, op. cit.

109. Ibid.; Woods, *Dying for Drugs*. For more recent information on this shocking case, see P. Rost, 'Dead Children, an Unapproved Drug, a Silenced Whistleblower, and a Secret Report', 5 August 2006, at http://www.huffingtonpost.com/dr-peter-rost/dead-children-an approv_b_20594.html. Rost, a former Vice President of Pfizer, who warned the company about their illegal marketing of growth hormones in January 2003, was likewise fired.

110. See Pfizer's website http://www.pfizer.ie/ under the section on values and community.

111. Medicines for All pamphlet [n.d.].

112. Communication with Lilian Collier, 13 September 2004.

113. Woods, *Dying for Drugs*.

114. Communication with Lilian Collier, 13 September 2004.

115. For an analysis of this dimension of state policy, see J. Abraham and G. Lewis, 'Citizenship, Medical Expertise and the Capitalist Regulatory State in Europe', *Sociology*, vol. 36, no. 1, 2002, pp. 67–88.

116. *Sunday Independent*, 5 September 2004.

117. Analysts refer to the 1980s as the 'Lost Decade' for countries of the South, as due to indebtedness, much of the socio-economic gains of the post-independence era were lost, especially in sub-Saharan Africa.

118. United Nations Development Programme, *UN Human Development Report 2003* (New York, 2004).

119. P. Cullen, 'Ireland Ranks Second in UN Poverty Index', *The Irish Times*, 16 July 2004.

Notes to Chapter 6

1. M. Barry, A. Heerey and J. Feely, 'Drug Reimbursement in Ireland', *Irish Medical Journal*, vol. 93, no. 3, 2000, pp. 71–74.

2. L. Tilson, B. McGowan and K. Bennett, 'The High Cost of Medicines in Ireland', *European Journal of Health Economics*, vol. 49, 2004, pp. 341–344.

3. General Medical Services Payments Board, *Report for the Year Ending 31st December 2004* (Dublin: GMS Payments Board, 2004) pp. 1–51.

4. Ibid.

5. Ibid.

6. M. Barry, 'Drug Expenditure in Ireland 1991–2001', *Irish Medical Journal*, vol. 95, no. 10, 2002, pp. 294–295.

7. J. Feely, 'The Influence of Pharmacoeconomic Factors on Prescribing Patterns in Ireland', *Pharmacoeconomics*, vol. 2, 1992, pp. 99–106.

8. L. Tilson, K. Bennett and M. Barry, 'The Potential Impact of Implementing a System of Generic Substitution on the Community Drug Schemes in Ireland', *European Journal of Health Economics*, vol. 50, 2005, pp. 267–273.

9. Ibid.

10. Ibid.

11. M. Barry, 'Pricing and Reimbursement of Medicines in Ireland', *Public Affairs Ireland*, vol. 32, 2006, pp. 14–15.

12. The Association of the European Self-Medication Industry, *Economic and Legal Framework for Non-Prescription Medicines*, June 2004. Available at *http://www.aesgp.be*.

Notes to Chapter 7

1. The General Medical Services (GMS) is a scheme to provide for the medical needs of the poorest in Irish society who are unable to provide for their own needs. Eligibility is determined primarily on grounds of insufficient income. Thus, for example, people entirely dependent on state benefits for their income are included. People entitled to full GMS cover do not have to pay for their medicines, as these costs are met by the state on their behalf. People without full GMS eligibility pay for the entire costs of their medicines, including pharmacists' dispensing fee, at the time of obtaining them. However, if they are registered for the Drug Purchase Scheme, the costs of any medicines supplied to them or their family in excess of €85 per month (as of February 2007) do not have to be paid by them but are refunded to the pharmacist on their behalf by the state.

2. Under this agreement, the state will receive a 35 per cent reduction in the price of off-patent drugs and new drugs prices will be based on the price of drugs in a wider basket of EU countries, including Spain, Austria and Belgium (where drug prices had, traditionally, been lower). However, under the agreement, Ireland will not introduce an automatic health economics assessment requirement on the introduction of all new drugs (as other countries such as the UK and Canada have done) and there will be no restriction on doctors' or patients' choice of medicines. The IPHA have welcomed the agreement as providing more 'headroom' to afford more innovative medicines.

3. C. Bradley, E. Holme Hansen and S. Kooiker, 'Patients and their Medicines', in E. Mossialos, M. Mrazek and T. Walley (eds.), *Regulating Pharmaceuticals in Europe: Striving for Efficiency, Equity and Quality* (Maidenhead: Open University Press, 2004), pp. 158–176.

4. Irish Pharmaceutical Healthcare Association, *The Value of Medicines* (Dublin: Irish Pharmaceutical Healthcare Association, 1999).

5. C. Chaix-Couturier et al., 'Effects of Financial Incentives on Medical Practice: Results from a Systematic Review of the Literature and Methodological Issues', *International Journal for Quality Health Care*, vol. 12, 2000, pp. 133–142.

6. The Medical Council is the regulatory body for the medical profession in Ireland. It was established under the Medical Practitioners Act, 1978 and it provides for the registration of medical practitioners and has responsibility for investigation and prosecution of allegations of professional misconduct. However, it may only investigate a doctor on foot of a specific complaint from a person or other legal entity (such as a limited company) and its determinations regarding whether or not a doctor is fit to practise are subject to judicial review by the High Court. It is, thus, restricted to investigation and prosecution of the most serious cases of professional misconduct in which a clear and specific allegation is made supported by sufficient evidence to prove the case against the doctor beyond reasonable doubt.

7. O. O'Donovan, 'Corporate Colonization of Health Activism? Irish Health Advocacy Organizations' Modes of Engagement with Pharmaceutical Corporations', *International Journal of Health Services*, Vol. 37, no. 4, 2007, pp. 711-733.

8. Irish Pharmaceutical Healthcare Association, *Facts and Figures 2006* (Dublin: Irish Pharmaceutical Healthcare Association, 2006).

9. Drug budgeting, or the Indicative Drug Target Scheme, was introduced in 1993 as a means to encourage GPs to help moderate prescribing expenditure within the GMS. Expenditure on drugs prescribed under the GMS exceeds all other costs of providing general medical services to eligible patients and at the time of the introduction of the scheme these costs were rising very steeply. Under the scheme, modelled on a similar scheme introduced in the UK, a doctor is assigned an indicative drug budget target for his or her GMS patients. Budgets are set with regard to the numbers of GMS patients and their ages and genders (allowing for the fact that older patients generally require more medicines). A GP whose prescribing incurs expenditure below the indicative target budget set is allowed to retain a proportion of the difference between the actual cost and the budget set for specified practice developments. The proportion allowed depends on how the doctors' prescribing costs compare to the target budget set for them. The scheme is renegotiated and refined in discussions with the Irish Medical Organisation (the doctors' union and representative body) on an ongoing basis.

10. J. Silcock et al., 'The Cost of Medicines in the United Kingdom: A Survey of General Practitioners' Opinions and Knowledge', *Pharmacoeconomics*, vol. 11, no. 1, 1997, pp. 56–63.

11. J. P. Kassirer, *On the Take: How Medicine's Complicity with Big Business Can Endanger Your Health* (Oxford University Press, 2005).

12. M. Angell, 'The Hard Sell . . . Lures, Bribes and Kick Backs', in M. Angell, *The Truth about Drug Companies: How They Deceive Us and What to Do About It* (New York: Random House, 2004), pp. 115–134; M. Angell, 'Marketing Masquerading as Education', ibid., pp. 135–155; and M. Angell, 'Marketing Masquerading as Research', ibid., pp. 156–172.

13. R. Moynihan, 'Who Pays for the Pizza? Redefining the Relationships between Doctors and Drug Companies. 1: Entanglement', *British Medical Journal*, vol. 26, 2003, pp. 1189–1192.

14. Irish Pharmaceutical Healthcare Association, *IPHA Code of Marketing Practice for the Pharmaceutical Industry*, 5th edition (Dublin: Irish Pharmaceutical Healthcare Association, 1999), p. 14.

15. Even a basic stethoscope would cost the doctor at least €20 and a basic sphygmomanometer would be at least €30 (2007 prices).

16. J. Lexchin, 'Interactions Between Physicians and the Pharmaceutical Industry: What Does the Literature Say?', *Canadian Medical Association Journal*, vol. 149, 1993, pp. 1401–1407.

17. R. Quinn and C. O'Neill, 'Attitudes of General Practitioners to Their Interactions with Pharmaceutical Companies: A Qualitative Study', *Irish Medical Journal*, vol. 95, 2002, pp. 199–200.

18. J. P. Kassirer, 'Influenced by Gifts? Not I!', in J.P. Kassirer, *On The Take*, pp. 63–78.

19. R. V. Gibbons et al., 'A Comparison of Physicians' and Patients' Attitudes Toward Pharmaceutical Industry Gifts', *Journal of General Internal Medicine*, vol. 13, 1998, pp. 151–154.

20. R. Adair, 'Hidden Costs of Free Samples', *Virtual Mentor Ethics Journal of the American Medical Association*, vol. 8, no. 6, 2006, pp. 367–371.

21. Irish Pharmaceutical Healthcare Association, *Code of Marketing Practice*, 1999, p. 14.

22. A. Harding, 'European and US Groups Draw Up Standards for CME', *British Medical Journal*, vol. 328, 2004, p. 1279.

23. A. Fugh-Berman and S. Batt, ' "This May Sting a Bit": Cutting CME's Ties to Pharma', *Virtual Mentor Ethics Journal of the American Medical Association*, vol. 8, no. 6, 2006, pp. 412–415; Editorial, 'What's Wrong with CME?', *Canadian Medical Association Journal*, vol. 170, 2004, p. 917.

24. Payments to doctors for entering patients into clinical studies can range from the order of €100 to more than €1,000 *per patient* entered, usually depending on the complexity of the study and the amount of effort deemed to be required from the participating clinician. In some clinical departments, such funds are used to fund other non-sponsored research or to pay other expenses of researchers (such as travel to scientific meetings), but there is no absolute obligation on clinicians to place these funds at the disposal of their institution.

25. J. E. Bekelman, Y. Li and C. P. Gross, 'Scope and Impact of Financial Conflicts of Interest in Biomedical Research: A Systematic Review', *Journal of the American Medical Association*, vol. 289, 2003, pp. 454–465; J. Lexchin et al., 'Pharmaceutical Industry Sponsorship and Research Outcome and Quality: Systematic Review', *British Medical Journal*, vol. 326, 2003, pp. 1167–1170.

26. C. Medawar and A. Hardon, 'Regulatory Dependencies', in C. Medawar and A. Hardon, *Medicines Out of Control? Antidepressants and the Conspiracy of Goodwill* ([Amsterdam]: Aksant Academic Publishers, 2004), pp. 133–158.

27. R. Moynihan, 'Cochrane at Crossroads over Drug Company Sponsorship', *British Medical Journal*, vol. 327, 2003, pp. 924–926.

28. J. Lenzer, 'New Cochrane Policy Tightens Limits on Industry Funding', *British Medical Journal*, vol. 328, 2004, p. 976.

29. Payment for participation in simple market research (e.g. by filling in a questionnaire) would not usually exceed €20 or €30.

30. M. Angell, 'Marketing Masquerading as Research', pp. 156–172.

31. J. P. Kassirer, 'Blatant Promotion of Off-label Drugs?, in J.P Kassirer, *On the Take*, pp. 27–28.

32. J. P. Kassirer, 'Institutional Conflicts of Interest?, in J.P. Kassirer, *On the Take*, pp. 57–58.

33. Irish Pharmaceutical Healthcare Association, *Facts and Figures*.

34. L. Tilson et al., 'Generic Drug Utilisation on the General Medical Services (GMS) Scheme in 2001', *Irish Medical Journal*, vol. 96, no. 6, 2003, pp. 176–179.

35. All medicines have a non-proprietary (or generic) name and most are available under one or more brand name. When medicines are first launched on the market (and are still under patent), there is only one brand available, so that, even if the medicine is prescribed by its generic (or non-proprietary) name, the branded product will have to be dispensed. However, when the drug comes off patent, a number of brands of the same medicine may become available. Generic brands are typically cheaper (sometimes much cheaper) than the original brand. In some countries, generic substitution is allowed whereby a pharmacist can (and is usually encouraged to) dispense the cheapest brand available, even when the doctor has used a brand name–although such systems do allow the doctor to insist, usually by some additional endorsement on the prescription, on a particular brand being prescribed (i.e. a generic substitution not being made).

36. Generic prescribing rate refers to the proportion of drugs prescribed in their non-proprietary form.

37. J. Feely et al., 'Low Rate of Generic Prescribing in the Republic of Ireland Compared to England and Northern Ireland: Prescribers' Concerns', *Irish Medical Journal*, vol. 90, 1997, pp. 146–147.

38. Tilson et al., 'Generic Drug Utilisation'

39. Ibid.

40. E. Donnellan, 'Generic Drugs Could Save State "Millions"', *The Irish Times*, 12 July 2005.

41. See *www.ipha.ie/htm/mediacentre/download/issue_documents/Generic_ Medicines.pdf. Accessed on 8 March 2007.*

42. Quinn and O'Neill, 'Attitudes of General Practitioners'.

43. B. O'Mahony, 'Interactions Between a General Practitioner and Representatives of Drug Companies', *British Medical Journal*, vol. 306, 1993, p. 1649.

44. M. Houston, 'Doctors and Drug Firms: An Unhealthy Alliance?' *The Irish Times*, 6 April 2004.

45. Irish Pharmaceutical Healthcare Association, *Code of Marketing Practice for the Pharamaceutical Industry*, 6th edn (Dublin: Irish Pharmaceutical Healthcare Association, 2006); Irish Pharmaceutical Healthcare Association, *Code of Standards of Advertising Practice for the Consumer Healthcare Industry*, 4th edn (Dublin: Irish Pharmaceutical Healthcare Association, 1999).

46. Medical Council, *A Guide to Ethical Conduct and Behaviour* (Dublin: Medical Council, 2004), p. 23.

47. Irish College of General Practitioners, *Pharmaceutical Sponsorship of ICGP Accredited Meetings: Guidelines* (Dublin: Irish College of General Practitioners, 2003).

Notes to Chapter 8

1. T. Lynch, *Beyond Prozac: Healing Mental Distress,* 2nd edition (Cork: Mercier Press, 2005). The first edition of this book was published under the title *Beyond Prozac: Healing Mental Suffering Without Drugs* (Blackrock: Marino, 2001). The British edition was published under the title *Beyond Prozac: Healing Mental Distress* (Ross-on-Wye: PCCS Books, 2004).

2. Government of Ireland, Department of Health and Children, *A Vision for Change: Report of the Expert Group on Mental Health Policy* (Dublin: Stationery Office, 2006).

3. R. J. Quinn and C. O'Neill, 'Attitudes of General Practitioners to their Interactions with Pharmaceutical Companies: A Qualitative Study', *Irish Medical Journal*, vol. 95, 2002.

4. A. Rynne, 'Special Relationships between Doctors and Drug Companies', *Irish Medical News*, 16 August 2004.

5. Ibid.

6. RTÉ, *Prime Time*, 17 May 2004.

7. Ibid.

8. Ibid.

9. Extract from letter from me to Irish Medicines Board, 19 October 2002.

10. Extract from letter to me from the Irish Medicines Board, 14 November 2002.

11. See www.socialaudit.org.uk.

12. C. Medawar, *Power and Dependence: Social Audit on the Safety of Medicines* (London: Social Audit, 1992); C. Medawar, 'Antidepressants: Hooked on the Happy Drug', *What Doctors Don't Tell You* (London: Social Audit, 1998).

13. Medawar, *Power and Dependence.*

14. The DSM-III, which is published by the American Psychiatric Association, is the main diagnostic reference of health professionals in the USA.

15. DSM-VI (1994).

16. Medawar, http://www.socialaudit.org.uk.

17. RTÉ, *Prime Time,* 17 May 2004.

18. The Cochrane Collaboration is an international non-profit and independent organisation, dedicated to making up-to-date, accurate information about the effects of healthcare readily available worldwide. It produces and disseminates systematic reviews of healthcare interventions and promotes the search for evidence in the form of clinical trials and other studies of interventions. See www.cochrane.org.

19. RTÉ, *Prime Time,* 17 May 2004.

20. Ibid.

21. Ibid.

22. M. Copty, *Mental Health in Primary Care* (Dublin: Irish College of General Practitioners and the South West Area Health Board, 2004).

23. RTÉ, *Prime Time,* 17 May 2004.

24. Ibid.

25. P. Thomas and P. Bracken, 'Time for Openness on Antidepressants', *The Guardian*, 4 March 2002; C. Chilvers et al., 'Antidepressant Drugs and Generic Counselling for Treatment of Major Depression in Primary Care: Randomised Trial with Patient Preference Arms', *British Medical Journal*, vol. 322, 2002, p. 772.

26. House of Commons Health Committee, *The Influence of the Pharmaceutical Industry* (HC 42–1), 5 April 2005.

Notes to Chapter 9

1. Health Canada is the federal department responsible for helping the people of Canada maintain and improve their health. In partnership with provincial and territorial governments, it provides national leadership to develop health policy, enforce health regulations, promote disease prevention and enhance healthy living for all Canadians. The TPD only approves and monitors prescription and non-prescription drugs derived from chemical manufacturing and medical devices; the Biologics and Genetic Therapies Directorate (BGTD) is responsible for biological and radiopharmaceutical drugs, including blood and blood products, viral and bacterial vaccines, genetic therapeutic products, tissues, organs and xenografts. While responsible for different types of products, both directorates function in an almost identical manner and for purposes of this chapter the term TPD will be used for both.

2.   M. M. Atkinson and W. D. Coleman, *The State, Business, and Industrial Change in Canada* (University of Toronto Press, 1989).

3.   See TPD News at www.hc-sc.gc.ca/hpfb-dgpsa/tpd-dpt.

4.   KPMG Consulting LP, *Review of the Therapeutic Products Programme Cost Recovery Initiative*, vol. 1 (Ottawa, June 2000).

5.   G. W. Lawson, *Impact of User Fees (i.e. Drug Industry Fees) on Changes Within the FDA* (University of La Verne, College of Business and Public Management, 2005). Accessed 26 March 2005 at www.fdastudy.com.

6.   Assessed prior to being publicly broadcast.

7.   D. M. Michols, *Drugs and Medical Devices Programme Quality Initiative Bulletin*, no. *2* (Ottawa: Health Protection Branch, 1997).

8.   Therapeutic Products Directorate, *Business Transformation Progress Report* (Ottawa: Health Canada, [no date]), p. 1.

9.   Government of Canada, *The Canada We Want: Speech from the Throne to Open the Second Session of the Thirty-Seventh Parliament of Canada* (2003). Accessed 6 July 2004 at www.sft-ddt.gc.ca/vnav/07_e.htm.

10.   External Advisory Committee on Smart Regulation, *Risk Management* [no date]. Accessed 2 February 2004 at http://www.pco-bcp.gc.ca/smartreg-regint/en/05/01/i4–01.html.

11.   Health Canada, *Health Protection Legislative Renewal: Detailed Legislative Proposal* (Ottawa: 2003).

12.   Royal Society of Canada, *Elements of Precaution: Recommendations for the Regulation of Food Biotechnology in Canada: An Expert Panel Report on the Future of Food Biotechnology* (Ottawa: Royal Society of Canada, 2001), p. 200.

13.   Ibid.

14.   M. E. Wiktorowicz, 'Shifting Priorities at the Health Protection Branch: Challenges to the Regulatory Process', *Canadian Public Administration*, vol. 43, 2000, pp. 1–22.

15.   All figures are in Canadian dollars except where otherwise indicated.

16.   Department of Finance, Canada, *Building the Canada We Want. Budget 2003: Investing in Canada's Health Care System* [cat. no. F1–23/2003] (Ottawa, 2003). Accessed 6 July 2004 at www.fin.gc.ca/budget03/booklets/bkheae.htm.

17.   Health Canada, *Improving Canada's Regulatory Process for Therapeutic Products: Building the Action Plan* (Ottawa: Public Policy Forum Multistakeholder Consultation, 2003). Accessed 6 July 2004 at www.ppforum.ca/ow/ow_e_05–2003/Presentation%20_Overview_of_Action_Plan.pdf.

18.   The Speech from the Throne is delivered at the start of a new parliamentary session and outlines, in general terms, the government's legislative goals for that session.

19.   N. S. B. Rawson, 'Timeliness of Review and Approval of New Drugs in Canada from 1999 Through 2001: Is Progress Being Made?', *Clinical Therapeutics*, vol. 25, 2001, pp. 1230–1247.

20. Patented Medicine Prices Review Board, *Annual Report 2001* (Ottawa, 2002).

21. The brand-name companies are generally the large multinational firms marketing patented medications.

22. Canada's Research-Based Pharmaceutical Companies, *Improving Health Through Innovation: A New Deal for Canadians* (Ottawa: Rx&D, 2002).

23. Green Shield Canada, *Drug Cost Analysis, 1997–2001* (Toronto, 2002).

24. Business Coalition on Cost Recovery, *Roy Cullen Congratulated on Passage of C-212* (Toronto, 2004). Accessed 6 July 2004 at www2.cdn-news.com/scripts/ccnrelease.pl?/2004/03/26/0326095n.html?cp=baystreet2.

25. Adverse drug reactions are reported on a voluntary basis by either healthcare professionals or patients to either the manufacturer or Health Canada. The manufacturer has a legal obligation to forward on to Health Canada any reports that it receives.

26. Progestic International Inc., *Final Report for the Financial Models Project* (Ottawa: Health Canada, 2004).

27. Adverse drug reaction reporting forms contain a number of fields for different types of information. The 'causality' field is the one used to assign the likelihood that the reaction being reported is actually due to the drug being taken.

28. 'Adverse Drug Reaction Reporting–1998', *Canadian Adverse Drug Reaction Newsletter*, vol. 9, no. 2, 1999, pp. 5–6.

29. 'Adverse Reaction Reporting–2005', *Canadian Adverse Drug Reaction Newsletter*, vol. 16, no. 2, 2006, pp. 2–3.

30. Abnormal heart rhythms.

31. 'Cisapride: Arrhythmia Awareness', *Canadian Adverse Drug Reaction Newsletter*, vol. 6, no. 3, 1996, pp. 1–2.

32. 'Cisapride (Prepulsid®): Interactions with Grapefruit and Drugs', *Canadian Adverse Drug Reaction Newsletter*, vol. 10, no. 1, 2000, pp. 1–3.

33. 'The Top 200 Drugs of 1997', *Pharmacy Practice*, vol. 13, no. 12, 1997, pp. 29, 30, 32, 34, 36, 39, 40; 'The Top 200 Drugs of 1999', *Pharmacy Practice*, vol. 15, no. 12, 1999, pp. 39–42, 44, 46, 47.

34. J. Abraham and C. Davis, 'A Comparative Analysis of Drug Safety Withdrawals in the UK and the US (1971–1992): Implications for Current Regulatory Thinking and Policy', *Social Science and Medicine*, vol. 61, 2005, pp. 881–892.

35. Ibid.

36. Office of Inspector General, *FDA's Review Process for New Drug Applications: A Management Review* [OE1–01–01–00590] (Washington: Department of Health and Human Services, 2003).

37. P. Lurie and S. M. Wolfe, *FDA Medical Officers Report Lower Standards Permit Dangerous Drug Approvals* (Washington: Public Citizen, 1998).

38. Office of Inspector General, FDA's Review Process.

39. Drugs go through three phases of testing before they are marketed. In Phase One they are tested in healthy volunteers to determine the metabolic and

pharmacological actions of the drug in humans, the side effects associated with increasing doses and, if possible, to gain early evidence on effectiveness. Phase Two testing takes place in several hundred people and consists of controlled clinical studies conducted to obtain some preliminary data on the effectiveness of the drug for a particular indication or indications in patients with the disease or condition. Phase Three testing usually involves several hundred to several thousand patients and is intended to gather the additional information about effectiveness and safety that is needed to evaluate the overall benefit–risk relationship of the drug. Post-marketing studies are referred to as Phase Four tests.

40. L. D. Sasich, P. Lurie and S. M. Wolfe, *The Drug Industry's Performance in Finishing Postmarketing Research (Phase IV) Studies: A Public Citizen's Health Research Group Report* (Washington: Public Citizen, 2000).

41. Biologics are derived from living sources and include blood products, vaccines and products that come from the use of biotechnology.

42. Food and Drug Administration, *Report to Congress: Reports on Postmarketing Studies* [FDAMA 30] (Washington, 2002).

43. 'Lessons from Cisapride', *Canadian Medical Association Journal*, vol. 164, 2001, p. 1269.

44. 'Postmarketing Drug Surveillance: What It Would Take to Make It Work', *Canadian Medical Association Journal*, vol. 165, 2001, p. 1293.

45. Women and Health Protection (WHP) is a coalition of community groups, researchers, journalists and activists concerned about the safety of pharmaceutical drugs. The group keeps a close watch over the proposed changes in the federal health protection legislation and examines the impact of those changes on women's health.

46. Colleen Fuller, *Women and Adverse Drug Reactions: Reporting in the Canadian Context* (Toronto: Women and Health Protection, 2002).

47. House of Commons Standing Committee on Health, *Opening the Medicine Cabinet: First Report on Health Aspects of Prescription Drugs* (Ottawa, 2004).

48. International Working Group on Transparency and Accountability in Drug Regulation, *Statement* (Amsterdam: Health Action International, 1996).

49. T. O. McGarity and S. A. Shapiro, 'The Trade Secret Status of Health and Safety Testing Information: Reforming Agency Disclosure Policies', *Harvard Law Review*, vol. 93, 1980, pp. 837–888.

50. International Working Group on Transparency and Accountability in Drug Regulation, *Statement*; T. O. McGarity and S. A. Shapiro, 'The Trade Status of Health and Safety'.

51. J. Lexchin and B. Mintzes, 'Transparency in Drug Regulation: Mirage or Oasis', *Canadian Medical Association Journal*, vol. 171, 2002, pp. 1363–1365.

52. Researchers a priori designate certain outcomes from clinical trials as either primary or secondary, depending on their significance.

53. In a clinical trial patients typically are randomised to receive either the product being tested, a comparator medication or a placebo. Each group is referred to as a 'treatment arm'.

54. Health Canada, *Health Protection Legislative Renewal: Detailed Legislative Proposal* (Ottawa, 2003), pp. 76–77.

55. Laurence Hirsch, 'Randomized Clinical Trials: What Gets Published and When?', *Canadian Medical Association Journal*, vol. 170, 2004, pp. 481–483.

56. This was a committee established by the Science Advisory Board to inform itself on the drug review process. The Committee was charged with reviewing existing reports about the drug approval process and the process itself and to report back to the Science Advisory Board.

57. Science Advisory Board Committee on the Drug Review Process, *Report to Health Canada* (Ottawa, 2000), p. 9.

58. Ibid.

59. House of Commons Standing Committee on Health, *Opening the Medicine Cabinet*.

60. Government of Canada, *Food and Drugs Act* [C.01.044]. Accessed on 23 October 2004 at http://lois.justice.gc.ca/en/F-27/C.R.C.-c.870/125114.html.

61. J. Lexchin, 'Enforcement of Codes Governing Pharmaceutical Promotion: What Happens When Companies Breach Advertising Guidelines?', *Canadian Medical Association Journal*, vol. 156, 1997, pp. 351–357.

62. J. Lexchin and I. Kawachi, 'Voluntary Codes of Pharmaceutical Marketing: Controlling Promotion or Licensing Deception', in P. Davis (ed.), *Contested Ground: Public Purpose and Private Interest in the Regulation of Prescription Drugs* (New York: Oxford University Press, 1996), pp. 221–235.

63. Government of Canada, *Food and Drugs Act*.

64. D. M. Michols, *The Distinction Between Advertising and Other Activities* (Ottawa: Health Canada, Therapeutic Products Programme, 1996); L. B. Rowsell, *Advertising Campaigns of Branded and Unbranded Messages* (Ottawa: Health Canada, Therapeutic Products Directorate, 2000).

65. D. M. Gardner, B. Mintzes and A. Ostry, 'Direct-to-Consumer Prescription Drug Advertising in Canada: Permission by Default', *Canadian Medical Association Journal*, vol. 169, 2003, pp. 425–428.

66. CBC-TV Undercurrents, *The Battle Over a Drug Ad* (transcript) (Toronto: Canadian NewsDisc, 2001).

67. Second-line agents are drugs kept in reserve and only used when there is either no or an inadequate response to the most appropriate treatment choice.

68. Barbara Mintzes, personal communication, November 2003.

69. J. Lexchin and B. Mintzes, 'Direct-to-Consumer Advertising of Prescription Drugs: The Evidence Says No', *Journal of Public Policy and Marketing*, vol. 21, 2002, pp. 194–201.

70. R. A. Bell, M. S. Wilkes and R. L. Kravitz, 'The Educational Value of Consumer-Targeted Prescription Drug Advertising', *Journal of Family Practice*, vol. 49, 2000, pp. 1092–1098.

71. B. Mintzes et al., 'Influence of Direct to Consumer Pharmaceutical Advertising and Patients' Requests on Prescribing Decisions: Two Site Cross Sectional Survey', *British Medical Journal*, vol. 324, 2002, pp. 278–279.

72. Cross-sectional surveys are used to gather information on a population at a single point in time.

73. S. Findlay, *Prescription Drugs and Mass Media Advertising, 2000* (Washington: National Institute of Health Care Management, 2002).

74. K. E. Lasser et al., 'Timing of New Black Box Warnings and Withdrawals for Prescription Medications', *Journal of the American Medical Association*, vol. 287, 2002, pp. 2215–2220.

75. A. Wood, 'The Safety of New Medicines: The Importance of Asking the Right Questions', *Journal of the American Medical Association*, vol. 281, 2000, pp. 1753–1754.

76. Health Canada, *Health Protection*.

77. Canada's Research-Based Pharmaceutical Companies, *Advertising Prescription Medicines in Canada: Why It Makes Sense* (Ottawa: Rx&D, 2002).

78. S. Cordon, 'Lift Ban on Drug Ads, Newspaper Group Says,' *The Windsor Star*, 11 June 2003, p. A11.

79. D. Wong-Rieger, 'Antiquated Drug Advertising Laws Need to Get With the Times', *Globe and Mail*, 2 June 2000, p. B9.

80. Canadian Treatment Action Council, *Position Paper on Direct to Consumer Advertising (DTCA) of Prescription Medications* (Toronto, 1999); B. Mintzes and R. Baraldi, *Direct-to-Consumer Prescription Drug Advertising: When Public Health Is No Longer a Priority* (Toronto: Women and Health Protection, 2001).

81. 'Ads and Prescription Pads', *Canadian Medical Association Journal*, vol. 169, 2003, p. 381.

82. Gardner, Mintzes and Ostry, 'Direct-to-Consumer Prescription Drug Advertising'.

83. The TGA is the equivalent of the TPD.

84. H. Lofgren and R. de Boer, 'Pharmaceuticals in Australia: Developments in Regulation and Governance', *Social Science and Medicine*, vol. 58, 2004, pp. 2397–2407.

85. L. A. Suydam and M. J. Kubic, 'FDA's Implementation of FDAMA: An Interim Balance Sheet,' *Food and Drug Law Journal*, vol. 56, 2001, pp. 131–135.

86. House of Commons Health Committee, *The Influence of the Pharmaceutical Industry: Fourth Report of Session 2004–05*, vol. 1 [Report no. HC 42–1] (London: Stationery Office, 2005).

87. *Reorienting European Medicines Policy* (Paris: Prescrire International, June 2002).
88. International Society of Drug Bulletins, *ISDB Assessment of Nine European Public Assessment Reports Published by the European Medicines Evaluation Agency (EMEA)* (Paris, 1998).
89. *Reorienting European Medicines Policy.*
90. IMS Health, *U.S. Data Indices – Promotion, 2003* (IMS Health Inc., 2004). Accessed 4 August 2005 at *http://www.imshealth.com/ims/portal/front/indexC/ 0,2773,6599_44304752_0,00.html.*
91. General Accounting Office, *FDA Oversight of Direct-to-Consumer Advertising Has Limitations* (Washington, 2002).
92. S. Coney, 'Direct-to-Consumer Advertising of Prescription Pharmaceuticals: A Consumer Perspective From New Zealand', *Journal of Public Policy & Marketing*, vol. 21, 2002, pp. 213–223.

Notes to Chapter 10

1. Selective serotonin reuptake inhibitor.
2. Much of this account is based on Charles Medawar and Anita Hardon, *Medicines Out of Control? Antidepressants and the Conspiracy of Goodwill* ([Amsterdam]: Aksant, 2004); House of Commons Health Committee, *The Influence of the Pharmaceutical Industry* (HC 42–1), 5 April 2005; and www.socialaudit.org.uk, especially the 'What's New?' section.
3. C. Medawar and A. Hardon, *Medicines Out of Control?*
4. Ibid., p. 138 ff.
5. D. Healey, *Let Them Eat Prozac* (Toronto: James Lorimer, 2003).
6. Since 1964, doctors have been asked to report suspected adverse reactions to drugs on special 'Yellow Cards' to the CSM. These forms are widely distributed, e.g. in the British National Formulary and the MHRA website. The reports that the CSM considers 'serious' are tabulated and analysed and are the mainstay of its pharmacovigilance programme. The results are intended to provide better information to health professionals and the public on the use of marketed medicines; warnings are issued, a few drugs are withdrawn from the market.
7. J. S. Price et al., 'A Comparison of the Post-marketing Safety of Four Selective Serotonin Reuptake Inhibitors including the Investigation of Symptoms Occurring on Withdrawal', *British Journal of Clinical Pharmacology*, vol. 42, 1996, pp. 757–763.
8. C. Medawar et al., 'Paroxetine, *Panorama* and User Reporting of ADRs: Consumer Intelligence Matters in Clinical Practice and Post-marketing Drug Surveillance', *International Journal of Risk and Safety in Medicine*, vol. 15, no. 4, 2002, pp. 161–169. (published in May 2003). Available at http://www.socialaudit.org.uk/IJRSM-161–169.pdf.
9. See Medawar and Hardon, pp. 161–162.
10. MIND (www.mind.org.uk) is the National Association for Mental Health, the leading mental health charity in the UK.

11. C. Medawar and A. Herxheimer, 'A Comparison of Adverse Drug Reaction Reports from Professionals and Users, Relating to Risk of Dependence and Suicidal Behaviour with Paroxetine' *International Journal of Risk & Safety in Medicine*, vol. 16, 2003/4, pp. 3–17. Available at http://www.socialaudit.org.uk/YELLOW%20CARD%20REVIEW.pdf.

12. For full quotations, see House of Commons Health Committee, *The Influence of the Pharmaceutical Industry.*

13. Efexor is produced by Wyeth.

14. C. Martinez, S. Rietbrock, L. Wise, D. Ashby, J. Chick, J. Moseley, S. Evans and D. Gunnell, 'Antidepressant Treatment and the Risk of Fatal and Non-fatal Self Harm in First Episode Depression: Nested Case-Control Study', *British Medical Journal*, vol. 330, 2005, pp. 389–393.

15. Medawar and Herxheimer, 'A Comparison of Adverse Drug Reaction Reports.'

16. See Social Audit website, February 2007.

17. Social Audit Ltd is a small non-profit organisation in London. 'Social audits' are analogous to financial audits: reports on the way any organisation is performing its duty to everyone affected by what it does. Social Audit Ltd 'aims to ask timely questions about the organisations whose decisions and actions shape public life. What, in social terms, do these organisations give to and take from the community, and how do they explain and justify what they do? Social Audit papers and reports seek to explain why these questions seem worth asking and what the answers to them seem to be. In recent years Social Audit has focused mainly on medicines policy. Social Audit's concern applies to all organisations and to any government, whatever its politics. The issues may differ, but the conclusions always tend to be the same: 'there is not enough accountability in the major centres of power. There is too much secrecy in the organisations that direct and manage our lives. These organisations go to great lengths to persuade us that they mean well and do good – but all too often they also suppress evidence of the harm they do. Unless and until there is proper accountability, these organisations will tend to operate by standards that suit them.'

18. GlaxoSmithKline Inc, Philadelphia Pa., Letter, 'Dear Healthcare Professional', IMPORTANT PRESCRIBING INFORMATION, April 2006.

19. www.socialaudit.org.uk.

20. Much of this account is based on House of Commons Health Committee, *The Influence of the Pharmaceutical Industry.*

21. On 29 January 2007 BBC's *Panorama* broadcast a further documentary about paroxetine, 'Secrets of the Drug Trials'. It revealed that GlaxoSmithKline attempted to show that the drug worked for depressed children despite failed clinical trials, and that ghostwriters employed by the company influenced 'independent' academics who advocated off-label use of the drug. All this emerged as a result of legal action by bereaved families in the US, in which GSK was forced to open its confidential internal

archive. The MHRA began a criminal investigation into GSK in October 2003, and in January 2007 told *Panorama* that 'the investigation has been given substantial additional resources and remains a high priority'. A review of the *Panorama* programme by Joe Collier appears in the *British Medical Journal* of 27 January 2007, p. 209.

22. Medawar and Hardon, 2004, op. cit., p. 208.
23. In June 2006 I submitted a detailed application to analyse Yellow Card data concerning possible interactions between SSRI antidepressants and alcohol, about which very little is known. The application was not acknowledged and, when I enquired about this six months later, I received an apology but was told that the committee had not yet been able to deal with my application and had just been enlarged with seven new members, who had met only for an induction. In January and February 2007 there has been no substantive communication, only repeated regrets and apologies. This suggests muddle and indecision and is no way to encourage much needed research into adverse effects.
24. MHRA, 'Always Read the Leaflet: Getting the Best Information with Every Medicine (London: MHRA, 2005). (downloadable from http://medicines. mhra.gov.uk/inforesources/publications/Alwaysreadtheleaflet.pdf).
25. J. Collier, 'New Arrangements for the Medicines and Healthcare Products Regulatory Agency', *British Medical Journal*, vol. 330, 2005, p. 917.
26. House of Commons Health Committee, 2005, op. cit.
27. See http://www.official-documents.co.uk/document/cm66/6655/6655.pdf.
28. See report in Hansard, Parliamentary debates, at http://www.publications. parliament.uk/pa/cm200506/cmhansrd/cm051208/debtext/51208–14.htm.
29. See www.gsk.com/media/paroxetine/briefing_doc.pdf.
30. The transcripts of all four *Panorama* programmes are available on the website: http://news.bbc.co.uk/1/hi/programmes/panorama/current_ archive/default.stm.

Notes to Chapter 11

1. This is a modified version of an article originally published in *International Journal of Health Services*, vol. 37, no. 4, 2007, pp. 735-744.
2. The BSE Inquiry, 2000. Available at http://www.bseinquiry.gov.uk.
3. E. Topol, 'Arthritis Medicines and Cardiovascular Events – "House of Coxib"', *Journal of the American Medical Association*, vol. 29, 2005, pp. 366–368; 'Comment Eviter les Prochaines Affaires Vioxx', *Revue Prescrire*, vol. 259, 2005, pp. 222–225; and 'The Vioxx Debacle', *The Network's Drug Bulletin*, vol. 13, 2004, pp. 3–13.
4. Health Insurance Commission, Health Statistics, Pharmaceutical Benefits Scheme, at <http://www.hic.gov.au/providers/health_statistics/statistical_ reporting/pbs.htm>. Accessed 27 April 2005.
5. S. Kerr et al., 'Lessons from Early Large-scale Adoption of Celecoxib and Rofecoxib by Australian General Practitioners', *Medical Journal of Australia*, vol. 179, 2003, pp. 403–407; L. Graudins, 'Celecoxib Prescribing: Drug

232

Use Review in a Sydney Teaching Hospital'. Available at the Quality Use of Medicines Mapping Project at http://www.qummap.health.gov.au/. Accessed 3 November 2005.

6. P. Langton, G. Hankey and J. Eikelboom, 'Cardiovascular Safety of Rofecoxib (Vioxx): Lessons Learned and Unanswered Questions', *Medical Journal of Australia*, vol. 181, 2004, pp. 524–525.

7. Australian Government, Department of Health and Ageing, 'National Medicines Policy 2000' (Canberra: 1999). Available at http://www.health.gov.au/internet/wcms/publishing.nsf/Content/nmp-objectives-policy.htm/$FILE/nmp2000.pdf.

8. Therapeutic Goods Administration (TGA), 'Common Technical Document'. Available at http://www.tga.health.gov.au/docs/html/eugctd.htm. Accessed 30 October 2005.

9. C. Bombardier et al., 'Comparison of Upper Gastrointestinal Toxicity of Rofecoxib and Naproxen in Patients with Rheumatoid Arthritis', *New England Journal of Medicine*, vol. 343, 2000, pp. 1520–1528.

10. F. E. Silverstein et al., 'Gastrointestinal Toxicity with Celecoxib vs Nonsteroidal Anti-inflammatory Drugs for Osteoarthritis and Rheumatoid Arthritis: The CLASS Study: A Randomized Controlled Trial', vol. 284, *Journal of the American Medical Association*, 2000, pp. 1247–1255; J. Hrachovec et al., 'Reporting of 6-month vs 12-month Data in a Clinical Trial of Celecoxib', *Journal of the American Medical Association*, vol. 286, 2001, pp. 2398–2399.

11. US Food and Drug Administration – Center for Drug Evaluation and Research, 'Application Number 021042 & 021052', 20 May 1999; US Food and Drug Administration – Center for Drug Evaluation and Research, 'Application Number 20–998', 31 December 1998.

12. Bombardier et al., 'Comparison of Upper Gastrointestinal Toxicity'.

13. 'COX-2 Inhibitors Update: Do Journal Publications Tell the Full Story?', *Therapeutics Letter*, vol. 43, Nov/Dec 2001/Jan 2002. Available at http://www.ti.ubc.ca/pages/letter43.htm.

14. D. Mukherjee, S. Nissen and E. Topol, 'Risk of Cardiovascular Events Associated with Selective COX-2 Inhibitors', *Journal of the American Medical Association*, vol. 286, 2001, pp. 954–959.

15. 'Rofecoxib, Celecoxib and Cardiovascular Risk', *ADRAC Bulletin*, vol. 22, 2003, p. 18. Available at http://www.tga.gov.au/adr/aadrb/aadr0310.htm#1.

16. T. Greenhalgh, O. Kostopoulou and C. Harries, 'Making Decisions About Benefits and Harms of Medicines', *British Medical Journal*, vol. 329, 2004, pp. 47–50.

17. J. Abraham, 'The Science and Politics of Medicines Control', *Drug Safety*, vol. 26, 2003, pp. 135–143; 'L'Agence Française des Produits de Sante: Est-elle Avant Tout au Service des Patients, ou au Service des Firmes Pharmaceutiques?' *Revue Prescrire*, vol. 25, 2005, pp. 793–796.

18. J. Abraham and G. Lewis, 'Harmonising and Competing for Medicines Regulation: How Healthy are the European Union's Systems of Drug Approval', *Social Science and Medicine*, vol. 48, 1999, pp. 1655–1667.

19. Union of Concerned Scientists, *FDA Scientists Issued Early Warnings on Drug Approvals*. Available at http://www.ucsusa.org/news/press_release/fda-scientists-issued-early-warnings-on-drug-approvals.html. Accessed 30 October 2005.

20. Transcript of Jonathan Holmes' Report into the Vioxx Controversy, Four Corners. Australian Broadcasting Corporation, 11 April 2005. Available at http://www.abc.net.au/4corners/content/2005/s1340327.htm.

21. Progestic International Inc., *Final Report for the Financial Models Project* (Ottawa: Health Canada, 2004).

22. Australian Government, Department of Health and Ageing, 'Relief for Half a Million Arthritis Sufferers: Wooldridge'. Available at http://www.health.gov.au/internet/wcms/Publishing.nsf/Content/health-mediarel-yr2000-mw-mw20048.htm. Accessed 31 October 2005.

23. K. Harvey, 'Securing the Future of the Pharmaceutical Benefits Scheme?' *Digest* [serial on the Internet], June 2002. Available at http://www.econ.usyd.edu.au/drawingboard/digest/0206/harvey.html.

24. J. Richardson, 'Financing Health Care: Short Run Problems, Long Run Options', paper presented to the Health Reform Forum, Melbourne Business School, 19 September 2002. Centre for Health Program Evaluation, Working Paper 138, April 2003.

25. Kerr et al., 2003, 'Lessons form Early Large-scale Adoption of Celecoxib and Rofecoxib'.

26. M. Fisher et al., 'Medicaid Prior-authorization Programs and the Use of Cyclooxygenase-2 Inhibitors', *New England Journal of Medicine*, vol. 351, 2004, pp. 2187–2194; D. Marshall, D. Willison and K. Sykora, 'Impact of Administrative Restrictions for Coxibs in Quebec (PQ), Ontario (ON) and British Columbia (BC)', *Pharmacoepidemiology and Drug Safety*, vol. 13 (S1), 2004, S24 (abstract).

27. M. B. Hamel and A. M. Epstein, 'Prior-authorization Programs for Controlling Drug Spending', *New England Journal of Medicine*, vol. 351, 2004, pp. 2156–2158.

28. Kerr et al., 'Lessons'.

29. The National Institute for Health Care Management Research and Educational Foundation (NIHCM), *Prescription Drugs and Mass Media Advertising* (NIHCM, November 2001). Available at http://www.nihcm.org/DTCbrief2001.pdf.

30. CBC Disclosure, 'Targeting Doctors'. Graph: top 50 drugs by total promotional dollars. Available at: www.cbc.ca/disclosure/archives/0103_pharm/resources.html. Accessed 30 March 2002.

31. Merck Sharp & Dohme [Advertisement 02-02VOX 01-AUS-248J] Headlines: 'Introducing once-daily Vioxx' 'A new world of GI safety in pain

relief providing ...' *Australian Family Physician,* vol. 30, issue 3, 2001, pp. 200-201.

32. P. Mansfield, 'Healthy Scepticism about Pfizer and Searle's Promotion of Celecoxib in Australia', *MaLAM International News,* vol. 18, 2000, pp. 3–4. Available at www.healthyskepticism.org/publications/editions/2000/IN0004.htm.

33. Pfizer [Advertisement PHA0198/CJB-AP] Headlines: 'This is the price thousands of patients are paying for arthritis relief.' 'Celebrex Life changing relief' *Australian Pharmacist,* vol. 21, 2002, pp. 256–257.

34. A. Vitry and E. Hurley, 'The Road to Consensus: Considerations for the Safe Use and Prescribing of COX-2-specific Inhibitors', *Medical Journal of Australia,* vol. 177, 2002, p. 572.

35. The Australian COX-2 Specific Inhibitor (CSI) Prescribing Group, 'Considerations for the Safe Prescribing and Use of COX-2-specific Inhibitors', *Medical Journal of Australia,* vol. 176, 2002, pp. 328–331.

36. Vitry and Hurley, 'The Road to Consensus'.

37. Australian Pharmaceutical Manufacturers Association (APMA), *Code of Conduct Annual Report 2000* (Australian Pharmaceutical Manufacturers Association, 2000).

38. FDA Warning Letter to Merck, 17 September 2001. Available at http://www.fda.gov/foi/warning.htm.

39. Medicines Australia, *2005 Code of Conduct Annual Report.* Available at http://www.medicinesaustralia.com.au/. Accessed 31 October 2005.

40. Medicines Australia, *Code of Conduct,* 14th edition. Available at http://www.medicinesaustralia.com.au/public/Code%200f%20Conduct%20Edition%2014%20-%20Jan%2003.pdf. Accessed 31 October 2005; E. E. Roughead, 'The Australian Pharmaceutical Manufacturers Association Code of Conduct: Guiding the Promotion of Prescription Medicines', *Australian Prescriber,* vol. 22, 1999, pp. 78–80.

41. S. Rossi (ed.), *Australian Medicines Handbook,* 2nd edition (Adelaide: Australian Medicines Handbook, 2000).

42. National Prescribing Service, 'Osteoarthritis-Have COX-2s Changed Its Management?', *NPS News,* 18 October 2001. Available at http://www.nps.org.au/site.php?content=/html/news.php&news=/resources/NPS_News/news18.

43. National Prescribing Service, 'Prescribing Practice Review 16: COX-2 Selective NSAIDs', December 2001. Available at http://www.nps.org.au/site.php?content=/html/ppr.php&ppr=/resources/Prescribing_Practice_Reviews/ppr16. Accessed 31 October 2005.

44. National Prescribing Service, 'Optimising Safe and Effective Use of Analgesics in Musculoskeletal Pain', *Prescribing Practice Review,* 22 July 2003. Available at http://www.nps.org.au/site.php?content=/html/ppr.php&ppr=/resources/Prescribing_Practice_Reviews/ppr22.

45. National Prescribing Service, 'Switching Patients from Vioxx' [factsheet], October 2004. Available at http://www.nps.org.au/resources/content/nps_factsheet_vioxx_20041001.pdf.

46. 'Rofecoxib (Vioxx): Un Antalgique AINS Decevant', *Revue Prescrire*, vol. 208, 2000, pp. 483–488.

47. US Food and Drug Administration – Center for Drug Evaluation and Research, 31 December 1998.

48. L. Gibson, 'Drug Company Sues Spanish Bulletin over Fraud Claim', *British Medical Journal*, vol. 328, 2004, p.188.

49. National Prescribing Service, Evaluation Report No. 7 (NPS December 2004). Available at http://www.nps.org.au/resources/evaluation/report_07.pdf.

50. R. Moynihan, 'Who Pays for the Pizza? Redefining the Relationships between Doctors and Drug Companies. 1: Entanglement', *British Medical Journal*, vol. 326, 2003, pp. 1189–1192.

51. B.B. McCormick et al., 'Effect of Restricting Contact Between Pharmaceutical Company Representatives and Internal Medicine Residents on Post-training Attitudes and Behaviour', *Journal of the American Medical Association*, vol. 286, 2001, pp. 1994–1999.

52. Silverstein et al., 'Gastrointestinal Toxicity'.

53. 'Medicines in Europe: The Most Important Changes in the New Legislation', *Prescrire International*, vol. 13, 2004, pp. 158–1–158–8.

Bibliography

Abraham, J., *Science, Politics and the Pharmaceutical Industry – Controversy and Bias in Drug Regulation* (London: Routledge, 1995).

—'The Pharmaceutical Industry as a Political Player', *The Lancet*, vol. 360, no. 9, 2002, p. 1498.

—'The Science and Politics of Medicines Control', *Drug Safety*, vol. 26, 2003, pp. 135–143.

—'Pharmaceuticals, the State and the Global Harmonisation Process', *Australian Health Review*, vol. 28, no. 2, 2004, pp. 150–160.

Abraham, J. and Davis, C., 'A Comparative Analysis of Drug Safety Withdrawals in the UK and the US (1971–1992): Implications for Current Regulatory Thinking and Policy', *Social Science and Medicine*, vol. 61, 2005, pp. 881–892.

Abraham, J. and Lawton, H. (eds.) *Regulation of the Pharmaceutical Industry* (London: Palgrave, 2003).

Abraham, J. and Lewis, G., 'Harmonising and Competing for Medicines Regulation: How Healthy are the European Union's Systems of Drug Approval', *Social Science and Medicine*, vol. 48, 1999, pp. 1655–1667.

—(eds.), *Regulating Medicines in Europe: Competition, Experts and Public Health* (London: Routledge, 2000).

—'Citizenship, Medical Expertise and the Capitalist Regulatory State in Europe', *Sociology*, vol. 36, no. 1, 2002, pp. 67–88.

Adair, R., 'Hidden Costs of Free Samples', *Virtual Mentor Ethics Journal of the American Medical Association*, vol. 8, no. 6, 2006, pp. 367–371.

ADRAC Bulletin, 'Rofecoxib, Celecoxib and Cardiovascular Risk', *ADRAC Bulletin*, vol. 22, 2003, p. 18.

Allen, R., *No Global. The People of Ireland versus the Multinationals* (London: Pluto, 2004).

Angell, M., *The Truth About Drug Companies – How They Deceive Us and What To Do About It* (New York: Random House, 2004).

Araga, Y., 'Keynote Address', in P. F. D'Arcy and D. W. G. Harron (eds.), *Proceedings of the Third International Conference on Harmonisation* (Belfast: IFPMA, 1996).

Arrighi, G., *The Long Twentieth Century* (London: Verso, 1994).

Atkinson, M. M. and Coleman, W. D., *The State, Business, and Industrial Change in Canada* (University of Toronto Press, 1989).

Australian COX-2 Specific Inhibitor (CSI) Prescribing Group, 'Considerations for the Safe Prescribing and Use of COX-2-specific Inhibitors', *Medical Journal of Australia*, vol. 176, 2002, pp. 328–331.

Australian Government, Department of Health and Ageing, 'National Medicines Policy 200' (Canberra; Department of Health and Ageing, 1999)

Australian Pharmaceutical Manufacturers Association, *Code of Conduct Annual Report 2000* (Australian Pharmaceutical Manufacturers Association, 2000).

Balasubramaniam, K., 'Access to Medicines: Patents, Prices and Public Policy – Consumer Perspectives', in P. Drahos and R. Mayne (eds.), *Global Intellectual Property Rights: Knowledge, Access and Development* (Basingstoke: Palgrave Macmillan, 2002).

Barry, M., 'Drug Expenditure in Ireland 1991–2001', *Irish Medical Journal*, vol. 95, no. 10, 2002, pp. 294–295.

—'Pricing and Reimbursement of Medicines in Ireland', *Public Affairs Ireland*, vol. 32, 2006, pp. 14–15.

Barry, M., Heerey, A. and Feely, J., 'Drug Reimbursement in Ireland', *Irish Medical Journal*, vol. 93, no. 3, 2000, pp. 71–74.

Bekelman, J. E., Li, Y. and Gross, C. P., 'Scope and Impact of Financial Conflicts of Interest in Biomedical Research: A Systematic Review', *Journal of the American Medical Association*, vol. 289, 2003, pp. 454–465.

Bell, R. A., Wilkes, M. S. and Kravitz, R. L., 'The Educational Value of Consumer-Targeted Prescription Drug Advertising', *Journal of Family Practice*, vol. 49, 2000, pp. 1092–1098.

Bhagwati, J., *In Defence of Globalisation* (Oxford University Press, 2004).

Bluhm, G. B., Smith, D.W. and Mikulaschele, W. M. 'Radiologic Assessment of Benoxaprofen Therapy in Rheumatoid Arthritis', *European Journal of Rheumatology and Inflammation,* vol. 5, no. 2, 1982, pp. 186-197.

Bodewitz, H., Buurma H. and de Vries, G., 'Regulatory Science and the Social Management of Trust in Medicine', in W. Bijker, T. Hughes and T. Pinch (eds.), *The Social Construction of Technological Systems. New Directions in the Sociology and History of Technology* (Cambridge, Mass: MIT Press, 1987).

Bombardier, C., Laine, L., Reicin, A., Shapiro, D., Burgos-Vargas, R., Davis, B., Day, R., Ferraz, M., Hawkey, C., Hochberg, M., Kvien, T. and Schnitzer, T., 'Comparison of Upper Gastrointestinal Toxicity of Rofecoxib and Naproxen in Patients with Rheumatoid Arthritis', *New England Journal of Medicine,* vol. 343, 2000, pp. 1520–1528.

Bradley, C., Holme Hansen, E. and Kooiker, S., 'Patients and their Medicines', in E. Mossialos, M. Mrazek, and T. Walley (eds.), *Regulating Pharmaceuticals in Europe: Striving for Efficiency, Equity and Quality* (Maidenhead: Open University Press, 2004), pp. 158–176.

Brezis, E. and Weiss, A., 'Conscientious Regulation and Post-regulatory Employment Restrictions', *European Journal of Political Economy*, vol. 13, 1997, pp. 517–536.

Brown, P. and Zavestoski, S., 'Social Movements in Health: An Introduction', in P. Brown and S. Zavestoski (eds.), *Social Movements in Health* (Oxford: Blackwell, 2005), pp. 1-16.

Canada's Research-Based Pharmaceutical Companies, *Improving Health Through Innovation: A New Deal for Canadians* (Ottawa: Rx&D, 2002).

—*Advertising Prescription Medicines in Canada: Why It Makes Sense* (Ottawa: Rx&D, 2002).

Canadian Adverse Drug Reaction Newsletter, 'Cisapride: Arrhythmia Awareness', *Canadian Adverse Drug Reaction Newsletter*, vol. 6, no. 3, 1996, pp. 1–2.

—'Adverse Drug Reaction Reporting – 1998', *Canadian Adverse Drug Reaction Newsletter*, vol. 9, no. 2, 1999, pp. 5–6.

—'Cisapride (Prepulsid®): Interactions with Grapefruit and Drugs', *Canadian Adverse Drug Reaction Newsletter*, vol. 10, no. 1, 2000, pp. 1–3.

—'Adverse Reaction Reporting – 2005', *Canadian Adverse Reaction Newsletter*, vol. 16, no. 2, 2006, pp. 2–3.

Canadian Medical Association Journal, 'Lessons from Cisapride', *Canadian Medical Association Journal*, vol. 164, 2001, p. 1269.

—'Postmarketing Drug Surveillance: What It Would Take to Make It Work', *Canadian Medical Association Journal*, vol. 165, 2001, p. 1293.

—'Ads and Prescription Pads', *Canadian Medical Association Journal*, vol. 169, 2003, p. 381.

Canadian Medical Association Journal Editorial, 'What's Wrong with CME?', *Canadian Medical Association Journal*, vol. 170, 2004, p. 917.

Canadian Treatment Action Council, *Position Paper on Direct to Consumer Advertising (DTCA) of Prescription Medications* (Toronto, 1999).

Catholic Agency for Overseas Development, *The Rough Guide to the WTO: A CAFOD Briefing* (London: CAFOD, 2001).

CBC-TV Undercurrents, *The Battle Over a Drug Ad* (transcript) (Toronto: Canadian News Disc, 2001).

Central Statistics Office, *National Income and Expenditure 1997* (Dublin: Central Statistics Office, 1998).

Chaix-Couturier, C., Durand-Zaleski, I., Jolly, D and Durieux, P., 'Effects of Financial Incentives on Medical Practice: Results from a Systematic Review of the Literature and Methodological Issues', *International Journal for Quality Health Care*, vol. 12, 2000, pp. 133–142.

Chang, H., *Kicking Away the Ladder: Development Strategy in Historical Perspective* (London: Anthem Press, 2002).

Chilvers, C., Dewey, M., Gretton, V., Miller, P., Palmer, B., Weller, D., Churchill, R., Williams, I., Bedi, N., Duggan, C., Lee A. and Harrison, G., , 'Antidepressant Drugs and Generic Counselling for Treatment of Major Depression in Primary Care: Randomised Trial with Patient Preference Arms', *British Medical Journal*, vol. 322, 2002, p. 772.

Collier, J., 'New Arrangements for the Medicines and Healthcare Products Regulatory Agency', *British Medical Journal*, vol. 330, 2005, p. 917.

Coney, S., 'Direct-to-Consumer Advertising of Prescription Pharmaceuticals: A Consumer Perspective From New Zealand', *Journal of Public Policy and Marketing*, vol. 21, 2002, pp. 213–223.

Consumers International, *Branding the Cure. A Consumer Perspective on Corporate Social Responsibility, Drug Promotion and the Pharmaceutical Industry in Europe* (London: Consumers International, 2006).

Copty, M., *Mental Health in Primary Care* (Dublin: Irish College of General Practitioners and the South West Area Health Board, 2004).

Cork County Development Board, *Integrated Strategy for the Economic, Social and Cultural Development of County Cork 2002–2011* (Cork County Development Board, 2001).

Correa, C. M., *Intellectual Property Rights, the WTO and Developing Countries: The TRIPs Agreement and Policy Options* (Penang: Third World Network, 2000).

Dawson, W., Boot J., Harvey, J. and Walker J., 'The Pharmacology of Benoxaprofen with Particular Reference to Effects on Lipoxygenase Product Formation', *European Journal of Rheumatology and Inflammation*, vol. 5, no. 2, 1982, pp. 61-68.

Democracy Commission, *Briefing Paper on Themes for the National Consultative Conference 2005. New Directions for Irish Democracy* (Dublin: Democracy Commission, 2005).

Department of Enterprise, Trade and Employment, *Building Ireland's Knowledge Economy – The Irish Action Plan for Promoting Investment in Research and Development to 2010* (Dublin: Government Publications, 2004).

Department of Finance, Canada, *Building the Canada We Want. Budget 2003: Investing in Canada's Health Care System* [cat. no. F1–23/2003] (Ottawa, 2003).

Di Masi, J., Hansen, R., Grabowski, H., and Lasagna, L., 'Costs of Innovation in the Pharmaceutical Industry', *Journal of Health Economics*, vol. 10, no. 1, May 1991, pp. 107–142.

Drahos, P., 'Global Property Rights in Information: The Story of TRIPs at the GATT', *Prometheus*, vol.13, no. 1, June, 1995, pp. 6-19.

Drahos, P. and Braithwaite, J., *Global Business Regulation* (Cambridge University Press, 2000).

Enterprise Strategy Report Group, *Ahead of the Curve. Ireland's Place in the Global Economy* (Dublin: Forfás, 2004).

European Commission, *Communication by the European Communities and their Member States to the Trips Council on the Review of Article 27.3(B) of the Trips Agreement, and the Relationship Between the Trips Agreement and the Convention On Biological Diversity (CBD) and the Protection of Traditional Knowledge and Folklore* (Brussels: Directorate-General for Trade, 2002).

Farmer, P., *Pathologies of Power – Health, Human Rights and the New War on the Poor* (Berkeley: University of California Press, 2003).

Fine Gael and the Labour Party, *Fine Gael/Labour Programme for Government* (Dublin: Fine Gael and the Labour Party, 1982).

Feely, J., 'The Influence of Pharmacoeconomic Factors on Prescribing Patterns in Ireland' *Pharmacoeconomics*, vol. 2, 1992, pp. 99–106.

Feely, J., McGettigan, P., O'Shea, B., Chan, R. and McManus, J., 'Low Rate of Generic Prescribing in the Republic of Ireland Compared to England and Northern Ireland: Prescribers' Concerns', *Irish Medical Journal*, vol. 90, 1997, pp.146–147.

Findlay, S., *Prescription Drugs and Mass Media Advertising, 2000* (Washington: National Institute of Health Care Management, 2002).

Fischer, M., Schneeweiss, S., Avorn, J., and Solomon, D., 'Medicaid Prior-authorization Programs and the Use of Cyclooxygenase-2 Inhibitors', *New England Journal of Medicine*, vol. 351, 2004; pp. 2187-2194.

Food and Drug Administration, *Guidelines for the Clinical Evaluation of Anti-Inflammatory and Anti-Rheumatic Drugs* (Washington DC: US GPO, 1977).

—*Report to Congress. Reports on Postmarketing Studies* [FDAMA 30] (Washington DC: US GPO, 2002).

Foreign Policy, 'Measuring Globalization: Who's Up, Who's Down?', *Foreign Policy*, January–February, 2003, pp. 60–72.

Fugh-Berman, A. and Batt, S., ' "This May Sting a Bit": Cutting CME's Ties to Pharma', *Virtual Mentor Ethics Journal of the American Medical Association*, vol. 8, no. 6, 2006, pp. 412–415.

Fuller, C., *Women and Adverse Drug Reactions: Reporting in the Canadian Context*, (Toronto: Women and Health Protection, 2002).

Gardner, D. M., Mintzes, B. and Ostry, A., 'Direct-to-Consumer Prescription Drug Advertising in Canada: Permission by Default', *Canadian Medical Association Journal*, vol. 169, 2003, pp. 425–428.

General Accounting Office, *FDA Oversight of Direct-to-Consumer Advertising Has Limitations* (Washington, 2002).

General Medical Services Payments Board, *Report for the Year Ending 31st December 2004* (Dublin: GMS Payments Board, 2004).

Gereffi, G. and Korzeniewicz, M. (eds.), *Commodity Chains and Global Capitalism* (Boulder, CO: Westport, 1994).

Gibbons, R. V., Landry, F., Blouch, D. Jones, D., Williams, F., Lucey C. and Kroenke, K., 'A Comparison of Physicians' and Patients' Attitudes Toward Pharmaceutical Industry Gifts', *Journal of General Internal Medicine*, vol. 13, 1998, pp. 151–154.

Gibson, L., 'Drug Company Sues Spanish Bulletin over Fraud Claim', *British Medical Journal*, vol. 328, 2004, pp. 188.

Government of Australia, *National Medicines Policy 2000* (Canberra: Department of Health and Ageing, 1999).

Government of Canada, *Food and Drugs Act* [C.01.044].

Government of Ireland, *Towards Better Regulation* (Dublin: Department of the Taoiseach, 2002).

—*Regulating Better – A Government White Paper Setting Out Six Principles of Better Regulation* (Dublin: Stationery Office, 2004).

—*A Vision for Change. Report of the Expert Group on Mental Health Policy* (Dublin: Stationery Office, 2006).

—*Houses of the Oireachtas Joint Committee on Health and Children, Eighth Report, The Adverse Side Effects of Pharmaceuticals* (Dublin: Stationery Office, 2007).

Green Shield Canada, *Drug Cost Analysis, 1997–2001* (Toronto, 2002).

Greenhalgh, T., Kostopoulou, O. and Harries, C., 'Making Decisions about Benefits and Harms of Medicines', *British Medical Journal*, vol. 329, 2004, pp. 47–50.

Hamel, M. B. and Epstein, A. M., 'Prior-authorization Programs for Controlling Drug Spending', *New England Journal of Medicine*, vol. 351, 2004, pp. 2156–2158.

Harding, A., 'European and US Groups Draw Up Standards for CME', *British Medical Journal*, vol. 328, 2004, p. 1279.

Hardon, A., 'Contesting Contraceptive Innovation – Reinventing the Script', *Social Science and Medicine*, vol. 62, issue 3, 2006, pp. 614–627.

Health Canada, *Health Protection Legislative Renewal: Detailed Legislative Proposal* (Ottawa: 2003).

—*Improving Canada's Regulatory Process for Therapeutic Products: Building the Action Plan* (Ottawa: Public Policy Forum Multistakeholder Consultation, 2–3 November 2003).

Health Action International Europe, *Patients' Reporting of Adverse Reactions.* (Amsterdam: Health Action International Europe, 2005).

Healey, D., *Let Them Eat Prozac* (Toronto: James Lorimer, 2003).

Henry, M., 'Vaccination and Clinical Trials', *Irish Medical News*, 16 November 2000.

Hirsch, L., 'Randomized Clinical Trials: What Gets Published and When?', *Canadian Medical Association Journal*, vol. 170, 2004, pp. 481–483.

Hoekman, B. and Kostecki, M., *The Political Economy of the World Trading System* (Oxford University Press, 1995).

House of Commons Health Committee, *The Influence of the Pharmaceutical Industry: Fourth Report of Session 2004–05*, vol. 1 [Report no. HC 42–1] (London: The Stationery Office Limited, 2005).

House of Commons Standing Committee on Health, *Opening the Medicine Cabinet: First Report on Health Aspects of Prescription Drugs* (Ottawa, 2004).

Hrachovec, J., Mora, M., Wright, J., Perry, T., Bassett, K., Chambers, G., Silversteini, F., Simon, L. and Faich, G., 'Reporting of 6-month vs 12-month Data in a Clinical Trial of Celecoxib', *Journal of the American Medical Association*, vol. 286, 2001, pp. 2398-2400.

Huskisson, E. C., 'Trials of Anti-Rheumatic Drugs', in C. Good and C. Clarke (eds.), *The Principles and Practice of Clinical Trials* (Edinburgh: Churchill Livingstone, 1976).

—'Editorial', *European Journal of Rheumatology and Inflammation*, vol. 5, no. 2, 1982, pp. 49–50.

—'Classification of Anti-Rheumatic Drugs', in E. C. Huskisson (ed.), *Anti-Rheumatic Drugs* (East Sussex and New York: Praeger, 1983).

Huskisson, E. C. and Scott, J., 'Treatment of Rheumatoid Arthritis with a Single Daily Dose of Benoxaprofen', *Rheumatology and Rehabilitation,* vol. 18, 1979, pp. 110–113.

Huskisson, E. C. Scott, J. and Dieppe, P., 'Benoxaprofen: a Clinical Trial with an Unusual Design', *Rheumatology and Rehabilitation,* vol. 17, 1978, pp. 254–258.

Ikenberry, J. and Kupchan, C., 'Socialization and Hegemonic Power', *International Organization,* vol. 44, no. 3, 1990, pp. 283–315.

Illich, I., *Limits to Medicine. Medical Nemesis: The Expropriation of Health* (London: Marion Boyars, 1976, 1995).

IMS Health, *U.S. Data Indices – Promotion, 2003* (IMS Health Inc., 2004).

Industrial Development Authority, *Vital Statistics* (Dublin: IDA, 2004).

—*Pharmaceuticals Ireland* (Dublin: IDA, 2004).

International Society of Drug Bulletins, *ISDB Assessment of Nine European Public Assessment Reports Published by the European Medicines Evaluation Agency (EMEA)* (Paris, 1998).

International Working Group on Transparency and Accountability in Drug Regulation, *Statement* (Amsterdam: Health Action International, 1996).

Irish College of General Practitioners, *Pharmaceutical Sponsorship of ICGP Accredited Meetings – Guidelines* (Dublin: Irish College of General Practitioners, 2003).

Irish Medicines Board, *Annual Report and Accounts 1997* (Dublin: Irish Medicines Board, 1998).

—*Newsletter,* October 2000.

—*Newsletter,* April 2001.

—*Annual Report 2004* (Dublin: Irish Medicines Board, 2005).

Irish Pharmaceutical Healthcare Association, *IPHA Code of Marketing Practice for the Pharmaceutical Industry,* 5th edn (Dublin: Irish Pharmaceutical Healthcare Association, 1999).

—*Code of Standards of Advertising Practice for the Consumer Healthcare Industry,* 4th edn (Dublin: Irish Pharmaceutical Healthcare Association, 1999).

—*The Value of Medicines* (Dublin: Irish Pharmaceutical Healthcare Association, 1999).

—*Submission to the Enterprise Strategy Group* (Dublin: Irish Pharmaceutical Healthcare Association, 2002).

—*Industry Report Pharma Ireland – Developing and Delivering Medicines* (Dublin: Irish Pharmaceutical Healthcare Association, 2005).

—'Ireland is World's Biggest Pharmaceutical Exporter', *Medicines Matter,* February, 2005.

—*Facts and Figures 2006* (Dublin: Irish Pharmaceutical Healthcare Association, 2006).

Jacobzone, S., 'Pharmaceutical Policies in OECD Countries: Reconciling Social and Industrial Goals' (Paris: OECD, 2000).

Johnson, C., *Blowback: The Costs and Consequences of American Empire* (New York: Holt Metropolitan Books, 2000).

Kassirer, J. P., *On the Take: How Medicine's Complicity with Big Business Can Endanger Your Health* (Oxford University Press, 2005).

Keogh, D., 'Ireland and 'Emergency' Culture, between Civil War and Normalcy, 1922 – 1961', *Ireland: A Journal of History and Society (Irish Democracy and the Right to Freedom of Information)*, vol. 1, no.1, 1995, pp. 4–43.

Kerr, S., Mant., Horn, F. McGeechanm K. and Sayerm G., 'Lessons from Early Large-scale Adoption of Celecoxib and Rofecoxib by Australian General Practitioners', *Medical Journal of Australia*, vol. 179, 2003, pp. 403–407.

Kirby, P., 'The Changing Role of the Irish State' in T. O'Connor and M. Murphy (eds.), *Social Care in Ireland* (Cork Institute of Technology, 2006).

Kirby, P. and Murphy, M., 'Ireland as a "Competition State"' in M. Adshead, P. Kirby and M. Millar (eds.), *Contesting the Irish State* (Manchester University Press, 2007) (forthcoming).

Klawiter, M., 'Risk, Prevention and the Breast Cancer Continuum: The NCI, the FDA, Health Activism and the Pharmaceutical Industry', *History and Technology*, vol. 18, 2002, pp. 309–353.

KPMG Consulting LP, *Review of the Therapeutic Products Programme Cost Recovery Initiative*, vol. 1 (Ottawa, June 2000).

Krimsky, S., *Science in the Private Interest. Has the Lure of Profits Corrupted Biomedical Research?* (Lanham: Rowman and Littlefield, 2003).

Langton, P., Hankey, G. and Eikelboom, J., 'Cardiovascular Safety of Rofecoxib (Vioxx): Lessons Learned and Unanswered Questions', *Medical Journal of Australia*, vol. 181, 2004, pp. 524–525.

Lanjouw, J. O. and Cockburn, I., 'New Pills for Poor People?: Empirical Evidence After GATT', *World Development*, vol. 29, no. 2, 2001, pp. 265–289.

Lanoszka, A., 'Global Politics of Intellectual Property Rights, WTO Agreement, and Pharmaceutical Drug Policies in Developing Countries', *International Political Science Review*, vol. 24, no. 2, 2003, pp.181–198.

Lasser, K., Allen, P., Woolhandler, S., Himmelstein, D., Wolfe, S. and Bar, D., 'Timing of New Black Box Warnings and Withdrawals for Prescription Medications', *Journal of the American Medical Association*, vol. 287, 2002, pp. 2215–2220.

Law, J., *Big Pharma. Exposing the Global Healthcare Agenda* (New York: Carroll & Graf, 2006).

Lawson, G. W., *Impact of User Fees (i.e., Drug Industry Fees) on Changes Within the FDA* (University of La Verne, College of Business and Public Management, 2005).

Lenzer, J., 'New Cochrane Policy Tightens Limits on Industry Funding', *British Medical Journal*, vol. 328, 2004, p. 976.

Levine, M. and Forrence, J., 'Regulatory Capture, Public Interest and the Public Agenda: Toward a Synthesis', *Journal of Law, Economics and Organisation*, vol. 6, 1990, pp. 167–198.

Lexchin, J., 'Interactions between Physicians and the Pharmaceutical Industry: What Does the Literature Say?', *Canadian Medical Association Journal*, vol. 149, 1993, pp. 1401–1407.

—'Enforcement of Codes Governing Pharmaceutical Promotion: What Happens When Companies Breach Advertising Guidelines?', *Canadian Medical Association Journal*, vol. 156, 1997, pp. 351–357.

Lexchin, J. and Kawachi, I., 'Voluntary Codes of Pharmaceutical Marketing: Controlling Promotion or Licensing Deception', in P. Davis (ed.), *Contested Ground: Public Purpose and Private Interest in the Regulation of Prescription Drugs* (New York: Oxford University Press, 1996), pp. 221–235.

Lexchin, J. and Mintzes, B., 'Direct-to-Consumer Advertising of Prescription Drugs: The Evidence Says No', *Journal of Public Policy and Marketing*, vol. 21, 2002, pp. 194–201.

—'Transparency in Drug Regulation: Mirage or Oasis', *Canadian Medical Association Journal*, vol. 171, 2002, pp. 1363–1365.

Lexchin, J., Bero, L., Djulbegovic, B. and Clarke, O., 'Pharmaceutical Industry Sponsorship and Research Outcome and Quality: Systematic Review', *British Medical Journal*, vol. 326, 2003, pp. 1167–1170.

Lofgren, H. and de Boer, R., 'Pharmaceuticals in Australia: Developments in Regulation and Governance', *Social Science and Medicine*, vol. 58, 2004, pp. 2397–2407.

Love, J., 'Access to Medicine and Compliance with the WTO TRIPs Accord: Models for State Practice in Developing Countries', in P. Drahos and R. Mayne (eds.), *Global Intellectual Property Rights: Knowledge, Access and Development* (Basingstoke: Palgrave Macmillan, 2002), pp. 74–89.

Lurie, P. and Wolfe, S. M., *FDA Medical Officers Report Lower Standards Permit Dangerous Drug Approvals* (Washington: Public Citizen, 1998).

Lynch, T., *Beyond Prozac: Healing Mental Distress*, 2nd edn (Cork: Mercier Press, 2005).

Mansfield, P., 'Healthy Scepticism about Pfizer and Searle's Promotion of Celecoxib in Australia', *MaLAM International News*, vol. 18, 2000, pp. 3–4.

Marshall, D., Willison, D. and Sykora, K., 'Impact of Administrative Restrictions for Coxibs in Quebec (PQ), Ontario (ON) and British Columbia (BC)', *Pharmacoepidemiology and Drug Safety*, vol. 13 (S1), 2004, S24 (abstract).

Martinez, C., Rietbrock, S., Wise, L., Ashby, D., Chick, J., Moseley, J., Evans, S. and Gunnell, D., 'Antidepressant Treatment and the Risk of Fatal and Non-Fatal Self Harm in First Episode Depression: Nested Case-control Study', *British Medical Journal*, vol. 330, 2005, pp. 389–393.

Maskus, K., *Intellectual Property Rights in the Global Economy* (Washington DC: Institute for International Economics, 2000).

Mayne, R., 'The Global NGO Campaign on Patents and Access to Medicines: An Oxfam Perspective', in P. Drahos. and R. Mayne (eds.), *Global Intellectual Property Rights: Knowledge, Access and Development* (Basingstoke: Palgrave Macmillan, 2002), pp. 244–258.

Mayoshi, M., '"Globalisation", Culture, and the University' in F. Jameson and M. Mayoshi (eds.), *The Cultures of Globalization* (Durham NC: Duke University, 1998), pp. 247-270.

McCormick, B., Tomlinson, G., Brill-Edwards, P. and Detsky, A., 'Effect of Restricting Contact between Pharmaceutical Company Representatives and Internal Medicine Residents on Post-training Attitudes and Behaviour', *Journal of the American Medical Association,* vol. 286, 2001, pp. 1994–1999.

McGarity, T. O. and Shapiro, S. A., 'The Trade Secret Status of Health and Safety Testing Information: Reforming Agency Disclosure Policies', *Harvard Law Review*, vol. 93, 1980, pp. 837–888.

McIntyre, A., *Key Issues in the Pharmaceutical Industry* (Chichester: John Wiley & Sons, 1999).

Medawar, C., *Power and Dependence: Social Audit on the Safety of Medicines* (London: Social Audit, 1992).

—'Antidepressants: Hooked on the Happy Drug', *What Doctors Don't Tell You* (London: Social Audit, 1998).

Medawar, C. and Hardon, A., *Medicines Out of Control? Antidepressants and the Conspiracy of Goodwill* ([Amsterdam]: Aksant, 2004).

Medawar, C. and Herxheimer, A., 'A Comparison of Adverse Drug Reaction Reports from Professionals and Users, Relating to Risk of Dependence and Suicidal Behaviour with Paroxetine' *International Journal of Risk and Safety in Medicine*, vol. 16, 2003–04, pp. 3–17.

Medawar, C., Herxheimer, A., Bell, A. and Jofre, S., 'Paroxetine, *PANORAMA* and User Reporting of ADRs: Consumer Intelligence Matters in Clinical Practice and Post-marketing Drug Surveillance', *International Journal of Risk and Safety in Medicine*, vol. 15, no. 4, 2002, pp. 161–169.

Medical Council, *A Guide to Ethical Conduct and Behaviour* (Dublin: Medical Council, 2004).

Medicines and Healthcare Products Regulatory Agency, 'Always Read the Leaflet: Getting the Best Information with Every Medicine (London: MHRA, 2005).

Merton, R. K., 'The Normative Structure of Science', in N. Storer (ed.), *The Sociology of Science: Theoretical and Empirical Investigations* (University of Chicago Press, 1942).

Michols, D. M., *The Distinction Between Advertising and Other Activities* (Ottawa: Health Canada, Therapeutic Products Programme, 1996).

—*Drugs and Medical Devices Programme Quality Initiative Bulletin*, no. 2 (Ottawa: Health Protection Branch, 1997).

Mintzes, B., *Educational Initiatives for Medical and Pharmacy Students about Drug Promotion: An International Cross-Sectional Survey* (World Health Organisation and Health Action International, 2005).

Mintzes, B. and Baraldi, R., *Direct-to-Consumer Prescription Drug Advertising: When Public Health Is No Longer a Priority* (Toronto: Women and Health Protection, 2001).

Mintzes, B., Barer, M., Kravitz, R., Kazanjian, A., Bassett, K.,Lexchin, J., Evans, R., Pan, R. and Marion, S., 'Influence of Direct to Consumer Pharmaceutical Advertising and Patients' Requests on Prescribing Decisions: Two Site Cross Sectional Survey', *British Medical Journal*, vol. 324, 2002, pp. 278–279.

Mossinghoff, G. and Bombelles, T., 'The Importance of Intellectual Property to American Research-intensive Pharmaceutical Industry', *Columbia Journal of World Business*, vol. 31, no. 1, 1996, pp. 38–48.

Moynihan, R., 'Who Pays for the Pizza? Redefining the Relationships between Doctors and Drug Companies. 1: Entanglement', *British Medical Journal*, vol. 26, 2003, pp. 1189–1192.

—'Cochrane at Crossroads over Drug Company Sponsorship', *British Medical Journal*, vol. 327, 2003, pp. 924–926.

Moynihan, R. and Cassels, A., *Selling Sickness. How the World's Biggest Pharmaceutical Companies are Turning Us All into Patients* (Vancouver/Toronto: Greystone Books, 2005).

Moynihan, R. and Henry, D., 'The Fight against Disease Mongering: Generating Knowledge for Action', *PLoS Medicine*, vol. 3, issue 4, 2006, pp. 1–4.

Mukherjee, D., Nissen, S. and Topol, E., 'Risk of Cardiovascular Events Associated with Selective COX2 Inhibitors', *Journal of the American Medical Association*, vol. 286, 2001, pp. 954–959.

Mullally, G., 'Challenging the Illusion of Powerlessness: Social Movements, the Transnational Pharmaceutical Industry and the State in the Republic of Ireland', unpublished MA thesis in the Sociology of Development, University College Cork, Department of Sociology, 1992.

National Drugs Advisory Board, *Annual Report 1980* (Dublin: National Drugs Advisory Board, 1981).

National Institute for Health Care Management Research and Educational Foundation, *Prescription Drugs and Mass Media Advertising* (Washington DC: NIHCM, November 2001).

National Prescribing Service, 'Optimising Safe and Effective Use of Analgesics in Musculoskeletal Pain', *Prescribing Practice Review*, 22 July 2003.

Navarro, V., 'Policy without Politics: The Limits of Social Engineering', *American Journal of Public Health*, vol. 93, no. 1, 2003, pp. 64–67.

Network's Drug Bulletin, 'The Vioxx Debacle', Network's Drug Bulletin, vol. 13, 2004, pp. 3-13.

O'Brien, W. M., 'Radiological Evaluation of Erosions: a Quantitative Method for Assessing Long-Term Remittive Therapy in Rheumatoid Arthritis', *British Journal of Clinical Pharmacology*, vol. 22, 1986, pp. 173S–182S.

O'Donovan, O., 'Corporate Colonization of Health Activism? Irish Health Advocacy Organizations' Modes of Engagement with Pharmaceutical Corporations', *International Journal of Health Service*s, vol. 37, no. 4, 2007, pp. 711-733.

O'Donovan, O. and Glavanis-Grantham, K., 'Researching the Political and Cultural Influence of the Transnational Pharmaceutical Industry in Ireland', *Administration*, vol. 52, no. 3, 2004, pp. 21–42.

Office of Inspector General, *FDA's Review Process for New Drug Applications: A Management Review* [OE1-01-01-00590], (Washington: Department of Health and Human Services, 2003).

O'Hearn, D., 'Economic Growth and Social Cohesion in Ireland', in M. Dauderstadt (ed.), *Economic Growth and Social Cohesion in Europe* (Bonn: Friedrich Ebert Foundation, 2001).

—*The Atlantic Economy. Britain, the US and Ireland* (Manchester University Press, 2001).

O'Mahony, B., 'Interactions Between a General Practitioner and Representatives of Drug Companies', *British Medical Journal*, vol. 306, 1993, p. 1649.

Oxfam, *Rigged Rules and Double Standards Trade: Globalisation and the Fight Against Poverty* (Oxford: Oxfam, 2002).

Panos Institute, *Patents, Pills and Public Health: Can TRIPs Deliver?*, Panos Report No. 46, 2002.

Patented Medicine Prices Review Board, *Annual Report 2001* (Ottawa, 2002).

Pharmacy Practice, 'The Top 200 Drugs of 1997', *Pharmacy Practice*, vol. 13, no. 12, 1997, pp. 29–40.

—'The Top 200 Drugs of 1999', *Pharmacy Practice*, vol. 15, no. 12, 1999, pp. 39–47.

Poggiolini, D., 'Research, Development and Regulation: A Background to Harmonization', in P. F. D'Arcy and D.W.G. Harron (eds.), *Proceedings of the First International Conference on Harmonisation* (Belfast: IFPMA, 1992).

Popper, K., *Objective Knowledge: An Evolutionary Approach* (Oxford: Clarendon Press, 1972).

Prescrire International, *Reorienting European Medicines Policy* (Paris: Prescrire International, June 2002).

—'Medicines in Europe: The Most Important Changes in the New Legislation', *Prescrire International*, vol. 13, 2004, pp. 158-1–158-8.

Pretorius, W., 'TRIPs and Developing Countries: How Level is the Playing Field?', in P. Drahos and R. Mayne (eds.), *Global Intellectual Property Rights: Knowledge, Access and Development* (Basingstoke: Palgrave Macmillan, 2002), pp. 183–200.

Price, J. S., Waller, P., Wood, S. and Mackay, A., 'A Comparison of the Post-marketing Safety of Four Selective Serotonin Reuptake Inhibitors including the Investigation of Symptoms Occurring on Withdrawal', *British Journal of Clinical Pharmacology*, vol. 42, 1996, pp. 757–763.

Progestic International Inc., *Final Report for the Financial Models Project* (Ottawa: Health Canada, 2004).

Quinn, R. J. and O'Neill, C., 'Attitudes of General Practitioners to their Interactions with Pharmaceutical Companies: A Qualitative Study', *Irish Medical Journal*, vol. 95, no. 7, 2002, pp. 199-200.

Raghavan, C., *Recolonization: GATT, the Uruguay Round and the Third World* (London and Penang: Zed/ and Third World Network, 1990).

Rawson, N. S. B., 'Timeliness of Review and Approval of New Drugs in Canada From 1999 through 2001: Is Progress Being Made?', *Clinical Therapeutics*, vol. 25, 2001, pp. 1230–1247.

Relman, A. and Angell, M., 'America's Other Drug Problem: How the Drug Industry Distorts Medicine and Politics', *The New Republic*, vol. 227, no. 25, 16 December 2002, pp. 27–41.

Revue Prescrire, 'Rofecoxib (Vioxx). Un Antalgique AINS Decevant', *Revue Prescrire*, vol. 208, 2000, pp. 483–488.

—'Comment Eviter les Prochaines Affaires Vioxx', *Revue Prescrire*, vol. 25, issue 259, 2005, pp. 222–225.

—'L'Agence Francaise des Produits de Sante est-elle Avant Tout au Service des Patients, ou au Service des Firmes Pharmaceutiques?' *Revue Prescrire*, vol. 25, issue 266, 2005, pp. 793–796.

Richardson, J., 'Financing Health Care: Short Run Problems, Long Run Options', paper presented to the Health Reform Forum, Melbourne Business School 19 September 2002.

Robinson, W., *Transnational Conflicts: Central America, Social Change, and Globalization* (London: Verso, 2003).

Rossi, S., (ed.), *Australian Medicines Handbook*, 2nd edn (Adelaide: Australian Medicines Handbook Pty Ltd, 2000).

Roughead, E. E., 'The Australian Pharmaceutical Manufacturers Association Code of Conduct: Guiding the Promotion of Prescription Medicines', *Australian Prescriber*, vol. 22, 1999, pp. 78–80.

Rowsell, L. B., *Advertising Campaigns of Branded and Unbranded Messages* (Ottawa: Health Canada, Therapeutic Products Directorate, 2000).

Royal Society of Canada, *Elements of Precaution: Recommendations for the Regulation of Food Biotechnology in Canada: An Expert Panel Report on the Future of Food Biotechnology* (Ottawa: Royal Society of Canada, 2001).

Rynne, A., 'Special Relationships between Doctors and Drug Companies', *Irish Medical News*, 16 August 2004.

Sasich, L. D., Lurie, P. and Wolfe, S. M., *The Drug Industry's Performance in Finishing Postmarketing Research (Phase IV) Studies. A Public Citizen's Health Research Group Report* (Washington: Public Citizen, 2000).

Scannell, Y., *Environmental and Planning Law in Ireland* (Dublin: Round Hall, 1995).

Schwarz, M. and Thompson, M., *Divided We Stand: Redefining Politics, Technology and Social Choice* (Hemel Hempstead, Herts: Harvester Wheatsheaf, 1990).

Science Advisory Board Committee on the Drug Review Process, *Report to Health Canada* (Ottawa, 2000).

Science Foundation Ireland, *Points of Excellence* (Dublin: Science Foundation Ireland, 2004).

Sell, S., *Private Power, Public Law: The Globalization of Intellectual Property Rights* (Cambridge University Press, 2003).

Sell, S. and Prakash, A., 'Using Ideas Strategically: The Contest Between Business and NGO Networks in Intellectual Property Rights', *International Studies Quarterly*, vol. 48, no. 1, 2004, pp. 143–175.

Shapiro, R. and Hassett, K., 'The Economic Value of Intellectual Property', report prepared for USA For Innovation, 2005.

Shukla, S. P., *From GATT to WTO and Beyond* (Helsinki: UNU World Institute for Development Economics Research, 2000).

Silcock, J., Ryan, M., Bond, C. and Taylor, R., 'The Cost of Medicines in the United Kingdom. A Survey of General Practitioners' Opinions and Knowledge', *Pharmacoeconomics*, vol. 11, issue 1, 1997, pp. 56–63.

Silverstein, F., Faich, G., Goldstein, J., Simon, L., Pincus, T., Whelton, A., Makuch, R., Eisen, G., Agrawal, N., Stenson, W., Burr, A., Zhao, W., Kent, J., Lefkowith, J., Verburg, K. and Geis, S., 'Gastrointestinal Toxicity with Celecoxib vs Nonsteroidal Anti-inflammatory Drugs for Osteoarthritis and Rheumatoid Arthritis: the CLASS Study: A Randomized Controlled Trial', vol. 284, *Journal of the American Medical Association,* 2000, pp. 1247–1255.

Sklair, L., *The Transnational Capitalist Class* (Oxford: Blackwell, 2001).

South West Regional Authority, *Regional Planning Guidelines* (Cork: South West Regional Authority, 2004).

Subramaniam, A., 'Putting Some Numbers on the TRIPs Pharmaceutical Debate', *International Journal of Technology Management*, vol. 10, no.2/3, 1995, pp. 252–268.

Suydam, L. A. and Kubic, M. J., 'FDA's Implementation of FDAMA: An Interim Balance Sheet, ' *Food and Drug Law Journal*, vol. 56, 2001, pp. 131–135.

The Network's Drug Bulletin, 'The Vioxx Debacle', *The Network's Drug Bulletin,* vol. 13, 2004, pp. 3–13.

't Hoen, E., 'TRIPs, Pharmaceutical Patents, and Access to Essential Medicines: A Long Way from Seattle to Doha', *Chicago Journal of International Law*, vol. 3, no. 1, 2002, pp. 27–46.

Therapeutic Products Directorate, *Business Transformation Progress Report* (Ottawa: Health Canada, [no date]).

Therapeutics Letter, 'COX-2 Inhibitors Update: Do Journal Publications Tell the Full Story?', *Therapeutics Letter*, vol. 43, Nov/Dec 2001/Jan 2002.

Thompson, J., Baird, P. and Downie, J., *The Olivieri Report* (Toronto: James Lorimer, 2001).

Tilson, L., Bennett, K. and Barry, M., 'The Potential Impact of Implementing a System of Generic Substitution on the Community Drug Schemes in Ireland', *European Journal of Health Economics*, vol. 50, 2005, pp. 267–273.

Tilson, L., McGowan, B. and Bennett, K., 'The High Cost of Medicines in Ireland', *European Journal of Health Economics*, vol. 49, 2004, pp. 341–344.

Tilson, L., McGowan, B., Ryan, M. and Barry, M., 'Generic Drug Utilisation on the General Medical Services (GMS) Scheme in 2001', *Irish Medical Journal*, vol. 96, issue 6, 2003, pp. 176–179.

Toop, L., Richards, D., Powell, T., Tilyard, M., Fraser, T. and Aroll, B., *Direct to Consumer Advertising of Prescription Drugs in New Zealand: For Health or For Profit?* (New Zealand Departments of General Practice, Christchurch, Dunedin, Wellington and Auckland Schools of Medicine, 2003).

Topol, E., 'Arthritis Medicines and Cardiovascular Events – 'House of Coxibs', *Journal of the American Medical Association*, vol. 29, 2005, pp. 366–368.

UNAIDS, *Report on the Global AIDS Epidemic* (Geneva: UNAIDS, 2004).

United Nations, *Human Development Report 2001* (Oxford and New York: United Nations Development Programme, 2001).

—*Human Development Report 2003* (Oxford and New York: United Nations Development Programme, 2004).

United States Congress, Hearings of the Intergovernmental Relations and Human Resources Subcommittee of the House of Representatives, *The Regulation of New Drugs by the FDA: The Drug Review Process* (Washington DC: US GPO, 3–4 August 1982).

University College Cork, Office of the President, *Growing Excellence* (University College Cork, 2003).

—*Careers Service Annual Report 2003* (University College Cork, 2004).

Van Egeraat, C., 'The Pharmaceutical Industry in Ireland: Agglomeration, Localisation or Simply Spatial Concentration?', NIRSA Working Paper no. 28 (Maynooth: National Institute for Regional and Spatial Analysis, 2006).

Velásquez, G., 'Bilateral Trade Agreements and Access to Essential Drugs' in J. A. Z. Bermudez and M. A. Oliveira (eds.), *Intellectual Property in the Context of the WTO TRIPS Agreement: Challenges for Public Health* (Rio de Janeiro: Escola Nacional de Saúde Pública/WHO, 2004).

Vitry, A. and Hurley, H., 'The Road to Consensus: Considerations for the Safe Use and Prescribing of COX-2-specific Inhibitors', *Medical Journal of Australia*, vol. 177, 2002, p. 572.

Wade, R., 'Is Globalization Reducing Poverty and Inequality?', *World Development*, vol. 32, no. 4, 2004, pp. 567–589.

Watal, J., 'Intellectual Property and Biotechnology: Trade Interests of Developing Countries', *International Journal of Biotechnology*, vol. 2, no.1/2/3, 2000, pp. 44–55.

Weedle, P. and Cahill, M., *Medicines and Pharmacy Law in Ireland* (Dublin: Kenlis Publishers, 1991).

Weissman, R., 'A Long Strange TRIPs: the Pharmaceutical Industry Drive to Harmonize Property Rules, and the Remaining WTO Legal Alternatives Available to Third World Countries', *University of Pennsylvania Journal of International Economic Law*, vol. 17, no. 4, Winter, 1996, pp. 1069–1125.

Wiktorowicz, M. E., 'Shifting Priorities at the Health Protection Branch: Challenges to the Regulatory Process', *Canadian Public Administration*, vol. 43, 2000, pp. 1–22.

Williamson, J., 'What Should the World Bank Think About the Washington Consensus?' *World Bank Research Observer*, vol. 15, no. 2, August 2000, pp. 251–264.

Wood, A., 'The Safety of New Medicines: The Importance of Asking the Right Questions', *Journal of the American Medical Association*, vol. 281, 2000, pp. 1753–1754.

...ld Development Movement, *Briefing on Regulating TNCs: Making Investment Work for People, an International Framework for Regulating Corporations* (London: World Development Movement, 1999).

...ing Paper on GATs (London: World Development Movement, 2002).

...Justice at Cancun? Why the WTO's Remit Should Not Be Expanded to ...ver the 'New Issues' (London: World Development Movement, 2003).

...alth Organisation, *14th Model List of Essential Medicines* (Geneva: ...O, 2005).

World Intellectual Property Organization (WIPO), *Implications of the TRIPs Agreement on Treaties Administered by WIPO* (Geneva: WIPO Publications, 1997).

Wren, M. A., *Unhealthy State – Anatomy of a Sick Society* (Dublin: New Island, 2004).

Zeng, K., *Trade Threats, Trade Wars: Bargaining, Retaliation, and American Coercive Diplomacy* (Ann Arbor: University of Michigan Press, 2004).

NEWSPAPER SOURCES

Beesley, A., 'Green Party Calls for Appointment of New EPA Director to be Terminated', *The Irish Times*, 28 August 2004.

—'"Cost is a Factor, But It's Certainly Not the Overriding One". No One is Safe From Unforgiving Forces of Business', *The Irish Times*, 9 February 2007.

Brennock, M. 'New Code Restricts Job Moves for Civil Servants', *The Irish Times*, 10 September 2004.

Bhagwati, J. and Panagariya, A., 'Bilateral Trade Treaties are a Sham', *Financial Times*, 13 July 2003.

Calnan, S., 'Nurse Urges Stricter Anti-depressants Regulation', *The Irish Times*, 28 June 2005.

Cordon, S., 'Lift Ban on Drug Ads, Newspaper Group Says', *The Windsor Star*, 11 June 2003.

Cullen, P. 'Ireland Ranks Second in UN Poverty Index', *The Irish Times*, 16 July 2004.

Deegan, G., 'Investigation Urged into Health Patterns after Firm is Fined', *The Irish Times*, 16 February 2006.

Donnellan, E. 'Generic Drugs Could Save State "Millions"', *The Irish Times*, 12 July 2005.

—'Oireachtas Body to Study Adverse Effects of Drugs', *The Irish Times*, 14 April 2006.

Dooley, C. 'Reports Says 2003 Set A Record for Industrial Peace', *The Irish Times*, 3 September 2004.

'Drug Output', *The Irish Times*, 27 July 2004.

Dundon, M., 'Pharmaceutical Giant Plans 1,000 Jobs in €650m Cork Investment', *Irish Examiner*, 28 July 2004.

—'1,000 Jobs Bonanza as Drugs Giant Expands', *Irish Examiner*, 28 July 2004.

Houston, M. 'Doctors and Drug Firms: An Unhealthy Alliance?', *The Irish Times*, 6 April 2004.

—'State gets its First Independent health website', *The Irish Times*, 27 April 2004.

Lucy, A., 'Cork Seen as Key to Future of South West', *The Irish Times*, 1 March 2004.

MacTaggart, B., 'Stealing from the mind', *The New York Times*, 9 July 1982.

Meek, J., 'Beginners Guide to Gene Patents', *The Guardian*, 15 November 2003.

Monbiot, G. 'A Truckload of Nonsense: The G8 Plan to Save Africa Comes with Conditions that Make it Little More than an Extortion Racket', *The Guardian*, 14 June 2005.

Mulqueen, E. 'The Price You Are Forced to Pay', *The Irish Times*, 27 January 2004.

O'Halloran, B., 'R&D is Vital to Sustaining Biotech Success', *The Irish Times*, 4 July 2003.

—'Looking Like the New IT', *The Irish Times*, 4 July 2003.

—'Spending is Key for Drug Firms to Develop Right Chemistry', *The Irish Times*, 23 April 2004.

Parsons, M. 'Sanofi-Aventis to Close Waterford Plant', *The Irish Times*, 15 March 2007.

Reid, L., 'Waste Issue Delays New Planning Bill', *The Irish Times*, 5 July 2006.

Roche, B., 'Why it's Boom Time in Pharmachem City', *The Irish Times*, 14 August 2004.

—'Munster suffers Loss of Hundreds of Jobs', *The Irish Times*, 8 March 2007.

Staunton, D. 'Bono Calls for "Conscientious Commerce"', *The Irish Times*, 27 January 2006.

Thomas, P. and Bracken, P., 'Time for Openness on Antidepressants', *The Guardian*, 4 March 2002.

Vidal, J. 'Mexico's GM Corn Shocks Scientists', *The Guardian*, 30 November 2002.

Wall, M., 'Price of 800 common medicines to fall 20%', *The Irish Times*, 1 March 2007.

Wong-Rieger, D., 'Antiquated Drug Advertising Laws Need to Get With the Times', *Globe and Mail*, 2 June 2000.

Index